The following are student evaluations:

"Thank you Ted for opening my mind to the endless possibilities in painting. You are the only teacher I know who does not expect us to paint the same way; rather you push us to paint from our heart and soul as you walk with each of us on that road less travelled." *Mary Jackson*

"Ted, What can I say? I'm always bragging about you! Wish there were more teachers like you." *Marilou La Chance*

" The best teacher ever!" *Ryan Mahony*

"Ted, thank you for giving me the path to find my way to the self I knew I was but couldn't reach." *Katrina*

"Ted Keller is the MOST AMAZING teacher I have ever had! His talent to teach and passion about art could make anyone fall in love with watercolor." *unsigned*

A couple more from my "bosses":

"Ted Keller is exceptionally talented at teaching students how to see. He has great respect for people's inherent talents and gifts, regardless of their level of proficiency or amount of formal training. Ted brings out the artist in everyone."
"It is never difficult to fill Ted's art classes. Students who take one course from Ted almost always sign up for another." *Chris Legore, Director University College at Thomaston, Maine (Chris took two classes from Ted).*

"Ted consistently inspires students to reach beyond preconceived notions and create new vision. He is an instructor, encourager, challenger. He models technique, excitement, experimentation in a classroom environment that honors each participant. Ted is able to teach students with a wide range of ability and self-confidence - in the same classroom. He is masterful in blending instruction and coaching so that students are productive and grow in their skills and creativity." *Joan Fink, Director University College at Thomaston, Maine.*

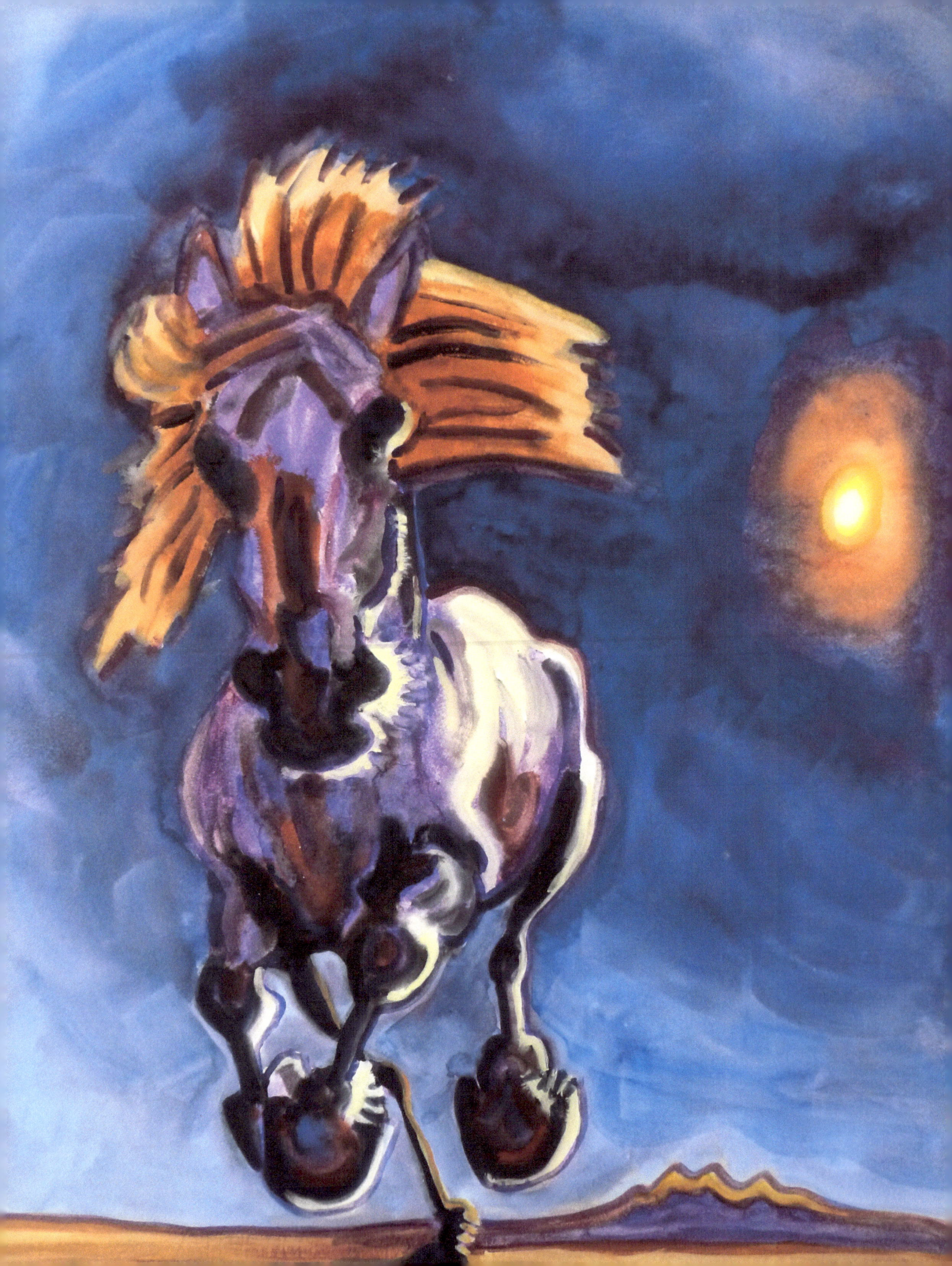

Watercolor

One Person's Teachings on Watercolor Painting and Becoming an Artist Along with a Gallery of His Work

Ted Keller

Pale Green Jade Press

Union, Maine
Taos, New Mexico

WATERCOLOR

One Person's Teachings on Watercolor Painting and Becoming an Artist Along With a Gallery of His Work

Grateful acknowledgments to Mary Olmsted Greene for her invaluable editing assistance.

ISBN - 13: 978-0692236253
ISBN - 10: 0692236252

Published by:

Pale Green Jade Press

40 Camino A Realidad
El Prado
New Mexico, 87529

For Chloe and Theo

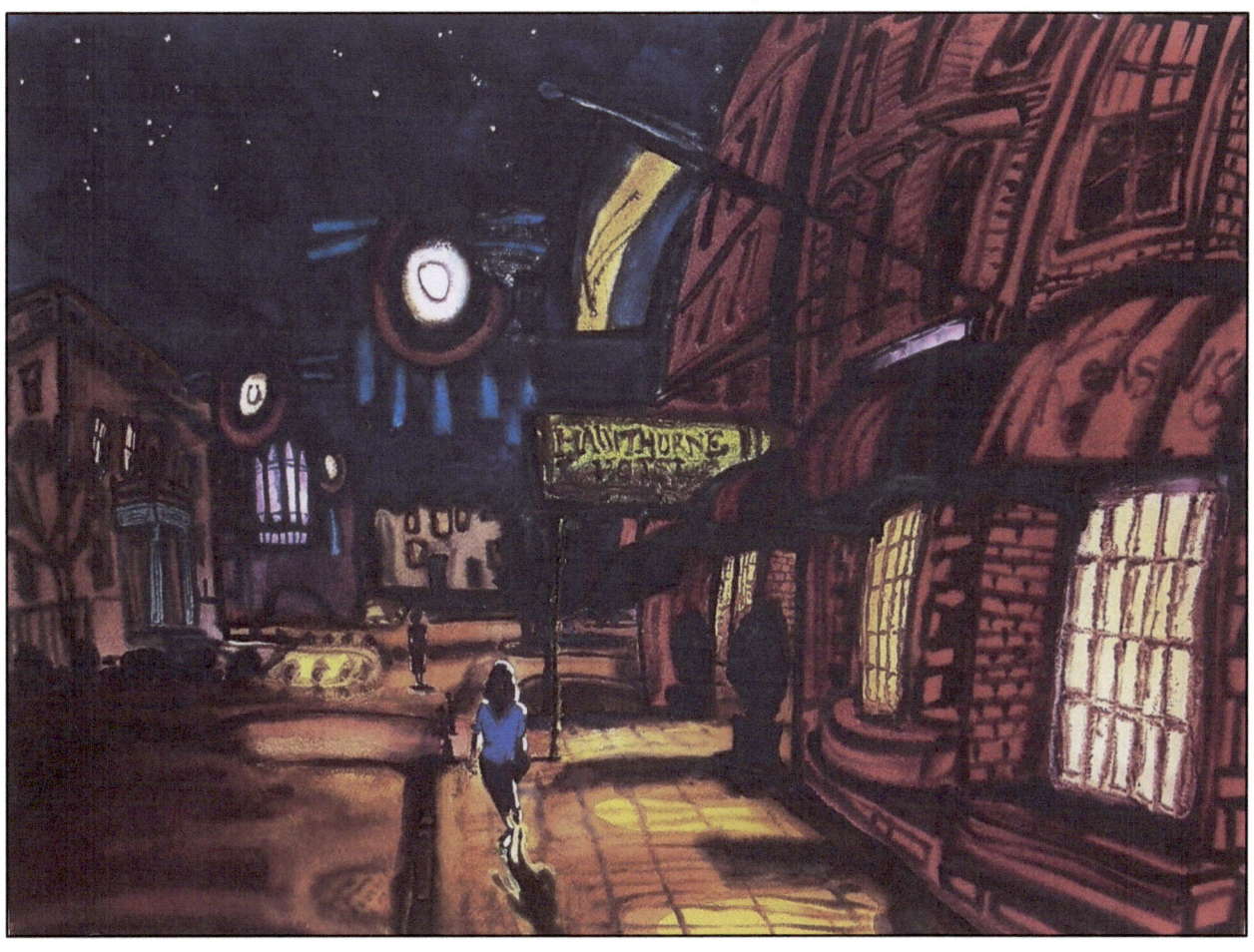

and Peggy

Table of Contents

The Teaching

The Gallery

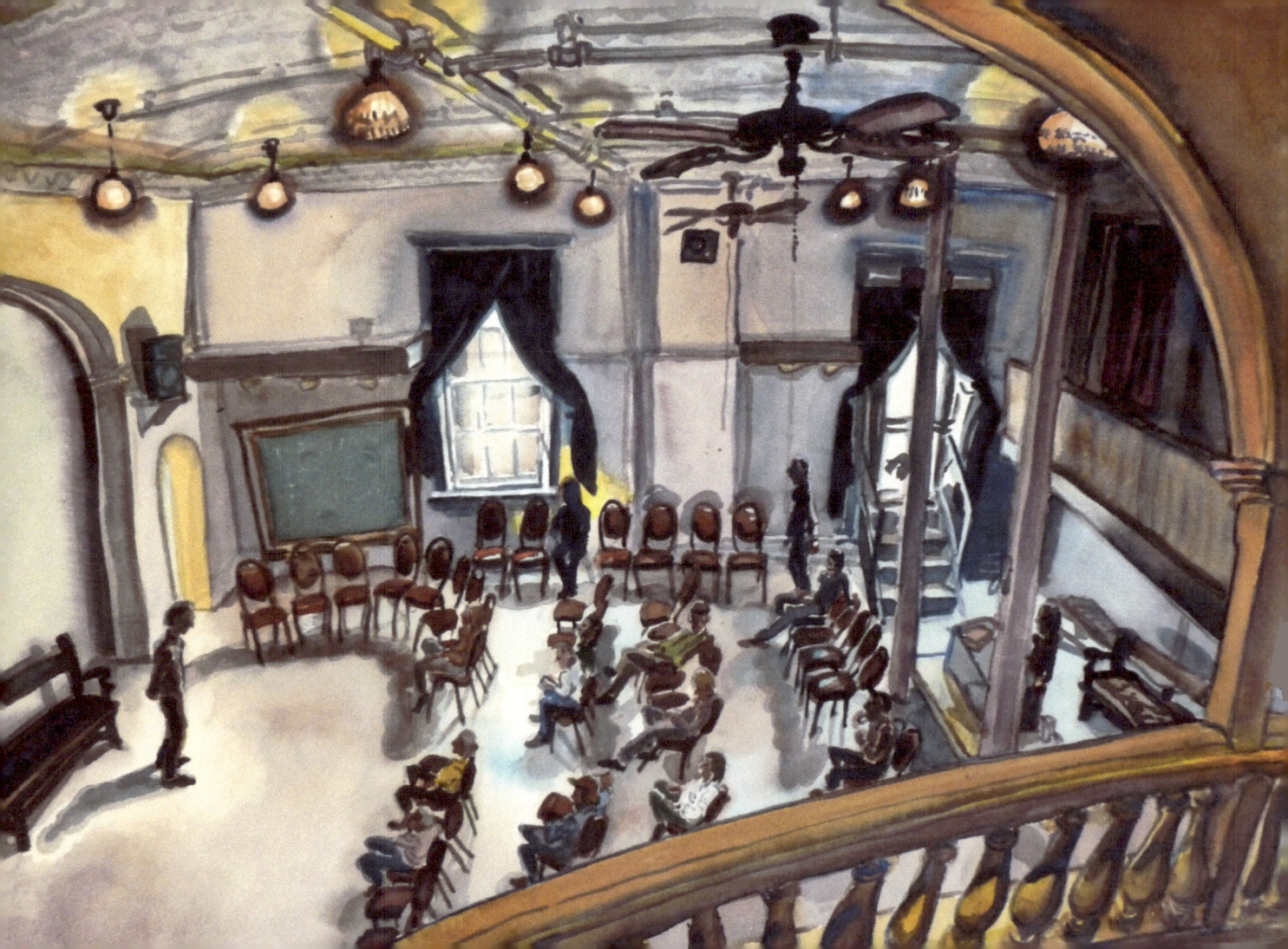

The teachings I have developed over the years are pretty much all here. How do you paint with this watercolor medium? What is a painting? What is talent? Art seems to be important, but why? What does it mean to be physical when you paint? What is artists' work? How does one produce 1,000 paintings? When are you ready to sell? How does that proceed? These and many, many more ideas are here. There are also a few exercises and a ton of very good technical, how to, and philosophical teachings. Things you really need to know about watercolor and becoming an artist.

If you have taken classes with me, here it is again. Everything you heard over and over again as you painted and I walked around class and said things. Every once in a while, I said something intelligent. The intelligent comments are here. If you have not been able to take art classes with a good teacher, this section is full of what that might sound like. Thanks. Enjoy!

Ted

The Teaching

Watercolor Materials

In watercolor painting, you need to be familiar with all of the materials. The paints, paper and brushes all need to be understood. It is more important to understand them in this medium than in other painting mediums. They have a big effect on your final product.

Watercolor Paints

Let's start with the paints. Paints are made from *pigments*. Different pigments make different colors. The same pigments, or colorants, mixed with different art mediums, make the different types of paints. Pigments mixed with oils become oil paints. Pigments mixed with acrylic medium become acrylic paints.

In watercolors, the pigments are mixed with glycerin, gum, and sometimes even a little honey. These are only binders that hold the paint pigments together. They have little effect on how the paint pigments act.

In oil or acrylic painting, all of the different colored paints work pretty much the same way. If a painter in these mediums paints with *thalo blue* (a turquoise blue), and then paints with *cobalt blue* (similar to blue jean blue), the colors look different, but they appear, as painted surfaces, pretty much the same.

Thalo blue and cobalt blue act very differently when used in a watercolor painting.

The first, thalo, is a very powerful, smooth, transparent color that penetrates and stains the paper. The cobalt blue forms an opaque, crystalline surface on the paper that glows blue. These are two very different results. Thalo, or phthalocyanine, and cobalt are names of the pigments that make these two different blues.

Pigments

Pigments that make paint colors are obtained from a number of different types of materials.

Colored earths: Dirts or hardened earths are used to make the earth colors. They have names like *yellow ochre* and *raw sienna*. These are the earthy browns, yellows, and reds that we see in the west. Earth colors tend to be opaque like muddy water, which is what they are.

Ground-up minerals: Minerals, or powdered stones, are also used. When treated in different ways, heated, etc., they make a whole range of colors. These are the *cobalt blues*, the *cadmium reds* and *cadmium yellows, chromium greens, manganese violets,* and even *lapis lazuli blue.* Lapis, a semiprecious blue stone, grinds up into a pale blue. Like stones, these pigments tend to sink or stay put in water when used as paint. Some of these minerals are a little toxic if swallowed.

Synthetics: Nowadays a lot of synthetics have been developed to replace old pigment colors. The new synthetic pigments are very good. Most are nontoxic. Many are transparent. Many are stains.

Many other old coloring agents, pigments used a long time ago, are no longer used. They have been replaced for good reasons.

Old Pigments: *Ivory black,* for instance, was made from burnt elephant ivory. It is now made from burnt bone.

Sepia, a very dark brown, was made from octopus ink. That has stopped.

The madders, such as *purple madder, rose madder,* and *alizarin crimson* were, and still can be, made from the roots of the madder plant. These red colors tend to fade in light. They have been replaced by light-fast synthetics.

Emerald green was made by a process that had the side effect of killing the artist. To this day, people still call a certain green color Poison Green.

A *purple* was made from a gland of a whelk mollusk. It took 12,000 mollusks to make one-and-one-half grams of dye.

My favorite old pigment was bull urine. It was used to make *indian yellow,* a deep orangey yellow. They made it by feeding bulls mango leaves, collecting their urine, and boiling it down. There's a job for that guy on TV who tries out the bad jobs.

There were some interesting old color making processes, most of them best left behind.

Paint Qualities

In watercolor painting, the paints have different working qualities depending on the pigments used to make them.

Transparent, semi-transparent or opaque: Watercolors are known for their lovely transparency. Light passes through the paint colors. It reflects off the white paper underneath, then back through the color. This makes the *transparent colors* glow a little. Artists call this glow *luminescence.* The transparent colors mix together well, forming new, clean color variations.

Transparent colors, the majority of watercolor paints, will not cover up mistakes or anything else that they are painted over. This requires the artist to be decisive about what's put on the paper.

Semi-transparent colors are less transparent.

The **opaque colors** in watercolor are a little more difficult to use. They include, along with some others, the earth colors and any manufactured colors made with white. When mixed together, the opaque colors tend to get muddy. Most do not glow; in fact, some seem to absorb light. Some artists will not use them because of this. The opaque colors are helpful to the watercolorist in building form, the illusion of three dimension. Opaque colors *will* cover over painting errors.

Flow: This is about how a color interacts with water. Some colors will explode when touched to a wet surface. They burst like a flat firework. Other colors sink in water. They stay put. All of the other paints, when interacting with water, will do something in between these two extremes.

Staining or easily lifted: Some of the colors are made from pigments that stain. These colors stain the paper. Watercolor papers are 100% cotton or a mix of cotton and linen. A cotton tee shirt will stain. So will cotton paper. Stains are hard to get out.

In watercolor it is possible to remove some color from the paper. The process is called *lifting.* The color to be removed is rewet and lifted off the page using something absorbent like a paper towel or a damp brush. Staining colors don't lift well, if at all. Other colors, like lapis blue, a ground-up stone, lift easily, sometimes completely, off the page. All of the paints stain or don't stain the page to varying degrees depending on what they are made from.

Granulation: Granulation happens with a few pigments. When these pigments are placed into a very wet surface, almost a puddle of water, they separate into granules. They dry to a granulated appearance. It's a very interesting effect. It only happens in watercolor.

Light fast vs fugitive: In paints the colors should not be affected by light. They should not fade when exposed to light. These non-fading paints are considered **light fast** or permanent. If the color fades when exposed to light, that is not good. If the paint fades, that color is considered *fugitive.* The color escapes.

Modern paints are mostly rated *excellent,* which means very permanent. The ratings for light fastness will be on the paint tube. There remain some red colors that are considered less than permanent, but they are still rated *very good.*

Many old pigments that were used to make watercolor paint are not used anymore. They were very fugitive. If you go to a museum and there is an exhibit of old watercolors, you might find it being held in a basement room with no windows, no outside light. Some of the paintings will have no bright colors; they look drab. This is because many of the paints used then were not good in light and have faded, or might still fade.

Watercolor painters learn how the paints work as they use them. It's not necessary to know all this beforehand or take notes. If a particular color does odd things, sooner or later the painter remembers that quality.

Buying Paints

Buying art supplies is a little like choosing wallpaper. There are too many choices. Let me break it down a little.

Watercolor paints come in two forms, **tubes** and **pans**. The pans are little tin cups of dry paint similar to what you remember from early school paints. There are *full pans* and *half pans.* They look a little like a wrapped piece of candy when you buy them. They are real paint and are not inexpensive. Pans are usually used in small paint trays when painting outside.

Most watercolor paints come in tubes. The tubes vary in size from 8 mls to 37 mls. Thirty-seven mls is the same size as an ordinary oil paint tube (about the size of a third of a large tube of toothpaste). The most common size in watercolor paint tubes is 15 ml. Be aware of the tube size when you are buying paint.

Most of the watercolor paint manufacturers make *two* qualities of paint: **artist quality**, more expensive, and **student quality,** less expensive. The companies often don't state the quality. They just give the two qualities different names. Windsor Newton, an old British paint company, makes *Windsor Newton* brand paints and *WN Cotman* paints. The first are artist quality; the second are student quality. Most of the companies use two names.

If you don't know which is which, it is easy to tell. *Student quality* tubes are usually all one smaller size and one price. They will include only the less expensive pigments; therefore, there is a smaller selection of colors.

A company will have a wide assortment of *artist quality* paint colors. They will have a range of prices. They will include the more unusual pigments. They are usually more expensive.

Watercolor paint also comes in kits of tubes or trays of dry color pans. Some of these are very inexpensive and not all that bad. They are fine for beginners.

One more note: watercolor paints can come in two forms. They can be made from an expensive pigment. If they are, they are named on the tubes as simply *cobalt blue* or *cerulean blue* or *viridian green,* etc. They may also have the word **genuine** after the name, such as *cobalt blue* **genuine**.

Paints may also be made to look like the more expensive pigments by mixing less expensive colorants to create a more or less close match of the expensive color. These will have the word **hue** added to the name on the tube. They will be called *cobalt blue* **hue,** *cerulean blue* **hue,** *viridian green* **hue,** etc. They will cost less.

These paints, with hue in the name, may look a little like the real pigment colors but they won't have their special qualities. Some hues may have white in their mixture. When you paint with them, the white may come to the surface and make a mess.

Watercolor Brushes

There is a lot to learn about watercolor brushes. They come in an almost endless variety of shapes, materials, and sizes. They are made by many different companies.

Shape: Watercolor brushes come in two basic shapes and a whole lot of variations on those shapes. The two shapes are **round** and **flat.** The round brushes are round in the belly of the brush. They are tapered to a point lengthwise. Round brushes are the classic art brush everyone has used since kindergarten. Flat brushes look like little house-painting brushes, except finer and not as thick. Large flat brushes are used for washes or wetting the paper.

Round brushes are very versatile. They come in many different sizes. The painter can do pretty much everything with them. Flat brushes make a characteristic square-edged mark on the paper. Some artists like this, some don't. Flat brushes are great for painting straight lines.

Size: Round brushes come in many sizes. They are numbered 000 thru about 20. As the number gets bigger, so do the brushes. The sizes are **not** standard. They change from company to company.

Flat brushes and wash brushes are sized in inches measured across the hairs.

Watercolor brushes have shorter handles than oil or acrylic brushes.

Hairs: Watercolor brushes are made from animal hair or synthetic hair. A good round brush should hold a point and spring back to its original shape. Hand-made *kolinsky sable* hair brushes are the very best. They are wonderfully responsive brushes. They can be expensive but some are not. *Sable hair* of any kind makes very good brushes.

Synthetic hairs are also used. There are lots of synthetic brushes on the market. Most are fine. They are not expensive, but they frizz after a while. *Squirrel hair* brushes flop around. I have

no idea how to use them. Pony hair brushes are awful. Bamboo-handled oriental brushes vary a lot. You will have to try them.

Choosing brushes is not easy. Go to an art store and look at what they have. Some stores will let you try them. Don't be too cheap. Generally, with brushes, you get what you pay for. I would start with two round brushes, a medium and a smallish one; a flat brush, three-quarters of an inch or so; and a one-and-one-half-inch wash brush.

The Paper

When choosing art painting surfaces, the artist always tries to use a material that will hold up for a long time. Most artists feel that some of the paintings they produce may have lasting value. Art materials that last are called **archival.**

Paper, Rag: Good watercolor paper is made from 100% cotton or a mix of cotton and linen. It is called **rag.** It is archival. When I talk of watercolor paper, I'm talking about rag. (The word *paper* is more familiar, so I use it.) Most ordinary paper is made from wood pulp. Over time, the acids in the wood pulp cause the paper to turn brown, then disintegrate. Place a sheet of newspaper (all wood pulp) in the sun for a day. It will turn yellow and quickly become brittle.

There are a number of things a painter needs to know about watercolor paper.

Size: It comes in many different sizes. No surprise there. **Full** sheets are always 22" x 30." Paper also comes larger or smaller than that. Many of the sheet sizes were established a long time ago. The paper sizes at one time had old British empire names like *Elephant* or *Double Elephant.* These names are not used anymore.

Manufacture: Some watercolor papers are hand made. Some are partly hand made. Some are machine made. Paper made by different processes will be of different quality. The surfaces will vary. They will also vary in price.

Good watercolor papers have something called **deckle edges.** These are rough edges that happen when paper is, at least partly, hand made. A deckle edge looks something like a hand torn edge. When watercolors are framed, this rough edging is often allowed to show.

Machine-made paper will have sharp edges and a mechanical looking textured surface. Hand-made paper has a more natural looking surface.

Surfaces: #1 **Hot press** - Hot press paper has a smooth surface. *Water tends to slide around on this surface.* When water moves around easily, it becomes hard to control. Some artists love that; some really don't. It is a beautiful paper surface, if hard to control.

#2 **Cold press** - Cold press paper is also called **not** as in *not* hot pressed. The cold pressed surface is textured with little bumps and dips. When used with water, the water flows into the dips and does not move around much. That makes painting on this paper *more controllable* than on a smooth hot pressed surface. Cold pressed paper is the most commonly used surface in watercolor painting.

#3 **Rough** - As the name implies, this surface is rough. It has larger bumps and dips than cold press. Some artists like that. I find it hard to use for small paintings, but good for large work.

Sizing: Good watercolor paper is usually all cotton. Painting on it would be like painting on a cotton tee shirt if nothing were done to change it. To alter it, something called **sizing** is added to the paper. Sizing is a glue-like substance, made from horses, I'm afraid ("the glue factory"). It stiffens the paper and lessens its ability to absorb liquids. Some watercolor papers are hard sized (lots of glue), while others are softer. The softer the paper the more absorbent. Painters try different papers and learn the ones they like to work on.

Weight: The paper comes in different weights. The weight refers to how much 500 full size sheets weigh. The more weight, the thicker the paper. 90# paper is thin. 140# paper is most commonly used. 300# paper is thick. It will buckle less when wet, but costs more.

There was a statement in a watercolor book I read. It said something like, "Life is too short to use poor quality watercolor paper." I agree. A full sheet, 22"x 30", of good 140# watercolor paper bought in bulk costs about five dollars (shop around). It can be torn into four 11"x 15" pieces. That is a nice size for a small painting. Enjoy good paper.

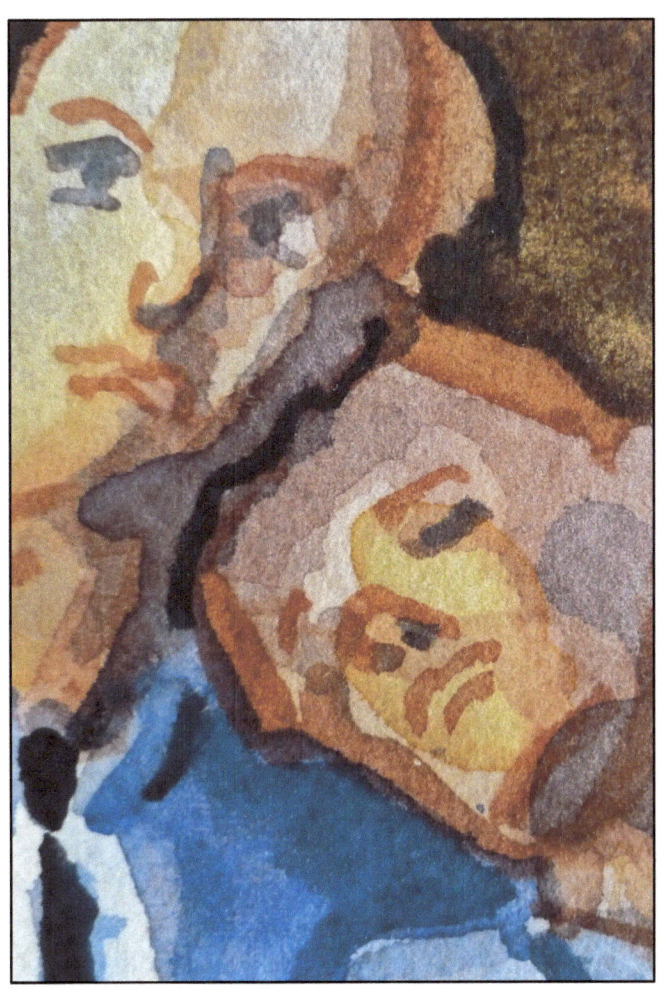

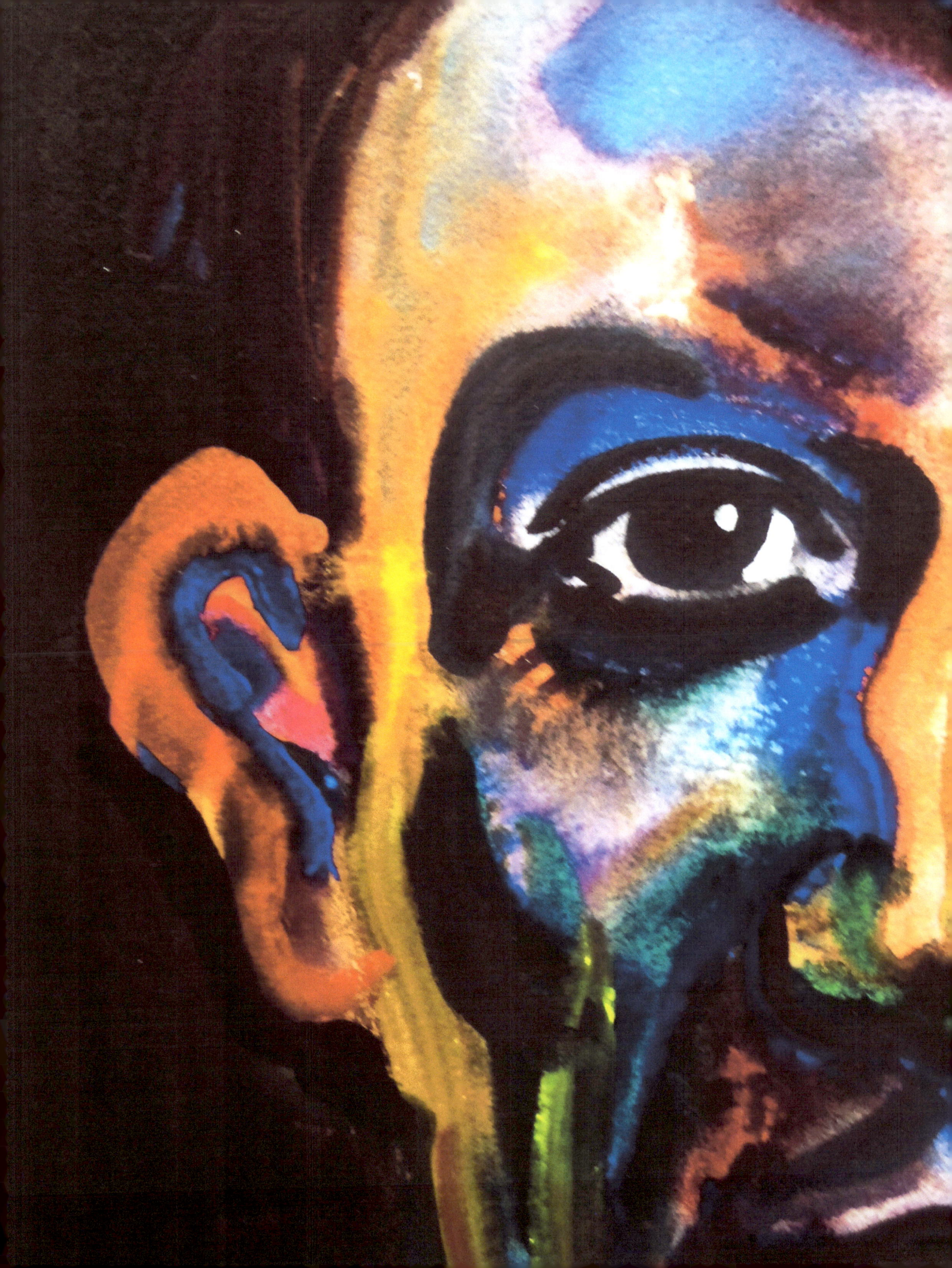

How to Paint

With interest and motivation, you can learn to paint. The skills needed are not that complicated. No matter what you want to paint, whether landscapes, faces, still lifes, abstracts, etc., it all comes to the same requirements.

You need some **drawing ability.** Most levels of drawing skills can be worked with. Everybody has some skill. Your ability will get better.

You must be able to see what's dark and what's light in whatever you are painting. Darks and lights are called **value** in artwork. When you paint, you make the *darks* that you see a *dark color.* You make the *lights, a light color.*

Then there is **color**. You learn to use the paints, the color, and the water. Then you make the drawings and the values in color.

Chapters on drawing, value and color follow these chapters on painting.

You get better at these skills by doing them. You learn to paint by painting. Books and teachers can help you with the basic art understandings as you learn. But mostly it's up to you. You need to cover a lot of square feet of paper with paint.

How Do You Start Painting?

I don't mean to be a wise guy on this, but really, you gather your courage and start painting. *You will do better than you think.* Most of what you need to learn about painting, you learn by painting. If you want to paint, and there seems to be real or imagined obstacles in your way, move through them. I don't know how else to say it.

There is much information in this book about working with watercolor. Get started painting. This book will help. Your interest will guide you.

Water

The name of the medium, **water***color, implies that water will have something to do with the process of painting. It does. It has some effect on every brush stroke. Water is your partner when you paint with watercolors.* **Water does water things.** *It doesn't care what you are doing.*

Water is not always controllable. This tends to scare some painters who want more control. How water works in watercolor painting is a very important understanding.

Pay attention here!
The key to painting with *water*colors is the **water.** It is not hard to understand how water works. Water seeks to be level, never hilly. Basically, *greater wetness (more water) will always flow into lesser wetness.*

A two-inch-thick puddle of water will flow into a one-inch-thick puddle of water and become level. A more wet area of paint will move into a less wet, or only damp area of paint, *if they touch.* If a wet area of paint touches a less wet, damp area on the paper, *the wet paint color will easily and quickly move into the damp area.* When that happens, the wet paint color will push aside or mix with whatever color is in the damp area. It will do this whether you want it to or not. This is called a *blossom.* A pretty name but sometimes a control problem.

The action of water doesn't only happen on wet areas on the paper. It also happens between the paint brush and the paper. If your paint brush is full of wet paint and the paper is only damp, less wet, the watery paint flows easily from the brush onto the paper. If your paint brush is just damp, and the paper is very wet, the water and paint on the paper will "lift" into the brush. *The brush acts like a mop.* More on lifting later.

*You move paint around, **and so does water.** Water can make paint flow around in a painting. You make a painting mark and the water might **move it!** This is controllable, if you need to control it.*

Work for a while with only water and paint on paper, no images, until you get a feel for what's going on.

Wet will not move into dry: The most needed and well used understanding about water in watercolor painting is that *wet paint will not move into dry areas of the paper.* Let me repeat that: *a wet painted area will not move into a dry area of the paper.* This is one way watercolorists use and control the action of water. If you want to keep an area of paint where you put it, leave the paper around it dry. Even a small line of dry paper will keep two wet areas from mixing.

Paper: Good paper, wet paper, damp paper, dry paper

Please use good paper. Use the best paper that you can afford. I use Arches 140# paper.

Watercolor is a very sensitive art medium. Oil or acrylic paints work fine and about the same when used on good paper, bad paper, canvas, wood, bricks, or most other surfaces. Watercolors don't. The paper makes a big difference. Starting with cheap paper is not a good idea if you want to learn to paint.

There is a choice to make at the start of a watercolor painting. You can choose to wet the paper a lot, a little, or start with it dry. I use all of these ways at different times.

Wet paper: If you **wet** the paper a lot before you paint, it stretches. It will buckle and form hills and valleys as it does. I lift the edges of the wet paper and move it up and down a little while it is doing this. Moving it releases it from the table top and allows it to stretch, get evenly wet, and finally mostly flatten out.

When you paint on wet paper, all your marks and colors move around and may spread some. How much it moves around depends on what colors you use. Some colors flow more than others. Control is not fully possible until the paper begins to dry out. On wet paper *you and the water are working together*. It's a fun and even helpful process, if you let it be.

Damp paper: You can start work on **damp** paper. Paper can be dampened by wetting it and then wiping off any extra water with a paper towel. Or better, just let the wet paper sit around till it dries some. Damp paper will still buckle.

I often dampen the paper just to *soften the surface* so it absorbs the paint colors better. Marks made and colors put on damp paper will *soften a little on the edges*. There is more control of what you are doing when working damp.

Dry paper: Starting with **dry** paper is fine. The water of watercolor will be added with every stroke. As the water is added, areas of the paper that are wet will stretch and form bumps.

On dry paper, the edges of your painting marks will be crisp and sharp. *The painting marks you make will stay where you put them on dry paper*. If you are careful, you can keep control of what's happening. If you are working quickly, everything gets wet or damp anyway and you will lose some control.

Good paper is, as I have said before, all cotton or cotton and linen. The paper acts like the cotton cloth that it is. It stretches when wet, then shrinks again when dry.

The Paints

If the paints are dry when you start (watercolors can be bone dry), it is a good idea to wet them with a spray of clean water. Wetting them will allow you to pick up more paint on the brush.

If you are working with tubes of paint and you want a lot of richness of color, squeeze some fresh paint from the tube onto your pallet. Painting with this wet paint and a little water will give you a lot of color.

Working with the different colors is covered in the chapter on color.

So How Do You Paint with this Stuff?

Let me take you through how a painting might proceed. Remember this is *water*color. Every paint stroke you make has something to do with water. *Water is your friend!*

As a teacher, I repeat this fact about water over and over. I do that because it is really important. I also repeat it because students seem to listen, and then go right back to worrying about the water. They start wondering if they should change to oil painting.

Knowing about how water works, we can look at how a painting might be made. The example here is an outdoor painting of trucks in front of trees, some distant buildings, sky and ground.

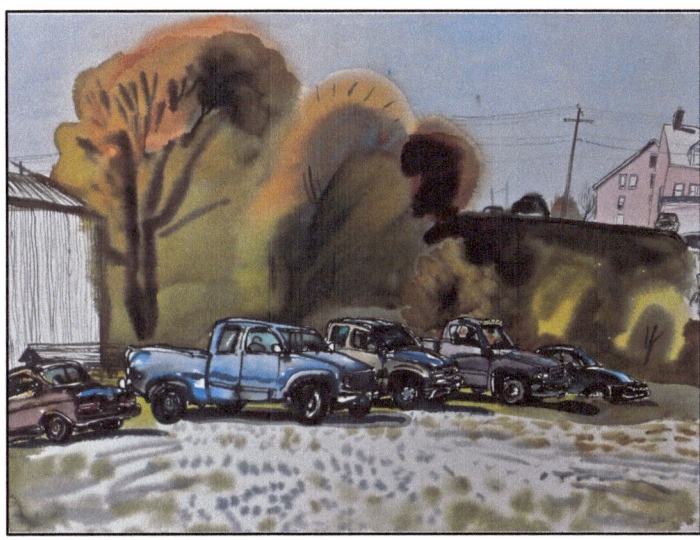

To begin this painting, the objects are drawn on dry paper in pencil. Then first, one by one, front to back, the trucks are painted.

While the trucks are drying or are dry, the buildings are painted. When the trucks and buildings are completely dry, the area where the trees will go is wet using plain water and a brush. The greens and oranges are painted into the wet area. They are quickly followed by the tree trunks and branches. The paints will move around some in the wetted area of the trees, *but not beyond it.*

The trees have been painted and are loose and wet looking. *The **water** has softened and blended the colors for you.* The loosely painted trees stayed inside the wet area. The colors did not move onto the dry paper or dry trucks. *Wet will not move into dry.* The wetness makes the area of trees interesting. You don't have to paint every leaf.

Next, the ground is made wet with clean water, and colors are added. By the time this is done, the trees have dried.

Finally, the sky is made wet and painted. *The wet paper will allow the sky's blue paint to flow and look even and smooth.* Since the trees and buildings are dry, the blue of the sky will stay where you want it to.

Step by step, the painting has been worked through. Some areas are detailed; some are vibrant and wet looking.

Water, wetted paper, makes watercolors flow softly and smoothly together. This can be lovely and you don't have to do anything. The *water* does the mixing for you. Because wet will not flow into dry, the painting is easily controlled.

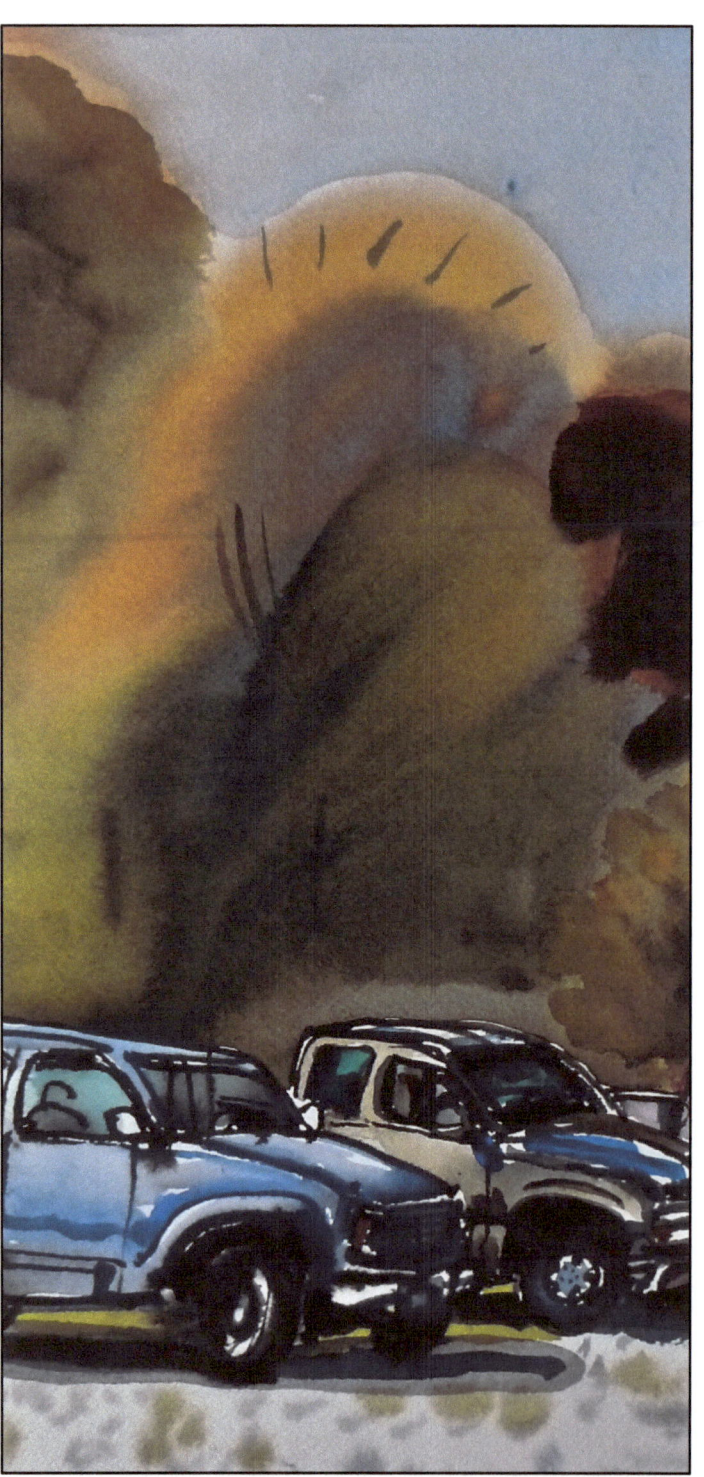

I read an article about a Georgia O'Keeffe watercolor. There was also a picture of the painting. The author was impressed with the thin white lines of unpainted paper left around each object O'Keeffe painted. He thought perhaps the white added "visual power" to the picture.

*As a watercolor painter, I have another thought as to why O'Keeffe left the thin dry unpainted areas around each object. She may have left them because she knew that the wet areas of paint she used would **not** move beyond the thin dry lines of paper. She may have wanted to keep painting without waiting to let areas dry.*

Watercolor painters often paint one wetted area, allow that one to dry, then wet and paint another area in the painting. Watercolors dry quickly. Watercolorists work their way one area at a time through a painting this way. This allows the artist to paint loose and wet. The water gets to help, and as long as the areas around the wet area are dry, the painter stays in control. It's easy.

Take some time and look at a watercolor painting closely. You might see that the painting is painted area by area. You might notice that a part of the painting that was obviously very wet when painted, will stop. There may or may not be a small space around it. Winslow Homer worked his way through a watercolor this way. If you look closely, you can see it in his work.

There are any number of ways to approach a painting, and this is a common one. When I teach, we start with this approach. It's a good, safe way to stay loose and learn how water and paint work together.

Control

People who start painting think that you take the paint, use a brush, and make an image. This works with a lot of paint mediums. Because of the water, watercolors are different.

When painting with watercolor, you are not alone or even fully in charge. It's you and the water making the painting.

Beginners should relax their desire to make a correct image and learn how the painting process works, how paint and water work. Good paintings come after you learn how to paint. *There is a lot to learn*. Give yourself the time to learn. Make paintings, but stay loose, *don't worry about the results*. Enjoy the paint. Enjoy the water.

***How** you paint is more important than **what** you paint.*

It is important to create for yourself some stressless space when learning to paint, so you feel free to screw up. *Making a mess* may be the best way to learn what to do and what not to do. No museums are going to come by today and check to see if you are doing things correctly. Stop worrying about the image; relax and enjoy what happens with the paint.

I gave myself three years (about 300 paintings) to learn how to paint before showing my work. I still use four dollar a sheet paper instead of eight dollar a sheet paper. When I mess up, it costs less. Find ways to de-stress the process and allow yourself to learn. Let go of control. Don't force results, *just paint*. The medium can be mastered, but only when you learn to work with how it works.

'Scary' Watercolor Control Problems

*There are two aspects of watercolor painting that scare people: the **water part** and the fact that the paints are **rewettable.***

The water again: Water is one of the control problems with watercolor. *It, by its nature, does what **water needs to do,** not what **you** think you need it to do.* Water must be worked with. Sometimes it needs to be *uncontrolled* and allowed to do water things. Sometimes it is *controlled* and made to do painting things. The water part of watercolor might be a little scary, but it can be a great help to painters.

*Water is part of watercolor painting that is not **you**. You work on making a painting. At the same time, something outside of you is working on the same painting: water.*

Rewettableness: Another control problem with this watercolor medium is that the paints *don't ever dry permanently.* They can always be rewet with water. Colors are rewet in a painting every time you paint over them. The colors can mix together and make a mess. Watercolor paints are *best put down on the paper and left alone.* You can rework areas sometimes, when you know what you are doing. In general, ***watercolor doesn't reward a lot of fussing.***

Common Watercolor Control Mistakes

Not using enough water: The thinking is, "since water is pretty uncontrollable, the less I use, the easier it will be for me." Beginners tiptoe around water. Not using enough water is trouble. *The paints don't work well without it*. It's *water*color; water must be part of every stroke. Take risks. You must learn what water does. It will be your friend.

Painting over and over an area: As you paint over a dry or drying area of color, the dry colors already on the paper will *rewet*. They will mix with the color you are putting down. This can be trouble. The more you try to control what is happening, the more mess you will make. The area will end up showing a lot of ugly brush work. The struggle will show in uneven areas of paint that are too thick or too thin. It might be better to just wet the whole area you want to change, lift it off and start over.

Trying too hard to control what's happening: This is not a problem made just by beginners. Generally, watercolor paintings are over-controlled. You will see some technically remarkable, highly realistic watercolors paintings. Realism in art is always understandable, admired and seductive. In many cases, I find that when a watercolor is controlled to this level, for me it dies a little. Sort of like training a wolf to fetch.

When you learn what water does, allow that to be, and work with it. Water allows life into your paintings. Let your painting process get out of control. When the process feels dangerous... that's good.

Control, the Mental Part

This next section is pretty subjective. It is directed at painters who want to feel freer when they work. They want something deeper. They want to loosen up.

All artists are different. Not all want to, or are even interested in, loosening up. Some artists are already deep, or too deep.

What follows are my thoughts and understandings.

'Release the Hounds!'

*Art may be a civilizing enterprise for a society. Art museums in cities seem very proper places. **Art is not an entirely civilized process for an artist.** To get your art to deeper, freer levels, areas where understanding comes more from the body than the mind, some releasing of boundaries is needed.*

In the beginning, most people who want to paint feel a responsibility to recreate accurately whatever it is they are looking at. They want to paint a visually understandable picture.

Starting there is fine. As a teacher, it is not easy to get painters to relax about this. It feels to students that that is what their task is. It is part of it, and there *is* a lot to learn. Reproducing accurately what you are looking at is an achievement. ***Is that art?***

Art is more than just a pursuit of technical excellence. Working for visual accuracy and realism is seductive, but it is often a dead end for painters. It is an achievable goal. There often needs to be more. *Technical excellence alone won't get you into museums or allow you your deepest expression.*

When you have attained good painting skills, maybe it's time to see if there is something more. In painting, might there be something more truthful, something more personal than being highly skilled?

*Without knowing what will happen, is it possible for you to examine what you've always believed to be true about art? Maybe the rules you have been following **are not real**. If you want to **loosen** up how you work, this might be how to approach it. **Art is a pursuit that, really, has no rules.**

Release

I do feel free when I work. I don't feel there is anything that I can't try.

Releasing or relaxing about art was, for me, a process. It happened step by step. When I realized I was free to not have to do something a certain way, I wrote it down on a sheet of paper. That paper went up on the wall as a reminder.

For example, after looking at Raoul Dufys' paintings, I realized that *colors can expand to areas beyond where they "belong."* They don't really "belong" anywhere. Keeping the colors in the lines felt like, but never was, a "rule."

With this new understanding, I could paint a little more freely. I became more intuitive about the whole idea of color. I could breathe a little more deeply.

You will need to find these "rules" within yourself. When you find them, you can then judge whether they are "true" or needed. Other artists have done this. This is artists' work. This is how they get to doing their **own** work.

Think About...

Releasing your training: It has been helpful up to this point, thank you. Now it's up to you to go further. Go further.

Releasing your responsibility to the scene you are painting: Artists are not cameras. Relax and respond to what you see. Paint, don't analyze. Paint like a kid.

Releasing your orderly mind: Allow the position and or size of objects to change. Look at Chagall's work.

People can be big. Cars can be small. Heads can be too big when you paint people. It's okay. Big heads actually makes some sense.

Relaxing compositional "rules:" Allow the painting to become more personal. Design the painting to be just like you feel it needs to be, not like you think it's supposed to be. Put things where you want them, if it works. *There is no way it is supposed to be.*

Releasing your drawing: Be brave. Learn to love and trust your own marks. Not all artists are architects when they draw. Let it flow a little. Be bold and *go with what appears*. Poor drawing skills are not a problem. Lack of courage can be. Your drawings will get better. When they do, you will have to work to release that.

Perspective: Perspective can be played with. Nothing hurts a painting more than bad perspective. Really accurate perspective can also harm a painting.

Perspective happens, but it's not really how we see things. You'll have to figure that out for yourself. There is more on perspective later in the book.

Releasing the colors: Here are the *hounds* of the title of this section. They are so beautiful. Let them loose.

Colors don't have to be accurate. Our color sense is very intuitive. *Pick your colors quickly.* Let the intuitive part of you have some say. It doesn't really matter what colors you pick. A face can be all blue. As you gain confidence and skill, it all is workable.

Start a painting with nothing: Nothing is really all you've got. Nothing is enough.

Take Risks

Do things that don't seem right. Fight your way out of the box that your ideas about how art should look has gotten you in. Make space for yourself and your paintings to roam around in. Risk-taking pushes out boundaries. It gives you a bigger playing field.

It doesn't matter what your paintings end up looking like. Art is free to look any way you want it or it wants to look. It matters that what you create is not hampered by pre-conceived ideas. Take risks. Makes messes. See how they work out. This is also artists' work. Work hard. Let the way you paint, *already there in every mark,* flower. Paint like you were born to paint.

Much of the subject of this book is how artists get to the place where they are painting how they should be painting, not how they think they should be painting. When painters paint just like themselves, they become artists. Their work begins to have value.

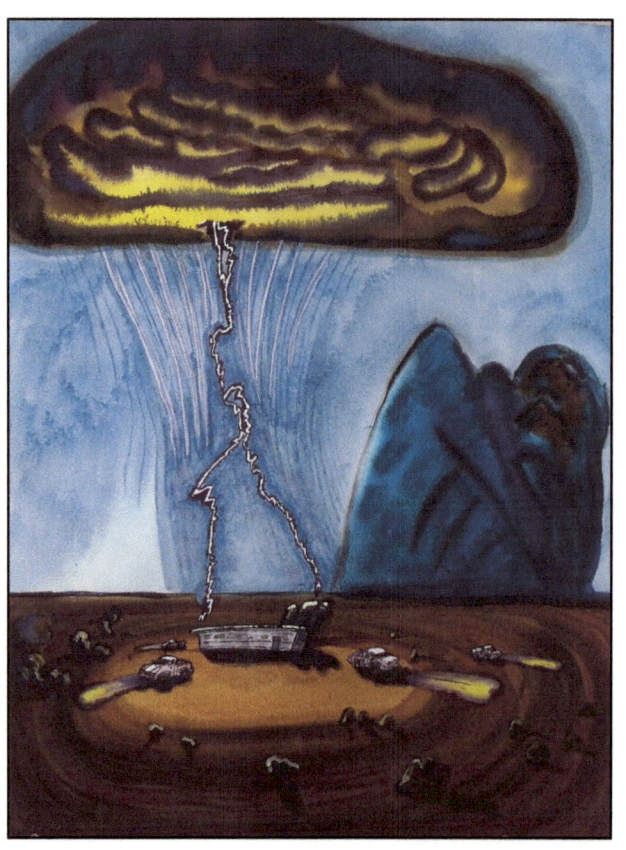

How I Paint

Before I start any painting, I spray the paints in my pallets lightly with water from a spray bottle. The water softens the paints. It lets me pick up a lot of paint on the brush when I'm working. I have two pallets. They hold 40 different colors total, 20 each.

Wet your paints before you start.

I usually work on fairly, or very, wet paper when I start a painting. I keep two delicate, non-staining violets on my palette. They are ultramarine violet, a blue violet, and manganese violet, a red violet (Da Vinci paints). I use these with a pointed brush to draw with. (I don't often use pencil.) The purples flow around a little on the wet paper. The imprecise wet marks actually help me visualize the images I'm drawing. The colors are *weak in staining power* so if I don't like what I've drawn, I just wash it away with water and a big brush. I can then start over.

I'm not good at making things up so I mostly work from something. It can be from life; for instance, a face, a still life, or a landscape. It can also be from a photo or a computer image. I use photographic images as visual information. I don't copy them exactly.

What I paint from doesn't make much difference any more in how the final paintings turn out. The paintings don't look like their source or sources. They just look like I did them.

Simple paintings: For a simple, direct painting, like a face, once the drawing is loosely made, I begin. I promise, at this point *I never know how to start. I just start.* **Get to painting. Don't get stuck before you start.**

For the first part of making a painting, I don't think or judge much, if at all. My hand picks up colors intuitively, quickly, and paints. It's a trusting, physical process. During this time I listen to music. Maybe it keeps my mind occupied and not continually judging what I'm doing.

The paper is often very wet. The colors move around by themselves some. I use a lot of paint because the water on the page will dilute the colors and make them paler. If I want a lot of color, I squeeze wet paint from the tube onto the pallet. Then paint with it. I use the empty areas of the pallet to wet and mix paints.

I work quickly; there is no reason not to. Working slowly allows more time for the conceptual mind to enter the process. I find the hand, at this point, is smarter that the mind.

As the paper dries some, after about an hour and a half, I slow down and pause. I'm usually tired after a period of painting this way. It's time to take a break and look at what has been painted.

The paper will dry. Everything I do then becomes more controllable. Over time, often a couple of days or longer, I correct what is wrong. I add detail where needed. The painting goes up on the wall. The painting will feel *unquiet* if it needs changes. When it no longer bothers me and is *quiet* for a long time, it is done.

Complex paintings: For a more complex painting, like one of the cafe scenes, I have to do more planning. Back when I started painting, I sat in cafes and did drawings. The cafe scenes were from real places. Now I more often work in the studio with images from a camera or computer.

I put the scenes together from a lot of separate pieces. A setting for the scene must be chosen. This may be a combination of places that I put together, a building chosen from one image, a street lamp from another. Each person sitting in the cafe must be selected and painted. Putting in and painting the cafe chairs can take a day.

Is it day time or night time? Are there cars on the street? What do they look like? Where is the light coming from? How are the shadows cast? The painting slowly builds. It gets filled with many things and then edited. I take out what

doesn't work. (You *can* edit watercolors when you learn how.) Sooner or later, it feels done.

Working flat: I work flat on a table top because I paint with a lot of water. This causes some problems. It's hard to stand back and see how you are doing. Objects in the painting can get distorted. Among other things, I find symmetrical objects, objects that have lefts and rights that are supposed to match, like two eyes, two ears, and the two sides of a bottle, don't always match. If I am painting a face, the chin may be made too small because it is close to me. The hair might be made too big because it is further away.

In the studio, I have a ladder and a big mirror. I climb the ladder, when the painting is wet, to look down on it from further away. When the painting is dry enough, I hold it up to the mirror. This also makes it look farther away and reverses it. Symmetrical objects, like faces, should look good reversed or not reversed. This helps you make the two sides of an object match.

As you paint, your mind accepts what you are doing. It thinks you are doing so well maybe you are a genius. The reversed mirror image helps you see the mistakes.

How it Feels to Do a Painting

Let me take you through a painting emotionally. These are my feelings. Your emotional process may be very different.

I mostly paint in the morning.

After the watercolor paper is laid out, but before I start painting, *I have a small hill to climb*, a barrier. **It's always there with every painting.** I don't know why, doubt of some kind. It's a possible stopping place and I haven't started painting. I climb over the hill and paint.

I have thoughts about what I am going to paint, or sometimes a pretty good vision. When I pick up the brush, *I have no idea what to do first.* I'm a blank. **Zero.** This is another possible stopping moment. Instead of stopping, I start.

I do trust from experience that I will make my way through the painting. *I know I'll get into trouble, but I'm not afraid of it.* I don't really think about it. I choose a color, right or wrong, and just begin.

From this moment and for a while I just paint. It's physical. My hand moves, colors are chosen, and marks are made. Thinking and judging are not important. They just slow things down. Too much thinking can bring the whole process to a halt. This proceeds till the paper dries out and I get tired. There is quite a bit of painting done in that time.

If the paper is dry enough, I hang it up and see what happened. I usually walk away for a while to let the intensity calm down.

That can be it for the day. The process of painting is underway. *I love having something to look at.* Often though, I come back from a short break and can see a lot of problems in the painting that need work. If they are obvious, I correct them. The **energy** from the earlier session is in the painting. *It now needs my eyes and mind to make it work. The painting process is no longer mostly in my body.* After these first needed changes are made, the painting goes back on the wall. It will be looked at and worked on as needed over the next period of time. There is plenty of wall space.

The next morning, I start again. I paint pretty much every day when I am painting.

It feels good to paint. It feels like work that I should be doing. It is rewarding in the same way that physical exercise is. I know I've done something good for myself.

After three or four hours of painting, I feel pretty empty, a little spacey. After a while that goes away.

I continue to paint for number of reasons. I want to be good. I know how to work. I'm curious about the whole process and idea of painting. I love seeing the work done and on the wall. I always feel there is more to do. I think what I am doing might have value.

Don't get stopped: You might find when you are painting that there are moments when you feel like stopping. Maybe you run out of courage. There are most likely many reasons. It is a common happening. If you want to paint, don't let yourself be stopped. Acknowledge whatever it is and keep going. Given time, you will get used to it.

For me, the same hill needs to be climbed every day I paint. I don't find painting to be easy. It is work. It is always a challenge.

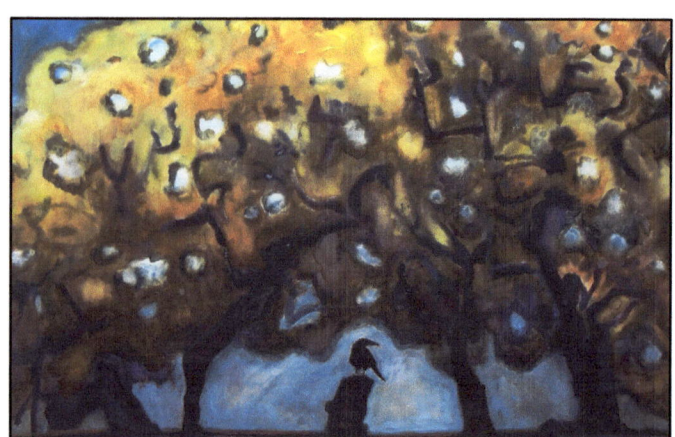

The Crow

I've heard it said that artists don't have a choice; they have to paint. That might be true for some. I have felt all along that I have a choice. I make the choice to paint. I make the same choice every day I paint. If you want to get good at painting, you have to paint.

Paint Like Yourself

As a long time art teacher, I have never encouraged students to paint like me. *I paint like me.* I want them to paint like themselves. Everyone has different energy in their hands. Some painters are energetic and impatient. Some are quiet, gentle, and thoughtful. Expecting these different energies to make paintings the same way is silly.

I tell students, "Make *100 paintings* and you will learn how to paint. Make *300 paintings* and you will learn how **you** paint." **How you paint** is there to some degree in every mark you make, but it takes time and persistence for your efforts and your process to flower.

You will know when it happens. When it does, your work begins to have worth. Galleries want paintings with a look that is unique to the artist. It's called a ***signature style.***

Signature Style

This idea of a signature style, is something I've thought a lot about. It is not a hard concept to understand. An artist's paintings should look like that artist's paintings. Gauguin's paintings all look like Gauguin paintings. Frida Kahlo's paintings all look like Frida Kahlo paintings.

Is a signature style just an odd way of painting? Is it something critical to "good" art? I'm not sure, but it is interesting to consider.

When I first started painting, I pinned that early work up on the wall. *My work looked like a group show.* I was making my paintings look like what I thought "good" art looked like. There were problems in doing that.

No matter what style or subject matter I painted, everything I painted had a cartoony look to it. I didn't like it, but there it was. How could any artist be taken seriously if his work looks cartoony?

I kept working. The cartooniness never went away. I began to like it, then love it. It is how I paint.

My cartooniness now makes simple sense to me. I honor it and trust it. Whether it is great art or whether it sells well doesn't matter. It is *my* style, and it feels true.

Moments of understanding and release come with *time, effort and frustration.* These moments allow you to relax about what you are doing. They help open your work to yourself. *How you paint* is always there in your work. If you want to find *it*, rather than make "*art*," you will.

All good artists sooner or later develop a recognizable style. They do it through some combination of hard work, skill, paint application, subject matter, composition, and so on. They end up with work that is their own, their signature style.

Don't try to "make art." Trust, and paint like yourself. See what happens.

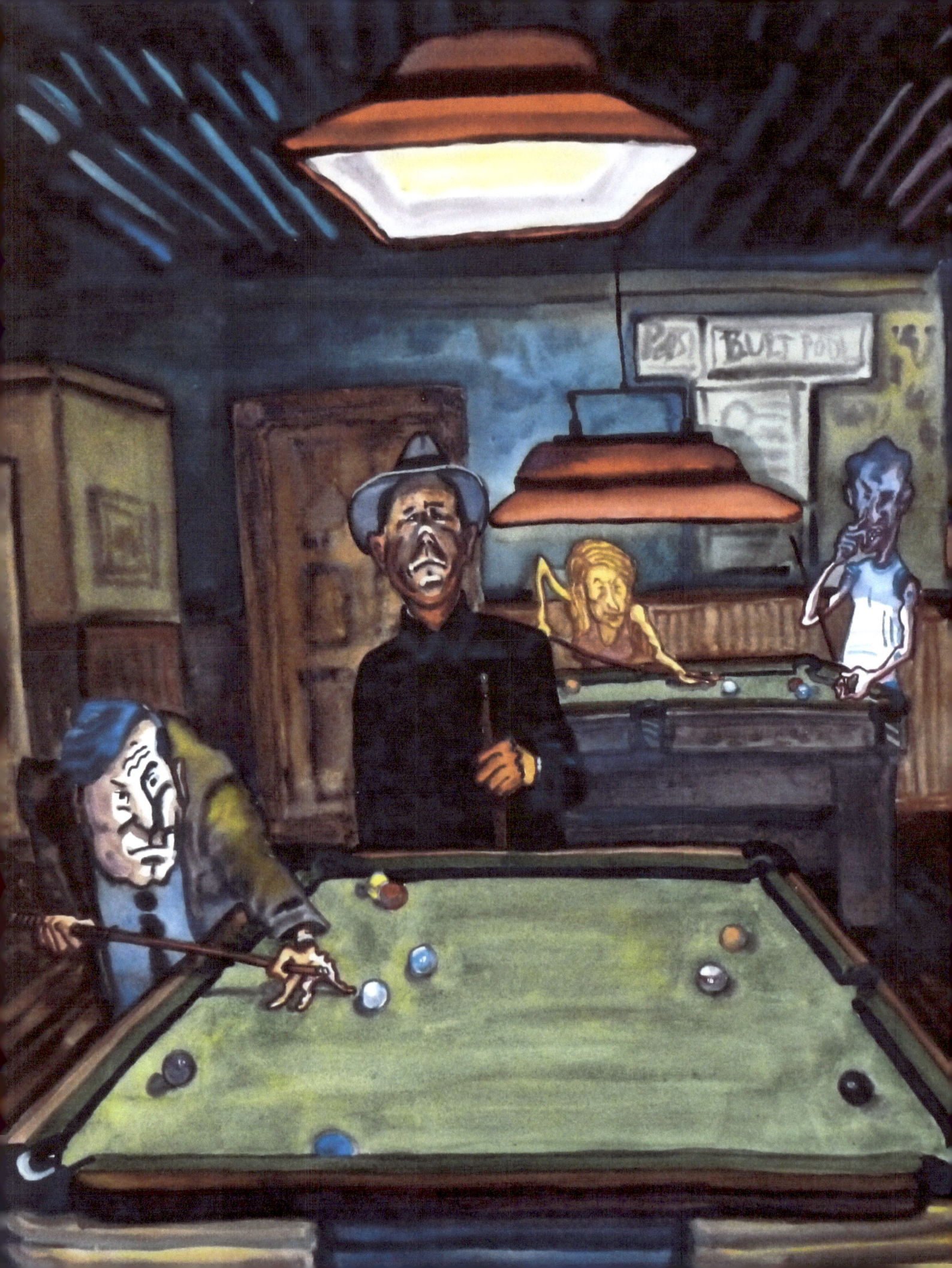

A Lot More About Painting

The following are understandings about painting that you are going to want to be very familiar with.

Some of what follows are big understandings. They take time and practice to learn. Subjects like linear perspective and creating the illusion of three dimension are often covered as part of semester-long college art classes. They will be covered only lightly in this book.

The Big Understandings

Mechanical 'Things'

There are **art** things that happen when you paint and there are **mechanical** things. The parts of painting that I, as a teacher, most want to help you with are the mechanical things. *Mechanical things* in painting means *how the painting marks you make work when you put them on the paper*. What do they do? Mechanical things are teachable. The art part of painting is less so.

Mastering **mechanical** techniques will include, among others, the following:

- Learning perspective that is good enough. It doesn't have to be great.
- Learning to see the different values. **Values,** as I have said, are the darks and lights you see. You will need to understand what it means to *push the values*. You make your darks darker and your lights lighter. There is a section in this book on value.
- How to make images that appear to advance or recede on the paper. This creates the illusion of depth.
- How to mix colors and quiet down colors.

The **art** in a painting includes what you choose to paint, the composition of the painting, and the the energy of your hands putting paint on paper.

I talk about art a lot, but prefer to leave the doing of it up to you, where it belongs.

Positive and Negative

In a painting there are the objects such as people, houses, trees, and so on; in other words, the *things* you draw or paint. In painting, these objects are considered the **positive.** The positive might be thought of as the things you can touch.

Then there is the *space* between objects. This is called the **negative** or the *negative space*. You can see space, but you can't touch it.

When you are drawing or painting, the positive and the negative have the **same** importance. They **both** need study and consideration.

Let's think of a face. There are the features – eyes, eye brows, nose, and mouth. These can be considered the *positive* objects of the face. When doing a portrait, each of these must be carefully drawn.

That is only half of the task. These features also have to be placed properly on the face. Good placement is achieved by studying the *spaces between* the features: between the two eyes, between the eyes and the brows, between the nose and the mouth. These areas are called *negative* spaces.

Equal consideration of the positive - the objects, and the negative - the space between the things - is one of the keys to good drawing. Good drawing is a big part of good painting.

Negative space is a big understanding. Life is full of empty spaces. These *nothings*, **no-things,** help make sense of things. One example is language. Language would make no sense without the spaces, the negative, between the positive words and sentences. **The negative helps make the positive useful.**

Another, opposite example is architecture. The walls, ceilings and floors are solid, positive things. They form rooms by enclosing space, the negative. That makes the space usable. **The positive helps the negative become useful.**

Artists of all mediums must acknowledge and understand the importance of the positive and the negative. The objects, or events of the world, and the spaces, or time between and around them, are part of *everything*.

The events, the positive, get all the attention. Without the organizing power of the negative, events, things, would be one big indecipherable jumble.

Warm vs. Cool

There are warm colors, the reds, oranges and most yellows. The warm colors can be understood as the colors of fire. The cool colors are most blues, many greens and some purples. The cool colors are not part of fire.

Warm colors tend to *advance* towards the viewer. They are energetic, emotional, and often inviting. The cool colors tend to *recede* into the painting, seem further away. They are usually quieter, calmer, and less emotional that the warm colors.

Warm and cool colors are more fully covered in the section of this book on color.

The words "warm" and "cool" can also reflect their other meanings in artwork.

A painting can be inviting, soft or emotive, and have a presence that comes towards you. This might be considered a *warm* painting. A warm painting is like a warm person.

A painting may also be quiet, distant, geometric, intellectual or unemotional. These attributes might be considered a cool painting. A cool person is thought of as unperturbed.

Creating or Denying Three-Dimensional Space

Watercolor paper is white and flat. It has no dimension. If you want what you are painting to have an illusion of three dimensions, there are things you need to learn.

A couple of easy examples are *size* and *overlap*. Perhaps you paint two cars in a painting. You make one car larger and the other car much smaller. The viewer will interpret this as the bigger car being nearer, and the smaller one further away. This is not magic. It is how people see things and interpret them every day.

If one object in a painting is in front of another, the object that *overlaps* the other is seen and understood as being the one in front.

There are other tools to help create the illusion of depth. They include, among others, perspective and atmospheric perspective. Both of these skills are talked of next and need to be studied and practiced.

The tools that create dimension have been part of art for centuries. It is not hard to find information on them. I have mentioned the ones I think are most important. There are a few others.

Look at the world around you. It looks three dimensional. Look at art work to see how these dimensional tools are used to give flat paintings the illusion of depth. Practice them. Incorporate them in your paintings if and when needed.

For the last 50 or 60 years, many artists have worked on flattening paintings, denying the illusion of dimension. That's just a matter of not doing what I am explaining.

All paintings start out flat. The artists who want to work flat make the choice to keep them that way.

Linear Perspective

Linear perspective is the very rigid understanding of how objects visually appear to get smaller as they recede from you. It is an exact study. As a painter you need to get *comfortable* with perspective. **You do not have to be perfect at it.**

Taking a class is very helpful in learning perspective. It takes a while. It can be fun to learn. It can be frustrating. There are books on it. I am not going to cover it in this one.

Atmospheric Perspective

Understanding atmospheric perspective is another way to create the feeling of space in a painting.

Atmospheric perspective in art is what appears to happen to objects **when they are looked at, from a distance, through a lot of atmosphere.** Looking through a lot of atmosphere, in art, makes the world look slightly foggy, soft and fuzzy, and a little blue.

Atmospheric perspective has simple rules. If the artist wants something to appear distant, to *recede* in the painting, like a mountain range, there is a way to do it. Make the mountains *softly defined or less sharp (fuzzy)*. Also *use less contrast (small changes of dark and light), and make them paler and bluer*. The song line "purple mountain majesties" talks of this. Mountains aren't purple (a bluish color). When mountains are far away they do appear bluer. The bluing and softening of distant objects is often easy to see if you look for it.

If some part of the painting needs to appear closer, make it *high in contrast (dark darks and light lights), crisp, (sharply defined), and use warmer colors (red, yellow, etc.).* Objects thus painted will appear to **advance** towards the viewer of the painting.

Take time to look at paintings and see how artists use these much used, and sometimes shamelessly used, *atmospheric perspective* tools.

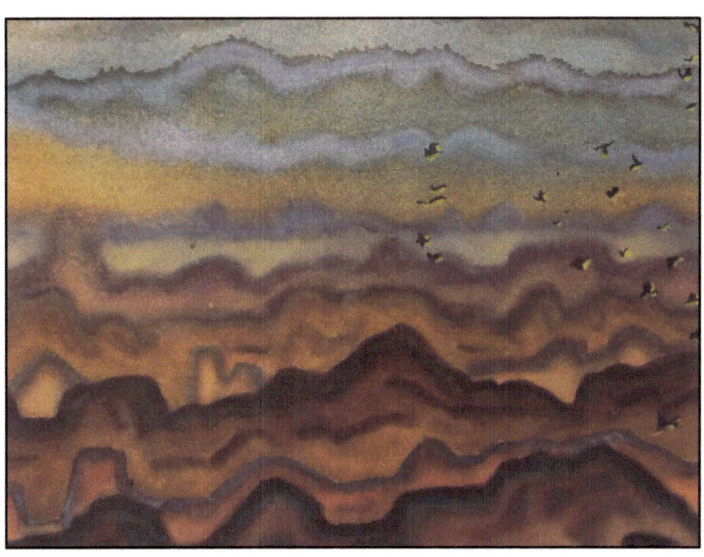

These perspective and dimensional tools work to create the illusion of depth because it is how we see things.

The artist makes the flat painting look like the world we see. If it is done well, the illusion of three dimensions happens.

Mixing Colors

Learning to mix colors in order to get variations on the colors that come in the paint tubes is something you will want to get good at. It comes with practice.

As you get better at painting, you will become more selective in your use of color. Color does powerful, *mostly emotional*, things to a painting. You will want to be at least partly in charge of what happens.

Some teachers teach beginners to mix *all* the colors from a *few* colors. This might be helpful. You *do* need to know how to mix colors.

I don't teach it that way. In the color section of this book, I describe what I think are the important things to know about mixing colors.

I like to buy and use a lot of different paint colors. I do this for a couple of reasons.

First, watercolor paints, unlike other paint mediums, don't all work alike. They work like the different materials they are made from. They have many different qualities as explained earlier. I keep about 60 tubes of different colors in the studio.

Second, having a lot of paints to use is visually exciting and more fun than grinding away with three or four colors.

Ways to Work the Painting

*Although a watercolor painting doesn't like a lot of fussing while it is in process, it can be worked on. Areas of the painting can be removed and then repainted. Colors can be altered. Major changes are possible when you learn how. The following are a few things that will help you **work** with watercolors.*

Glazing

Glazing is a useful watercolor technique. To glaze, you use a thin watery *wash* of a *transparent* color. Glazing is done quickly. A glaze is washed over a *bone dry* area of a painting. The painting must be *fully dry.* You need to work quickly, or the wet wash, *the glaze,* will rewet the colors under it. They will mix together and may get messy.

Glazing is used to slightly alter the color that is glazed over. A glaze, using a red over an area of yellow, will turn the yellow into an orange color. A yellow glaze over an area of blue will turn the blue to a green.

Glazing can be used to harmonize the colors in a painting. A glaze of orange can change the emotional quality of a whole painting. When all the warm and cool colors of a painting are glazed with a warm color, like orange, all the colors of the painting are made a little warmer. The painting might become easier to look at, less harsh, more inviting.

Glazing is not hard to do, but needs to be practiced before you try it on a painting.

Lifting

Learning to "lift" paint off the paper is a great tool for working a painting. I use it all the time. It helps me correct what's happening as I am painting. Lifting was talked about briefly in the **how to paint section.** I'm repeating myself here, but I think lifting deserves its own section.

The brush is used like a mop. A *damp, not wet* brush will sop up, or lift, wet paint off the paper. If an area you want to correct is not wet enough, *add water, rub the water around a little,* then lift it, mop it off.

Lifting is also used to correct *dried* areas that you don't like. The dry area is gently but thoroughly rewet with water and a brush to loosen the paint. The colors in error are lifted off the page with the dampened brush. When the brush is filled, squeeze it out and it will mop up more.

With watercolors it is hard to paint over other paint. Mopping off a layer of paint is one good way to prepare the painting to be corrected.

There are good pictures of this in the "Lincoln" painting section later in this book.

Scrubbing

If lifting with a brush doesn't get enough paint off the paper, it can be often be scrubbed off.

Wet well the area you want to remove. Use a *soft tooth brush, a flat watercolor brush,* or *soft bristle paint brush* and gently scrub the paint you want to remove. Blot once or twice with a paper towel. It usually will come off pretty well.

Don't repeatedly dab at the paper to remove the paint. That may push the paint into the paper fibers. It won't come out if that happens.

The paper surface will be changed where you have scrubbed. The paper fibers will be roughed up a little. It will take paint okay, but differently than when you started.

Other Helpful Things to Know About Painting

What follows, in no particular order, are more short writings that may help you further understand painting.

Composition

I know little about composition, and have made a choice as a teacher, not to teach it. *Composition is about how you design a painting.* There are no rules of composition that I know of that can't be broken. There are no compositional rules that haven't been broken.

There are a few parts of making a painting that I don't think should be taught. How you design your paintings is one of them. It is one of those **art** things. Beginners flounder a little when they are not given "rights and wrongs" about painting. There is nothing wrong with floundering. It can be a good way to learn.

When I started painting, I looked at a ton of paintings. I did this to absorb what paintings are and what they look like. This helped me. I talk about *what a painting is* later in this book.

Techniques

You can think of what I call a "technique" in painting as a short cut. A way, possibly, of doing sometime special with the brush to make marks that look like leaves or branches of a tree. Techniques are commonly shown on TV painting shows. They can look pretty good. Techniques might be fun, clever, and even helpful for a while, but they are *very* limiting.

My students often ask me to show them how to paint a tree. I don't know how to paint **a** tree. A tree isn't one thing. There are young trees, old trees, trees in the morning light, trees silhouetted at dusk, healthy trees, dying trees, trees with leaves, trees with needles, and on and on. How do you paint **a** tree? I don't know.

Good painting comes from hard-won skills. Skills earned are not limited. Skillful painters can figure out how to paint anything. An artist looks at a tree, sees what is happening visually, and paints it as it is.

Don't Lose the Big for the Little

This is another of my sound bites. It means don't lose track of big things that are happening in a painting when you are painting the little things.

Let me give an example. You are painting a night scene. Night and darkness are the **big things** that are happening. All the details of the painting, cars, buildings, people are the **small things.** To be a successful night painting, it better look like night. It better be pretty dark. The details are less important.

Losing the big for the little is a common mistake painters make. There is more on this later.

Painting Light

Where light and dark meet, the light is lighter and the dark is darker. Take a look, in daylight, out a window. Even if the sash, the wood around the window, in reality is painted white, you will see that the sash appears pretty dark. It's darkest right next to the light from the outside.

When you paint a window with light coming through it, you can't make the sash white even though it is. To a painter, it has to be painted a dark color because that is how it appears. All the walls around the window have to be painted fairly dark also. This will make it look like the window is bright.

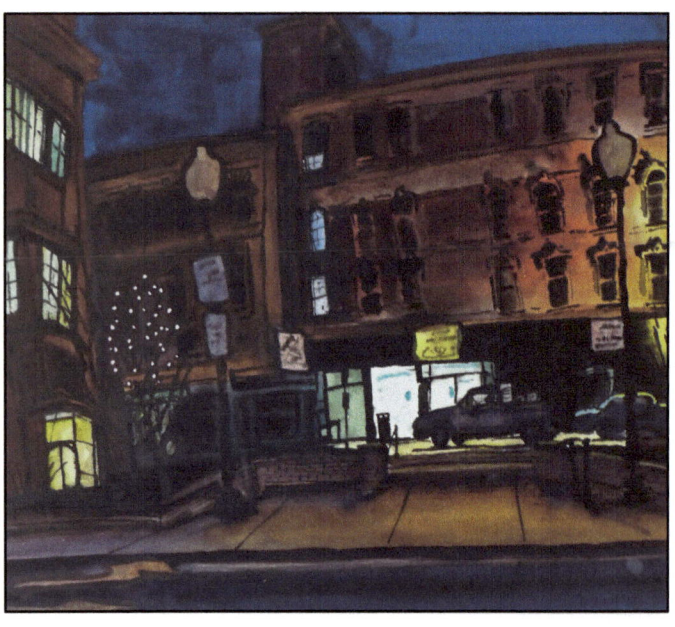

If you need something to look bright in a painting, the sun, a streetlight, and so on, you have to darken everything around it. That will make the lighted area look brighter.

I find some things feel right when working on a painting, and some things seem wrong. As I paint, I change the things that seem wrong.

If it's Wrong, Change it

One of my sound bites in painting class is, **" If it's wrong, change it. Change it until it's not wrong anymore."** When there is nothing wrong with the painting, you are done.

This may seem pretty simplistic. When you are painting, you make a zillion small or large choices before you are finished. The choices are personal and subjective. If something seems, *to you*, wrong, change it. This leads you to how you set up a painting and how you paint. **Trust yourself.** *No one else really cares or knows any better.* **It is your painting.**

Stretching the Paper

One way watercolor painters try to gain some control of what they are doing is to stretch the paper. The control comes because this flattens the painting surface.

The paper is soaked, sometimes in the bathtub. When it is thoroughly wet and fully expanded, it is taped with gummed tape to a flat surface. It then dries and shrinks. When dry, it is a tight, flat, promising surface.

Working carefully and fairly dryly, stretched paper does add some control to the painting process. Unstretched paper usually gets bumpy as you paint. A stretched surface will also buckle if it gets too wet.

I don't stretch my paper. I don't like doing those kinds of things. I'm comfortable being only partly in control. It fits how I paint. I don't mind painting on the bumps of buckled paper.

When you use water when you paint, the paper will stretch and buckle where it is wet. It'll make hills and valleys to paint on. It's not a big problem. It is something to get used to. I don't even think about it any more. It is just part of the process.

Flattening Paper

When a painting is finished, it is almost always not flat. The surface will have bumps even when dry. My technique for dealing with this is to just lay them in a pile of paintings. After a while they will flatten.

Framing shops often have devises to flatten artwork.

Another way to flatten watercolors is to iron them. They are cotton after all. Flip the painting over and wet it a little on the back. Iron out the bumps. It works pretty well.

There are other ways if you do a little research.

Wall Presence

Paintings are *decorative objects.* They live on walls. They should have what I call *wall presence.* Stop occasionally, when you are working. Put the painting up on a wall and look at it from a small distance. Does all that wonderful detail work you did when working up close, still work from ten feet away?

How does the energy of the painting feel on the wall? Is it too busy, too bold, too quiet, or too detailed? Good wall presence is a factor in good paintings. *Paintings should look good on walls.*

Watercolors have less of a presence on a wall than oil paintings. Oil paintings are more powerful. This is good and bad. Good oil paintings can look very good. Bad oil paintings can look very bad.

Watercolors are quiet on the wall. I think, though, that watercolors are very musical.

The Studio

Watercolor painting is not a real messy process. It cleans up easily with a little water. It can be done anywhere. If your interest is strong and you want to get good, it helps to have a place to call *the studio*; your own safe space to paint and to keep all your stuff.

There are a few things a studio needs. It needs a good work table with plenty of room and walls to pin up your work so you can see what you are doing. Sheet-rocked walls works fine if you don't mind the little holes the pins put in it. A studio also needs good day light and artificial light.

Workable Lighting

When watercolors are wet and in process, they will glisten and reflect light. The brightness of the reflections makes it impossible to see what you are doing.

Work with your artificial lighting until it just illuminates what you are doing. It shouldn't cast a shadow of your hand on the painting. It shouldn't cause reflections on the work. It is never easy to get your light just right.

For natural light, north windows are best. You want *indirect* light. Direct sunlight is too much light. It is too much light and too much shadow. Direct sunlight makes it really hard to see anything in a studio.

Direct sunlight can cause some paint colors to bleach out, the same way the sun bleaches fabric.

Adjust what you have for light, until the illumination is helpful.

When I look at paintings from a while ago, five or six years maybe, I don't know how they were done. How I paint has changed over time. I can do more with paint now.
As you learn about painting, things change. Change is fine. Change is part of the process.

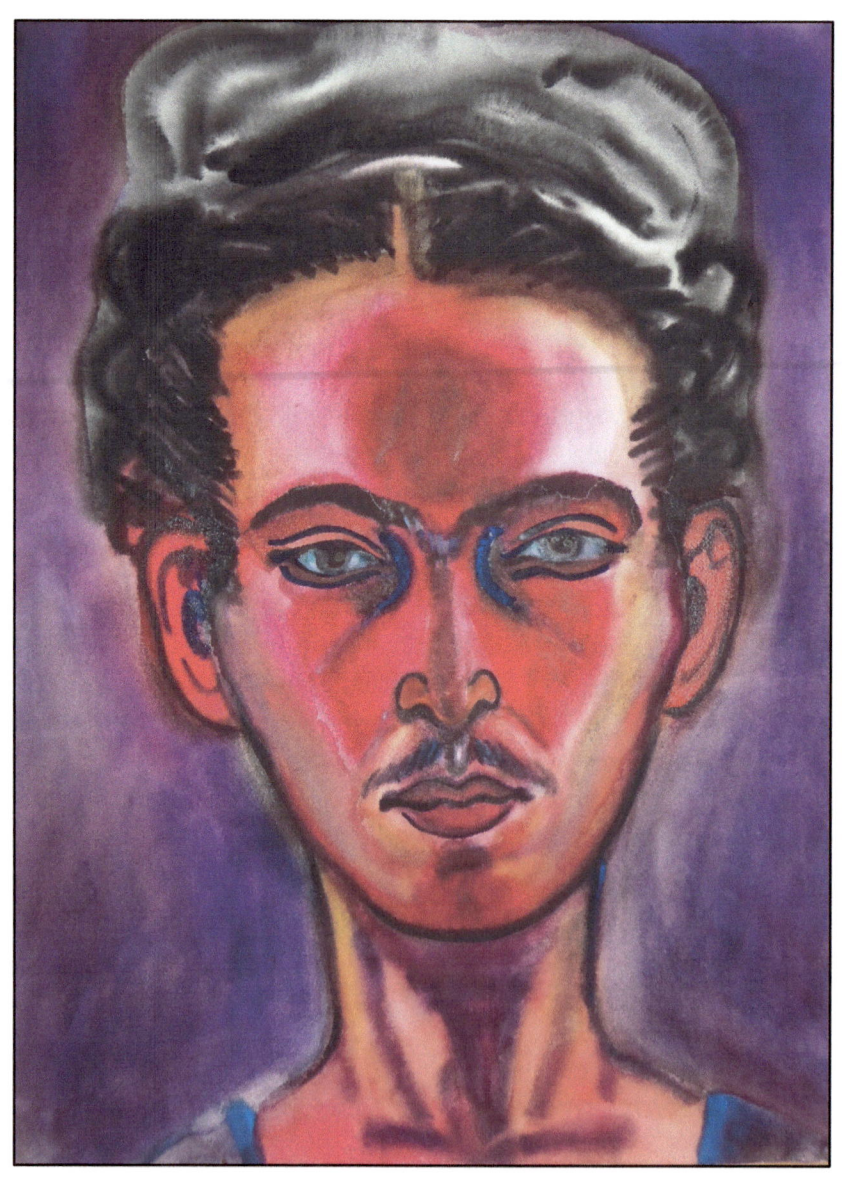

Frida then

There is making a picture, which is a dominantly mental process. Then there is painting, which is a physical process. The first comes from your mind, which is not very trustworthy. The second, painting, comes from your body. Your body can't lie. Allow some of the physical into the painting.

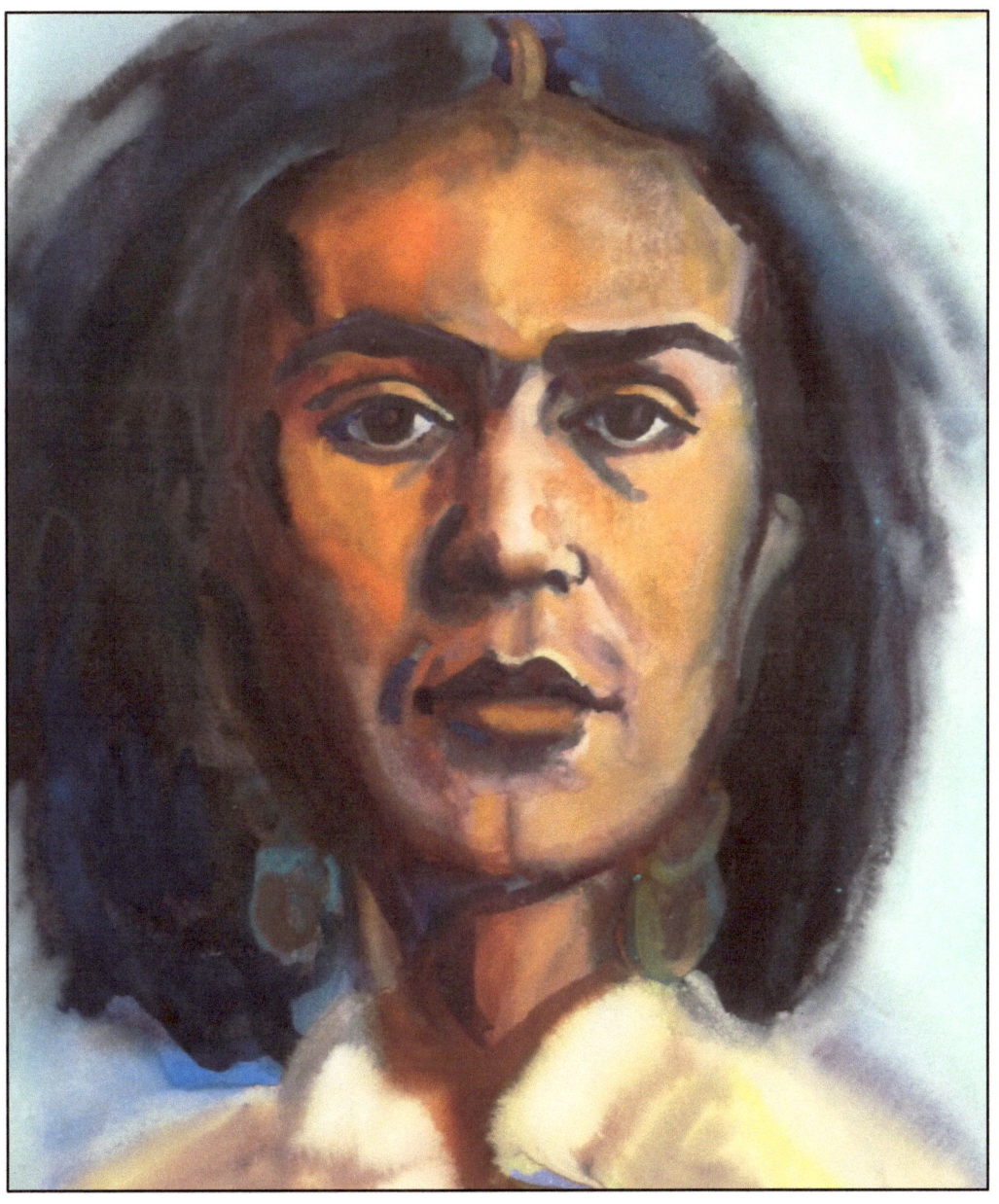

Frida now

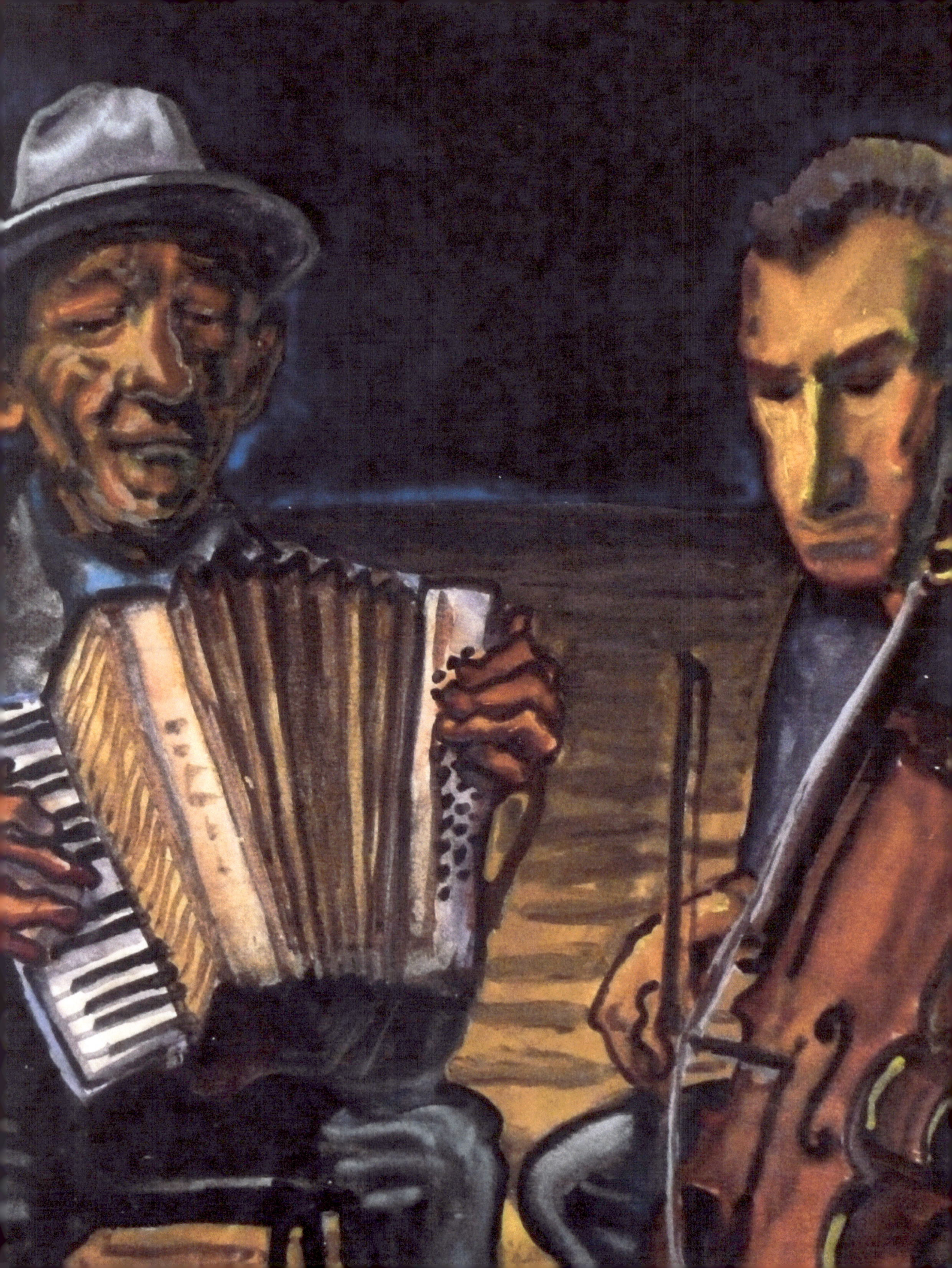

What to Paint

*After you finish with art school, or private classes, or you have just started painting, you have figure out for yourself **what to paint**. There are no more assignments. If you are expecting to do a thousand or more paintings, that is a lot of figuring. There are a number of ways to approach what to paint.*

Copying

In the beginning, if you are pursuing some form of realism, copying other artists' paintings is not a bad idea. Most people like to do it. Some schools teach classes doing just that. It is fairly stress free. Everything is right there in front of you. *You just need to make what you paint look like what you are copying.* It gives the beginning artist a chance to learn how to paint without having to be concerned with ideas and composition.

Working from other artists' good artwork also helps the beginner learn what art looks like. The paintings you make this way are not fully your own, but it is, and always has been, a worthwhile and common practice.

Working From Photos

It is okay to work from photos but be aware that photos are different than paintings. Copying a photograph is more suspect.

Cameras and humans see the world differently. Cameras **record** what they are pointed at. They do it with only *one* eye, the lens.

Humans **respond** to what they are looking at. They see things with *two* eyes. Because of this, photographic images can be quite different from what humans actually see.

We read photographs easily, but they are not our reality. They are photo reality. In picturing human reality, photos are pretty limited. Among many other things, photos sharpen up a soft round world, and they flatten and distort space.

Take a walk on a downtown street. As a human, you are responding to everything that's happening. That includes the store windows, people, cars, the unevenness of the sidewalk, litter, colors, smells, parking meters, telephone wires, textures, etc. While on your walk, take a moment to take a photo of where you are and look at it. You will see that the camera is seeing a very different scene from what you are experiencing. It is much emptier. It's okay to work with photographic images, as long as you are aware of their limitations.

Photos are camera things. Paintings are human things. Paintings can come closer to expressing what humans experience.

*Try not to get stuck copying photos for your art. Even your own photos are still photos. Don't trust them. **Paintings made from photos often look like photos, not paintings.** They are different.*

Let photographers turn their photographs into art, which they do very well.

En Plein Air

Many artists work *en plein air*. En plein air is a French expression that means painting outside in the open air. Plein air artists go outside, find something to paint, and they paint it.

Working en plein air can be quite a challenge. The air is moving, people might be around and interested, bugs are always around, cars come and go, the ocean tide changes, boats floating one way turn around and float the other way.

The sun moves quickly across the sky. Besides a chance of causing a sunburn, the sunlight and shadows keep moving. The plein air artist has about three hours maximum to work before the light on everything being painted changes too much. When the light on a scene changes, the whole scene looks different.

Creating plein air paintings is a busy, even frantic endeavor. They require all of the artist's attention and skill for a very short time.

I have done hundreds of plein air paintings. I started doing them when I started painting. It's a great way to force yourself to get something on the paper quickly without a lot of unnecessary judgement.

The first thing beginning artists who want to try plein air painting need is a comfortable place to set up and work. Perhaps this would be a shaded, secluded spot. Then, look around and see what there is to paint. There is always something to paint. I tell my students this because *how you paint is as important, or more so, than what you paint.*

Studio Work

After dealing with the challenges of painting outside, staying in the studio to work is very nice. It does take a different approach, though, when choosing what to paint.

For me, moving to the studio was a process. At first, I would paint only outside en plein aire. I didn't trust photos. Later, I would go outside and make a drawing on the watercolor paper and take photos of the scene. The drawing was to set up the scene on the paper. The photos were to record what was in the scene. Returning to the studio, I would put it all together and make the painting.

Presently I paint mostly in the studio. I often use photos I've taken, or images taken off the internet. I always compose the pictures myself. I don't trust how cameras set things up. The images I use are only to help me figure out what things look like. For example, what does a crow in flight look like or a 1964 cadillac?

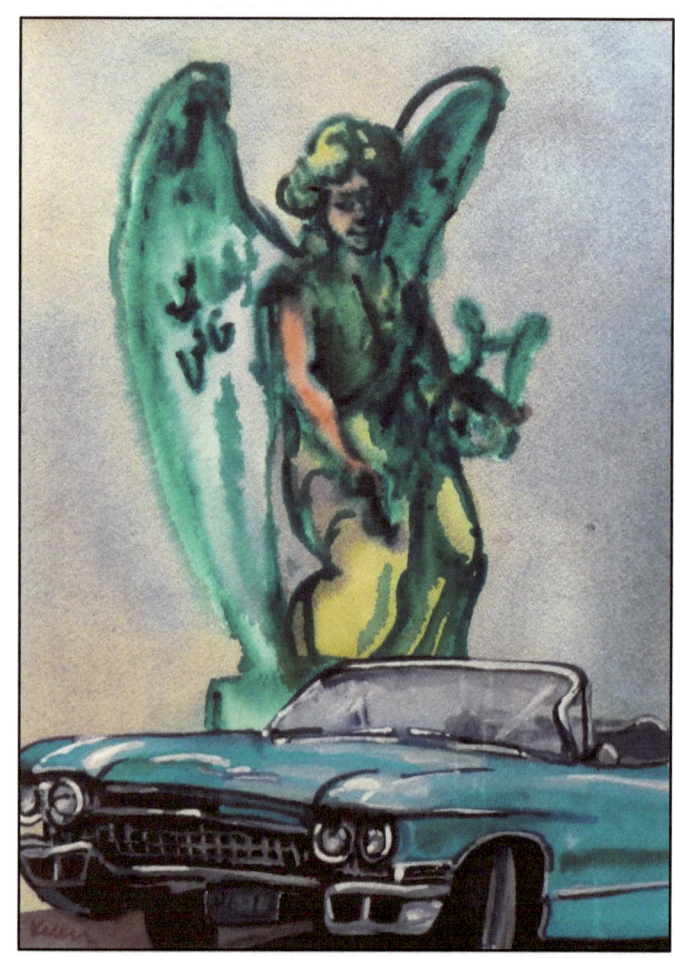

Still Lifes

Still lifes are a lovely thing to paint in the studio. They make still, quiet paintings. The key to good still lifes is the set up and good lighting. A well set up still life is enjoyable to paint. It allows you to take your time. It doesn't keep changing.

Some artists could, and do, make a career of painting them. Most artists do some still lifes.

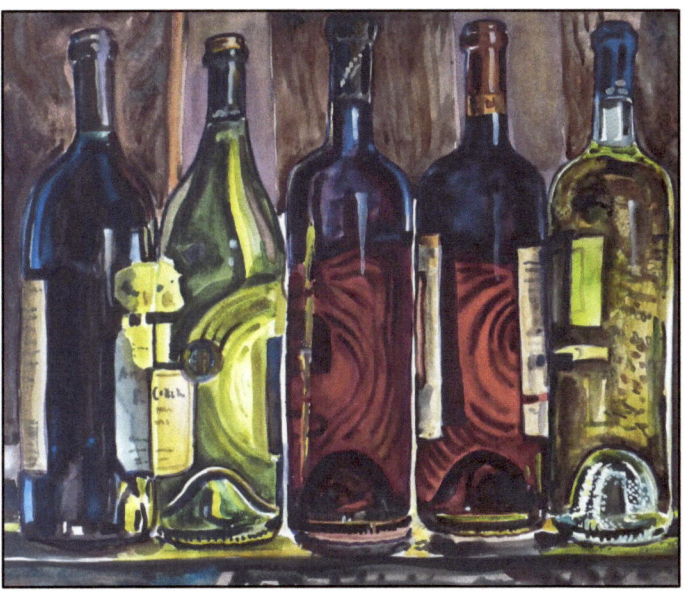

Painting Difficult Things

There are many things that you might want to paint that are quite difficult to draw, such as trees, horses, and children. These challenging parts of the world need a lot of practice to learn to draw well. Achieving some mastery with these difficult things is very rewarding. Mastery comes from repetition.

Painting People

Painting people is usually studio work. People move around a lot when you try to draw them outside.

It takes a strong commitment to learn to paint human figures. It is a challenge. It can't really be taught. Learning to do it just takes a lot of practice.

The human body is very complex and does many things. When you draw it enough, the knowledge gets into your body. Body knowledge in art helps your hand move and make the right marks.

Even when you are pretty good at drawing the figure, finding photos of people in the positions you want to paint them in is very helpful. I often google images like "man holding coffee cup."

In any painting with people in it, the people will strongly draw the attention of the viewer. For this reason, when I put people in a painting I always paint them early in the process. If they are poorly done, nobody who later looks at the painting will ever see anything else.

Draw people, draw people, draw people. It's the only way to learn to paint people.

In most communities there are figure drawing sessions you can join. These can be very helpful. Drawing living nude human bodies is almost spiritual. It engages the artist's empathy. Do as much of it as you can. Do it even if you want to paint abstract paintings.

The Human Face

Drawing and painting *human faces* is teachable and not too hard. It does take time to cover it as a teacher. My next book will be on the human face.

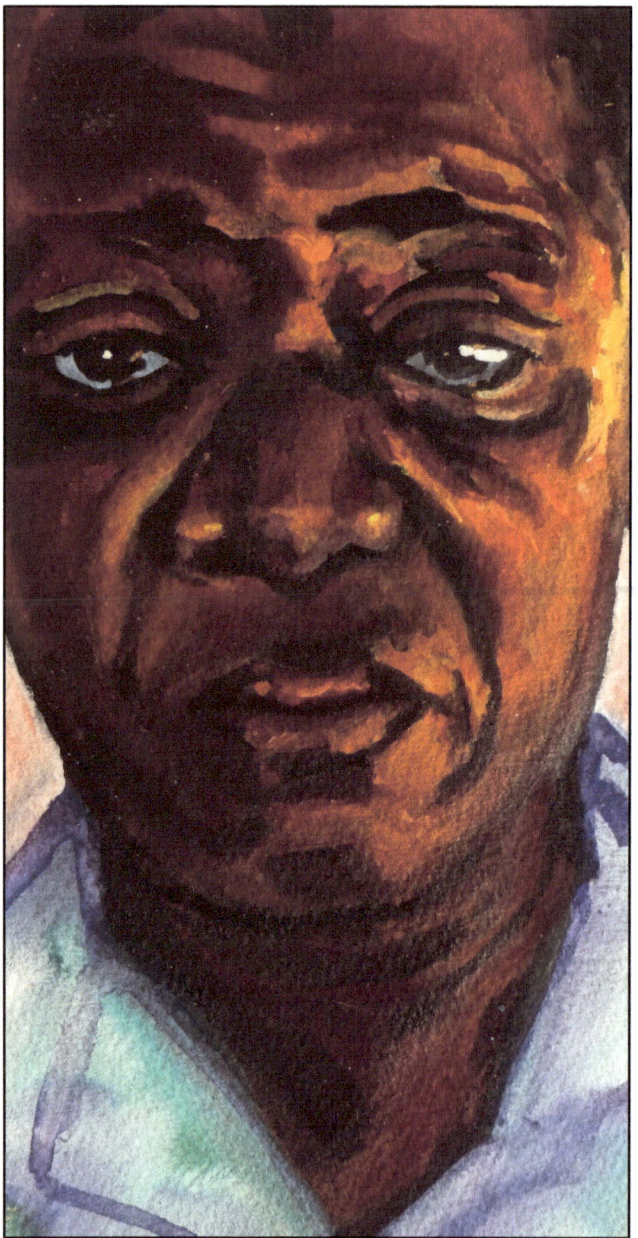

Louis Armstrong

Self-Portraits

I do a self-portrait about every year or so. It's very good practice. I often start with a self-portrait when I am transitioning back to painting after not painting for some time. It's a good way to start painting again when you haven't got a thought in your head about what to paint. You can always paint yourself.

There are a few self-portraits in this book.

Painting the Night and the Weather

I have found that people love and react strongly to night paintings. Night paintings are vibrant on the wall, with dark colors and sparkling lights.

The weather is also always interesting to paint. Wind, rain, and snow add a look to a painting that deepens the viewer's experience.

Adding weather or night to a painting is studio work. Figure it out. It can be worthwhile and fun.

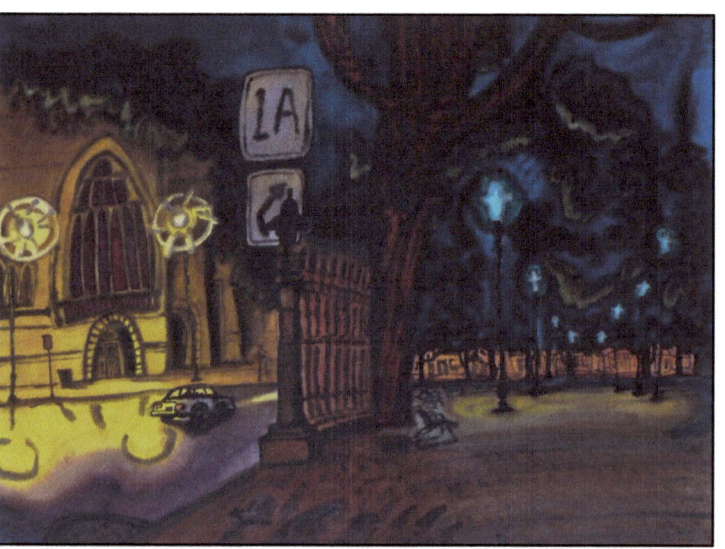

Salem Witch Museum

Abstract, or Non-Objective Work

Abstract work in painting is like music without words. It makes sense in its own way.

Abstract paintings, also called non-objective paintings, are paintings that are not based on realism. It is an area I'm finding more interesting as I grow older. It is a very wide open realm to explore. It is, by its nature, studio work. It takes commitment and time to develop something out of nothing.

There are many things that can be explored visually that don't need recognizable images. Color, heartbeats, heaven, darkness, strength, fear, math, clarity, texture, or no topic at all, might be some.

Music composers do fine without words. Many painters do fine without recognizable images. There are many ways to proceed.

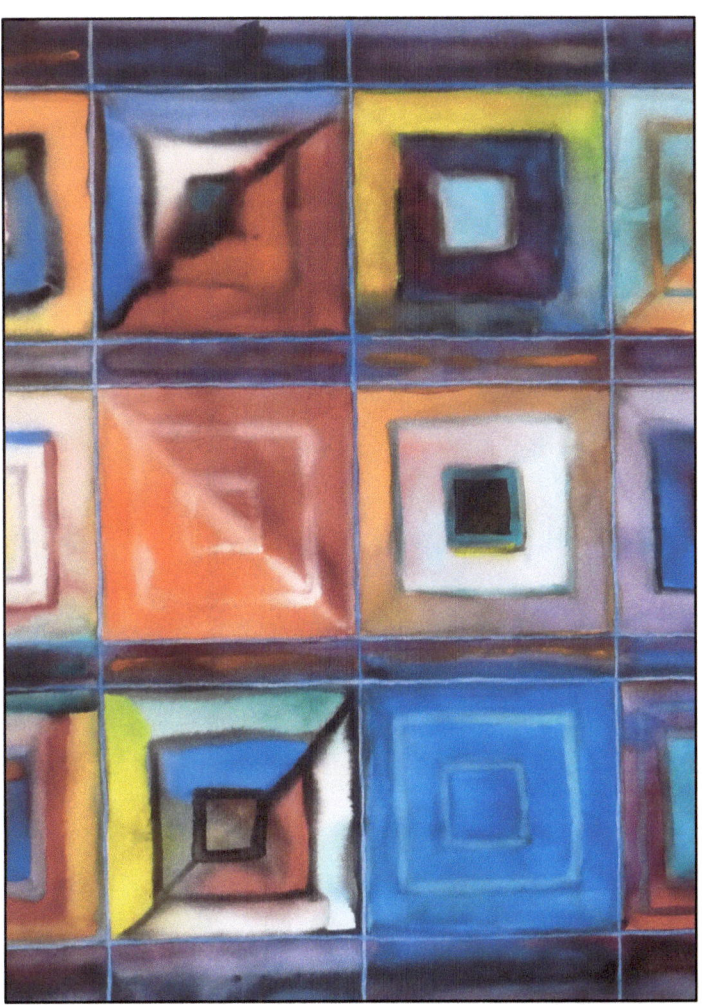

Ideas, Inspiration

Good paintings are rarely based on an *idea* alone.

There is often something that looks like an idea in a painting. "*Man screaming on a bridge,*" might be an example. A painting does start with something. Sometimes it is an idea. Good ideas may lead to good paintings and they might not.

Not all paintings need ideas to be made. A painting can just as easily start with nothing. The artist just starts making marks. The painting develops from that.

Inspiration is thought of as having something to do with artists and paintings. "*The artist was inspired.*" Inspiration is wonderful. **It does happen.** It can lead to inspired paintings. An inspired painting is one that seems to paint itself. It feels like everything just falls into place as you work.

Inspiration is a gift. The only problem is that you may have to wait around a long time for it to come along.

Ideas, *ways to proceed,* will come to you when you are working, actively making paintings. One painting often leads to the next painting. You will discover something in a painting that is interesting. That leads to the next painting. This in turn can lead to a number of paintings.

When you get what feels like a usable idea, *follow it for a while*. Let it develop painting to painting. It often takes a number of paintings for something really good to happen. Edward Munch painted four versions of "The Scream."

You will know when the idea runs out of energy.

The act of following one painting with the next painting is a very artistic process. Most artists do just this. If you want to do a lot of art work, do your best to keep something going in the studio.

Geniuses: This is Important

Artists, even geniuses, don't do one great masterpiece, then when that one is done, do the next great masterpiece. It does not happen that way.

I've heard it said that great artists are known for a dozen paintings. That's twelve paintings out of a thousand or thousands that were made. Think about it. Can you name twelve different works by Van Gogh? And he is easy.

The point that I am making here is don't put pressure on each painting to be great or even good. ***It's just a painting***. You can do the painting again if it deserves it.

There will be many more paintings. If you do enough, some will be good, and some may even be very good.

It's All the Same

No matter whether you paint landscapes, still lifes, abstracts, etc., it's really all the same process. Painting is painting. Paint what you want to paint.

If you want to get good at painting, it is important just to paint. Find a way to keep going. Everything you achieve will follow that.

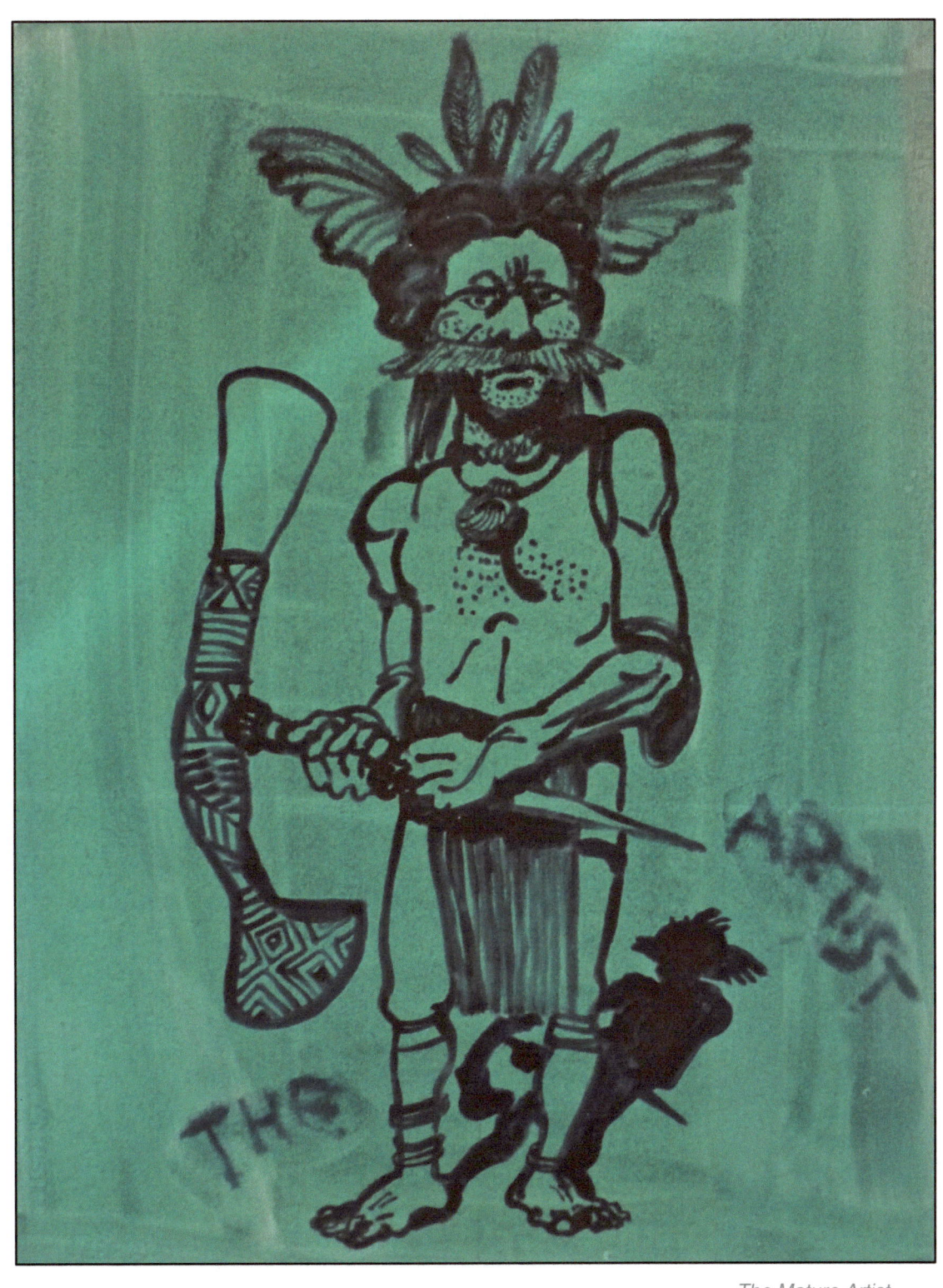

The Mature Artist

A person can learn to paint fairly quickly, especially with watercolors. When a person learns to not be afraid of, and work with, the water part of watercolor, good usable paintings follow in a short time. To get better at painting requires more and more from the artist. This goes on as long as you paint.

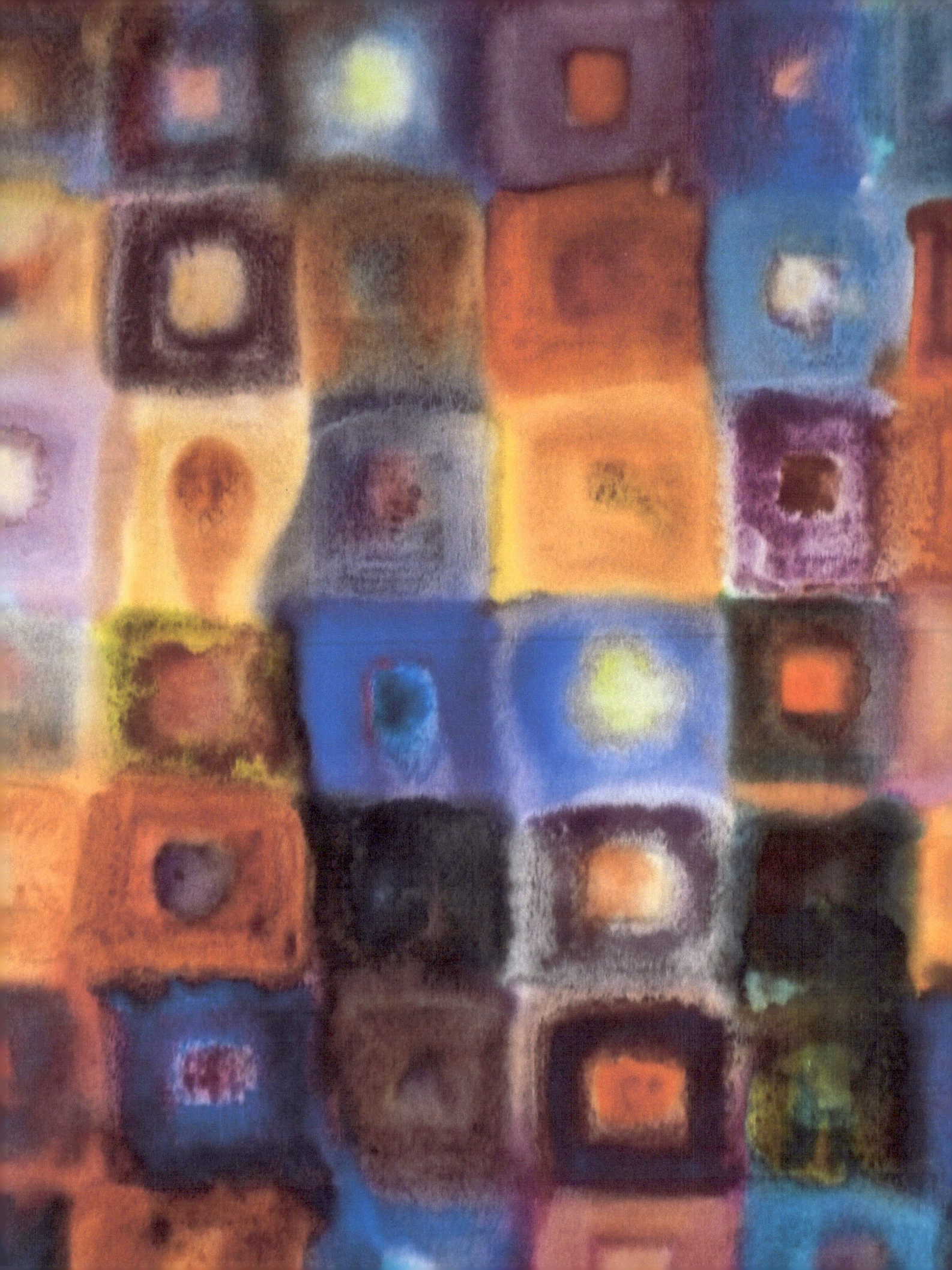

Color

Color is the music in a painting. It helps set the emotion in the work.

Colors and music are very similar. They both come at us in waves. The ears are our receptors for music. Our eyes receive the colors. Music affects us emotionally and so do colors.

Individual Colors and Emotion

Let's look at colors as emotional entities.

There are many possible variations of any color. For instance, a green can have a lot of yellow in it and become chartreuse. A green could also have a lot of blue in it and become a blue green or green turquoise.

It is easy to find charts on the emotional effects of color. Because of the color variations mentioned above, these charts are only somewhat useful, albeit fun.

Let me give you my thoughts on individual colors, keeping it simple.

YELLOW. Yellow reflects the most light of any color, except white. It is highly attractive. It can feel aggressive or happy. Yellow comes out at, or *advances,* toward the viewer. Yellow is often used in warning signs because of these properties.

ORANGE. I love orange. It is always warm and inviting. I keep two or three oranges on my pallet at all times. When orange is mixed with blues or greens, it makes them warmer. Blues and greens can feel cold in a painting. The color orange is capable of warming up a whole painting when used as a glaze.

RED. Red is said to be the most material, or worldly of colors. It is not subtle. It has strength. It *advances* toward the viewer.

Red gets a lot of attention. Babies react strongly to red. It is also used in warning signs.

Cars that are red supposedly say "red" things about the owner. The color red is bold and brave and maybe a little angry.

BLUE. Blue is understood to be the deepest, most spiritual color. It seems to *recede* into the painting. It can be soothing.

Blue is a cool color. Emotionally it tends to create feelings of equanimity, tranquility, stillness, and distance.

GREEN. Green is a mixture of outward flowing (*advancing*) yellow and inward flowing (*receding*) blue. It stills these opposite energies and is a quiet, calming color. Greens comfort us. When living things in the world are green, they are getting enough water, light, and nourishment.

Hospital rooms are painted pale green, "hospital green," in order to create a calm atmosphere.

PURPLE. Purple can be regal. Purple robes are worn by people in the highest places, like popes and kings.

Purples can be delicate. Purples and violets are always interesting colors. Being both warm and cool by nature, they fill a neutral color area for an artist. I use two on my pallet, warmer manganese violet and cooler ultramarine violet. I use them all the time. They feel a little like heaven to me. Purples can feel spiritual.

BROWN. Like the dirty orange colors that they are, browns are earthy and comforting. They are often made from colored dirts. They feel grounded.

BLACK. Black has formality and dignity. It has weight. It enhances other colors when used in a painting. Of course, it has darkness.

When black is mixed with a color, the color that results is called a **shade.** These shade colors tend to be somber.

WHITE. White symbolizes peace, illumination and innocence. White areas in a painting also enhance the other colors used.

When white is mixed with colors, the resulting colors are called **tints.** Tints are childlike, innocent, and sweet colors. People know them as *pastels.*

Mixing Color

Opposites

Colors are often presented in a circle called a **color wheel**. The main colors are red, yellow, and blue. These are called the *primaries.* Supposedly all other colors can be mixed from them.

The other three main colors on the wheel are green, orange, and purple. These are called the *secondaries.* They are mixed from the primaries. These six colors are arranged in a circle in this order: red, orange, yellow, green, blue and purple.

On the color wheel, the colors that are across from each other I call **opposites.** Red is across from, *opposite,* green. Blue is across from, *opposite,* orange. Purple is across from, *opposite,* yellow. This is important to know for two reasons.

First, **when opposites are placed next to each other, they enhance each other.** When blue is set next to orange, for instance, where the two colors meet, the blue will look more vibrant and so will the orange. They may seem to pop out at you and may even visually vibrate a little.

The old '60s psychedelic rock concert posters often used this color enhancing effect. Stripes of opposite colors would be put next to

each other throughout the poster. The result was a poster that seemed to pulsate with energy.

Much more useful is the second reason. **When opposites are mixed together, they neutralize each other.**

If you want to quiet down a green, (green paints almost always need some changing) add a little of it's opposite, red. The green will become quieter, less green, but still green. If you want to quiet down a red, add a little of it's opposite, green. The red will change and become a little more brown. The opposites blue and orange will do this to each other, as will purple and yellow.

Yellow is a good example of how useful this "opposite" understanding is for mixing colors. Yellow contaminates, changes, very easily. If the artist wants to quiet down a yellow and not change it to some other color, the only thing to add is a true, not a blueish, purple. If you add a blue to yellow it turns green. Red mixed with yellow turns the yellow to orange. Green added to yellow turns it to chartreuse. Adding a little of it's opposite, purple, turns a bright yellow into a quieter mustard yellow color.

There are a lot of lovely colors created when different amounts of yellow and purple are mixed. Try it, understanding that you need to add very little purple to the yellow to change it.

*The watercolor paints you buy come in a large array of colors. Finding exact opposites is not possible and not necessary. Keeping the **idea** of opposites in mind, try mixing colors and see what happens.*

Mixing Color: A Variety of Ways

The colors you buy in tubes or pans are in general pretty vivid. Except for certain things in a landscape like flowers, the natural world we look at is much more quietly colored. Artists must be able to mix colors. Understanding opposites, as I explained in the last section, is essential.

When mixing colors, there are usually a lot of ways to achieve the color you want. A brown, instance, can be mixed many ways. Red mixed with black will make a brown, and so will red mixed with green. Yellows and purples mixed together make some very nice browns. If you experiment with mixing three different colors together in order to get a brown, there are many combinations that will do it.

It would be silly to try and remember all the possible combinations of colors that, when mixed, make other colors. The possibilities may be close to infinite. Given time and experience, mixing the colors you want will become *intuitive*. You will find yourself just doing it.

Mixing colors is not hard. Many times the mix is quite obvious. Add a little red if you want the color to be redder. If the color seems too bright, add it's opposite or some black. The black will give the color some darkness and visual weight.

Mixing Transparent vs. Opaque Paints

When working with watercolor paints, it is important to keep in mind that not all colors mix easily and cleanly together. Most watercolor paint colors are transparent. Transparent colors usually mix well together.

Some watercolor paints are opaque. Mixing opaques colors together can get muddy. You will learn to spot opaque paint colors. They look like they have, and often do have, white paint mixed into them.

Mix away. *If you mix something that you don't like, don't use it*. Your particular method of mixing paint will become part of your process.

The Uses of Orange

I mix oranges with a lot of colors, especially greens. Greens, straight from the tube, are mostly awful. To make natural looking greens, orange (an almost opposite of green) mixed with the tube green paint helps a lot. When green leaves die, the green chlorophyll goes away and the leaves turn some shade of orange. The orange is already there. Try mixing in some orange when you use greens.

Tints and Shades

Tints and shades are valuable mixed color possibilities for the artist. Tints, as already stated, are made by mixing white with colors. Tints often feel light and youthful. When white is mixed with a color, it becomes opaque.

Shades are made by mixing black with colors. Shades of colors are somber and heavy. They are perfect for painting a murder scene. Mixing black with a color also makes it opaque.

Contamination

Yellow, orange, and white are colors that contaminate, change, easily with the addition of only a very small amount of another color. Almost no paint color mixes are 50 percent of this and 50 percent of that. Some paint colors are strong in tinting power; some are weak. Be sensitive to what happens when you mix colors. You will figure it out.

Some Exercises for Learning to Mix Color

There are a of couple good exercises which I use to help people learn to mix colors.

One is to look through a magazine and find interesting, odd, or subtle colors. Cut out small squares of these colors. Cut as many as you like. Tape them on a sheet of watercolor paper. Using the paint colors you have, work on mixing colors that match the cut-out squares colors.

You can try to remember how you got to certain colors, but as I've said, it's not important. Just mix the colors. *Mixing colors is about learning what colors do.* It's not about remembering formulas.

Here is another good exercise for mixing paints and developing your own color awareness.

Divide a sheet of watercolor paper into 100 or so spaces. Do that anyway you want. Squares are fine. Then fill each space, *mixing* colors for *each* space. Every color you use should be changed a little or a lot by mixing it with another color or colors. Work your way through the spaces one at a time. Allow your color sense to be intuitive; trust it. The results from this exercise are often lovely.

I call this the *Paul Klee exercise.* Klee was a well loved, one-of-a-kind artist. He said, "Color possesses me." If you are not familiar with his work, google him and take a look. You will enjoy it. He makes "music" with color.

Final Thoughts

White and Pale Colors

In watercolor most of the colors are transparent. This allows the white paper to show through thinly painted colors. The white of the paper lightens the colors. This is the usual way light colors are created in watercolor. The painting of Matisse on the next page has no white paint in it.

Using white paint to lighten watercolors is not often satisfying. It can make colors muddy.

Pigment vs Light

Let me say a little about *pigments* (paint colors) vs *light spectrum* colors (the **rainbow**).

Paint colors, when mixed together, move toward muddiness. Colored lights, when mixed together, move toward pristine white light.

The primary colors in pigments are red, yellow, and blue (magenta, cyan, and yellow to be exact). The primaries in light are red, blue, and green. When the three primary pigment colors are mixed together you get a *muddy brown color.* When the three primary light colors are mixed you get *pure white light.*

If you mix red light with green light, you get yellow light. You can do this at home with christmas lights. Hold a red light and a green light together and they will create an area of yellow light around them. Lights added to each other get lighter. If you mix red paint with green paint you get brown, a dirty yellow,.

The world is colored using light. Artists use *colored pigments* to try and match what they see.

Artists and Color

The more you paint, the more you will see what you are looking at in terms of pigment colors. For instance, if you wake and look at early morning light on snow you will see it has a turquoise color to it. An artist will think about matching that using cerulean blue paint.

A final reminder that *color is music* and can set a mood. There are no rules. Look at the landscapes of Camille Pissarro, an impressionist. You will see that he uses all manner of sky colors to set moods. In his paintings there are peach colored skies, also yellows, greens, all sorts of blues, and pink skies. When you look at his paintings they all look fine, not strange at all. These sky variations are easily accepted and even comforting.

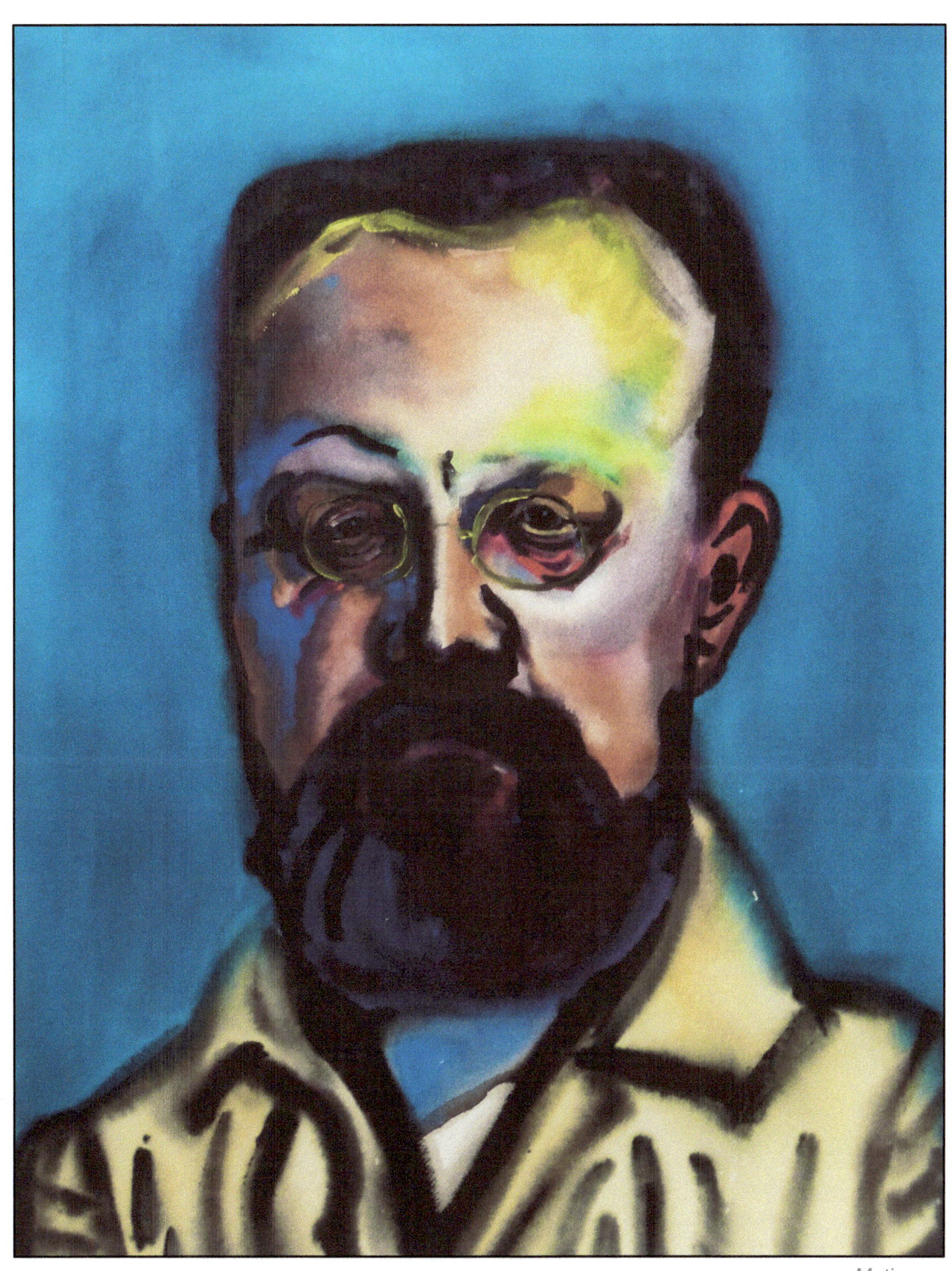

Matisse

Color doesn't have to always match what you see. Creative use of color is artist work.

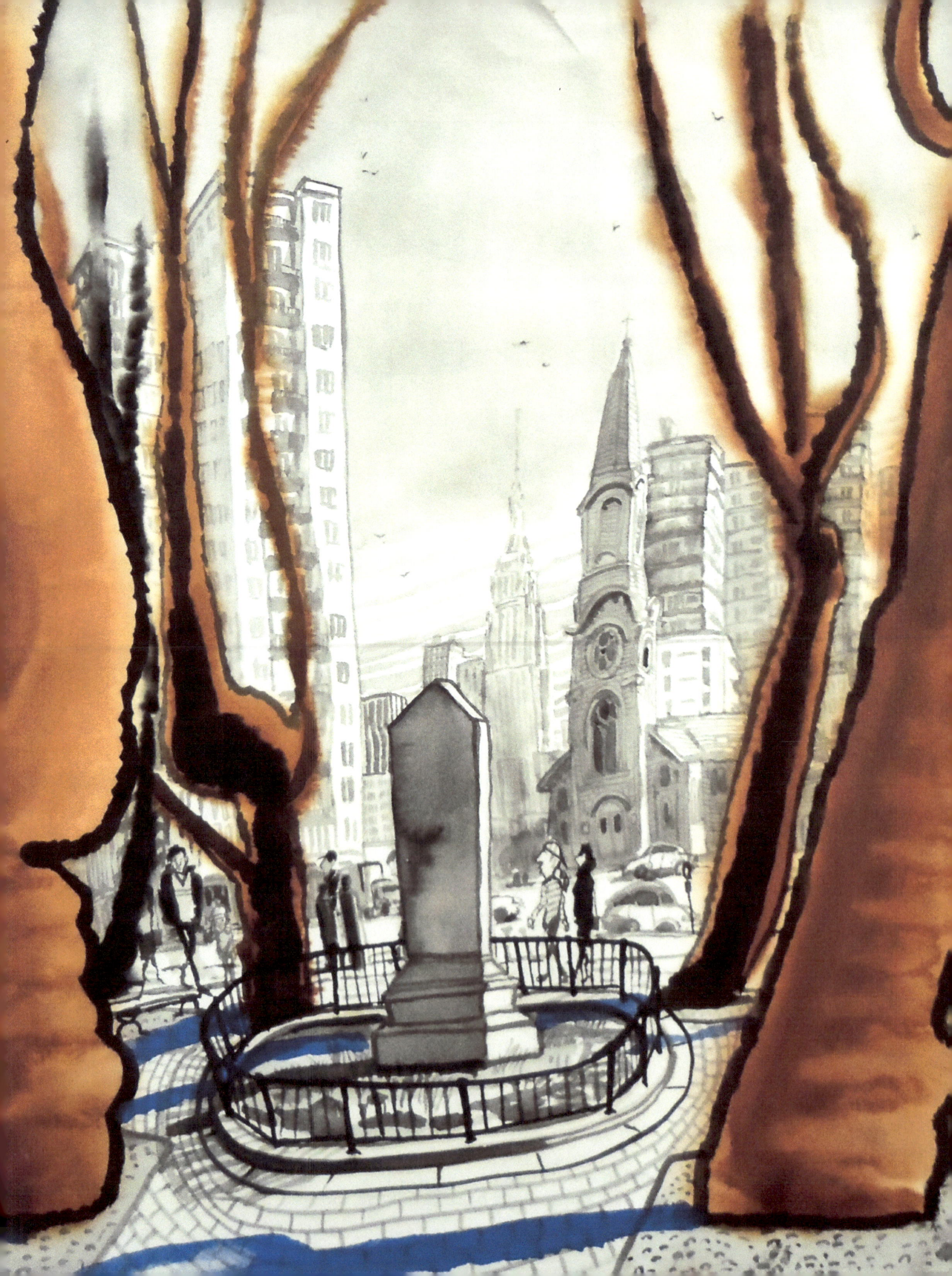

Drawing

Drawing is learned by practicing drawing. In many university art programs, Drawing 1 is a semester-long course. This is followed by Drawing 2 and 3, then Advanced Drawing and, all the while, Figure Drawing.

It takes time and practice to build the confidence and skill needed for putting usable images on paper.

I'll be covering this big part of art work in a couple of pages, hoping to give at least a taste of why artists need these skills and how they are used.

Overview

Seeing and Drawing

Do artists see the world differently from non artists? Probably, because they have to do something with what they are looking at. They need to be able to draw it.

Art is a visual pursuit and product. Being able to draw is, for the artist, like being able to put a sentence together for the writer.

Drawing is basically making marks on a surface. The marks may look like something or not.

Drawing is one way the artist expresses who he or she is into the artwork. Each person's unique energy flows onto the page in the marks the artist makes. The energy might be precise and quiet, energetic and chaotic, or anywhere in between.

Van Gogh is a good example of what I'm talking about. (I like to use Van Gogh as an example because his work is familiar to most people interested in art.) His rhythmic, moving, choppy energy is in every brushstroke and ink mark he makes. Beyond his subject matter, people can see who he is in his marks. They can feel the energy he brings to a painting.

Approaches to Drawing

Realism: Drawing realistically implies drawing from *one point of view*, the view point of the drawer. The picture, if done well, ends up looking like what the drawer is looking at. The images in realism are easily recognizable to the viewer.

Cubism: Drawing can be done from *several points of view* at the same time. The Cubists and others worked on this. It allows, for example, the showing of the front and back of a violin in the same picture. This type of drawing can be challenging to look at.

Architectural: Architects and builders make drawings for buildings by separating the buildings into many measured parts. They need to present a lot of visual information in a very specific, usable way.

Emotional: Drawing can be emotionally based. An artist can give a sense of importance to an object in the drawing by making it larger than everything else. Children will often do this. Mom, being the most important figure in their lives, will be the largest object in the drawing.

As I have said, when I draw people I always make their heads bigger than they really are. That just makes sense to me even though it's not realistic.

There are many other ways one can increase the emotional impact of an object in a drawing.

Abstract: Drawings can be abstract. They don't have look like anything recognizable. Non-objective, abstract drawings can portray movement, raw emotion, geometry, and about anything else.

For the purpose of this section on drawing, I will pretty much stick with realism. People are familiar with it and can judge whether it is well done or not. It is not as specific or subjective as other approaches.

Drawing Mechanics

My father, after he retired, took a beginners drawing class. The teacher went around class telling these novice drawers in a loud voice to "Make your mark! Make your mark!" The students had no idea what he was talking about. They were willing to make marks, but they wanted them to look like something. They didn't know how to do that.

A little history: Back about 500 years ago, during the Renaissance, western artists made a large change. Up until that point, their job had been pretty much to paint *stylized* biblical stories. How the world *really* looked was not important.

With the Renaissance came a new interest in humankind, and in fact the world in general. Artists wanted to paint what they were looking at as it *actually* appeared.

In order to see things properly and figure out the distortions that happen (square buildings with all 90-degree corners do not appear to be square from most viewpoints), they set up large rectangular frames. They placed strings vertically and horizontally on the frame to form a grid. Looking through these grids, the scene appeared to be on the surface of the grid. The scene was flattened. This is similar to looking through a window. You can pretend the image you see is a flat picture on the surface of the glass. What these Renaissance painters looked at could then be drawn as it appeared through the grid. The image was drawn square by square. This mechanical process helped painters figure out what was visually going on.

Some artists still use grids to help them draw when they want things to look very realistic. They may mark a grid on a photo, then reproduce it square for square onto a similarly gridded paper. This is a very mechanical approach. Artists can, but usually don't, use that type of gridded device when drawing a scene. Instead, they will *mentally flatten* what they are looking at, so they can draw it.

Pretend it's a photo: Drawing is learned by drawing. But, the process is not so mysterious that it can't be talked about. Many people who want to start doing some artwork think about doing outdoor scenes or landscapes. So let's start there.

The first understanding you have to make is that *drawing is a process of putting a three-dimensional scene onto a two-dimensional surface.* You are not sculpting or making a diorama of what you are looking at. You are making a *flat* drawing.

Think of what you are looking at as a *photograph of the scene,* rather than what it is: a three-dimensional scene. In doing that, you will mentally flatten what you are trying to draw. Once a scene is flattened, it is like being in your studio and having a photo to copy. Photos are easy to copy because everything has been flattened for you.

This pretend photo is right in front of you. If you have a ruler, you can reach out and measure everything in the photo (the scene). You can measure each *object* and the size of the *spaces between the objects.* Then you can transfer those measurements onto the drawing paper. The ruler method will help you to draw the objects in the scene the right size. It should also help you put them where they belong on the paper.

You may have trouble drawing some of the things in the scene. Drawing objects well comes with practice. Treating what you are drawing as a *flat photo* will help you create a fairly accurate, artistically usable, scene to paint.

Finger measuring: Artists will try to measure what they are looking at to help them draw the scene. You may have seen cartoons of artists drawing, looking out at the scene over their extended arm with their thumb up. The thumb alone is not very useful. Holding up the end of a paint brush, then using your thumb on the brush to set sizes in order to measure things, is more helpful.

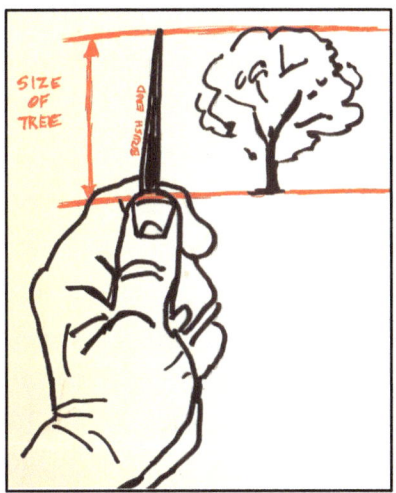

Artists will also look out at the scene they are drawing and measure things between their finger and their thumb. The tree is this big: the house is smaller, that big. The space between the two is this big.

*When you draw, it's important to remember that the spaces between objects, called **negative** spaces, are just as important as the objects themselves.*

When Drawing, Things Change

When, in your perception, you flatten the three-dimensional world you are looking at to two dimensions in order to draw it, *things change*. In two dimensions, *closer to you* becomes *lower* on the page. Likewise, *farther away* from you becomes *higher* on the page. Distant things, for example a house, may end up being much smaller

in the drawing than something in the foreground, like a lawn chair.

Relationship of Parts

Drawing what you see is actually pretty mechanical, and it is teachable. First, you visually flatten what you are looking at. Then you see that everything in the scene is in some *relationship* to everything else. An object in a drawing may be to the right or left, above or below, or larger or smaller in relationship to some other object in the drawing. If some relationships are hard to see, they can be measured. After a little practice it all begins to make sense.

Drawing Mechanics and Different Objects

Everything you draw, not just landscapes, can be approached mechanically.

When drawing a face, the corner of the mouth might be directly below the center of the eye. The space between the nose and the mouth is important to get right. Proper placement of the parts of the face constitute mechanical things.

When an object is difficult to draw, look at it mechanically. Where are things in relationship to other things? Mechanics will help you draw **anything**.

*In one sense everything you draw is **the same**. You are not so much drawing a person or a place or a still-life, as you are drawing certain things in relationship to other things.*

A Drawing

Let me take you through the start of a landscape drawing. This may be confusing, but the drawing at the end of this section will help.

To begin, I'll look out a window from the second story of my house here in New Mexico. The scene I'm looking at contains juniper trees, mountains, a driveway, a lawn chair, and a bird feeder. There are many other things, but let's get those five things on the page.

I **start** with *what is* **easy** *and what* **I see best**. There is a large juniper tree, with its usual lumpy shape, that will work to begin the drawing. I'll put it near the center of the page and a little to the left. Having done that, everything else I draw (trying for realism) is in *relationship* to that tree. As I've said, the other objects might be above or below it, bigger or smaller than it, to the right or left of it.

I draw the mountains next. They are behind the tree in the distance. That means that when I'm drawing them, they are above the tree on the paper... just like it looks. The tree *overlaps* them, covers part of them. The mountains stretch out across the whole sheet.

Now the driveway. This is harder, more distorted. It comes in from the right of the scene, never rising above the bottom third of the tree. As the driveway comes toward me it passes by the tree on the right, and as it drops down the page it bends slightly back to the left. As I look at the scene, I can see that it appears wider as it comes toward me. In my drawing it gets bigger, wider, as it moves down the paper. On the paper, the complete driveway ends up a skinny vertical shape. It is fatter near the bottom of the paper and has a bend near the top.

Finally, I put in the lawn chair and the bird feeder. They are next to each other but much closer to me than the tree and to the left of the driveway.

As I *mentally flatten* this scene into two dimensions, I see that the chair and the feeder are directly below the right edge of the juniper.

There is space between the juniper tree and the chair. I need to know how big that space is. I reach out with my fingers and measure the height of the tree (everything starts with the tree). I hold that size and drop my fingers down to check out the size of the space between the tree and the chair. The space is about one and a half tree heights.

I make a mark that distance below the tree on the paper. Below that mark is where the chair goes.

How big should I make the chair? Once again, I measure the tree height with my fingers. Hold that measurement and move my fingers to the chair. I find out the chair is about three quarters of the height of the tree. So now I know where the chair belongs on the page and approximately how big it is. I can now draw it.

The bird feeder goes next to the chair to the right.

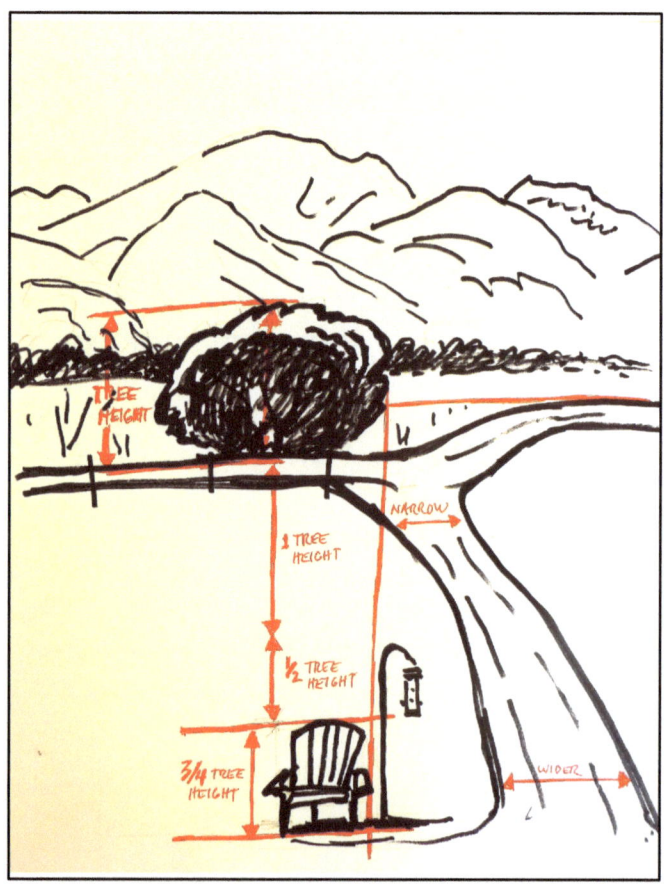

Drawing a landscape is a little like a construction. It is put together piece by piece.

Illusion of Three Dimensions

People are very used to looking at flattened 3D images. Photographs, magazines, TV, and movies are all examples. When the artist places objects in a drawing in the correct sizes and relationships to each other, the viewer reads the drawing easily. The two-dimensional drawing creates the illusion of a three-dimensional scene.

Drawing

To sum it up, drawing a scene is, in large part, a mechanical process. After a while, people who draw a lot don't think much about the mechanics that are involved. They just draw. I promise, though, they are constantly scanning the scene and the paper. They are checking vertical and horizontal relationships (above or below, to the right or left) of things. They are making sure *the space between things, the **negative space***, is the correct size. They are looking for visual overlapping, like fence posts in front of a bush, and so on.

When everything is pretty well placed on the paper and drawn well, the drawing is done.

To people who don't draw, it seems like a little magic has happened when the artist makes a successful realistic drawing. To the artist, it's just good visual skills, training, mechanics, and a lot of practice.

Drawing and Watercolor

Painting in watercolor is often very decisive and direct. The medium doesn't allow or reward a lot of fussing around. Mistakes can be corrected but the corrections don't always look that great. Good drawing skills really help to keep the paint brush moving. By that, I mean good drawing ability helps to keep the artist from losing confidence in what's happening in the painting.

Some artists, when they watercolor, begin with a lot of drawing. Winslow Homer comes to mind. You can easily see his pencil marks on the paper. He drew very precisely. After the drawing was made, he would then wet an area defined by the lines and fill it in with lovely loose wet watercolors. The structure in his paintings comes from his drawing ability. A friend of mine calls him an architect.

John Singer Sargent's drawing skills were excellent, other worldly. He was fearless when he watercolored. He did draw a little first. You can see the pencil lines. Then the painting happened with great bravado and daring. His watercolors are breathtaking achievements in the medium. He said of watercolor painting, *"Make the best of an emergency."*

If you choose to draw with pencil first, and most painters do, the lines will show. David Hockney, an excellent contemporary painter, sums it up well in this quote: *"With watercolor you can't cover up the marks. There's the story of the construction of the picture* [the pencil marks]*, and then the picture* [the painting part] *might tell another story."*

When I start a painting, I do draw first but I use a brush and paint. I often use a very weak purple color that lifts (erases) easily with water. I find drawing with paint and water is more fluid than pencil. If I don't like what I've done, I just take a brush full of water and wash it away and try again. The wet paper also helps me draw. The water moves the paint around as I put it on the paper. As the paint moves around I can, perhaps paradoxically, better see where the lines belong.

With pencil you can draw with the paper upright on an easel. That makes what you are doing easier to see. With the wet way that I work, the paper needs to be on a flat surface. That can cause some distortion.

Final Thoughts on Drawing

The final products of realism in drawings can have many different looks. They may be very *realistic,* which are easy for most viewers to understand and admire.

They may be *loose and childlike.* Loose and childlike drawing doesn't just happen because the artist is loose and childlike. It takes real confidence in your skills to work that way.

Drawings may be *cartoony*. Mine are.

There are ways to make paintings without the need to draw well. An example might be geometric paintings, like mandalas.

Learning to draw is not terribly difficult. It takes interest and practice. You can do it yourself or with a teacher. Learning to represent what you are looking at is mechanical and manageable.

You can learn to use paint while learning how to draw. You just need to be brave.

I had a meaningful moment in art school. I was taking a figure drawing class as a sophomore. There was a three-hour long figure study. I was doing what I thought was a Michelangelo quality drawing. It was very detailed with lots of fancy crosshatching. The teacher came by and said something was wrong. He sat down and erased the bottom half of the figure. He then drew in stick legs, leaned back and said "that's better". I couldn't believe it, and walked out.

I stewed for days about what had happened. When I went back to class something had changed. I started working larger with thick black chalks. I changed from making a drawing to just drawing.

Art to the artist is a fairly pedestrian process. It's work. It is compelling, but still work. It has been said that art is 5% inspiration and 95% perspiration. It is something like that.

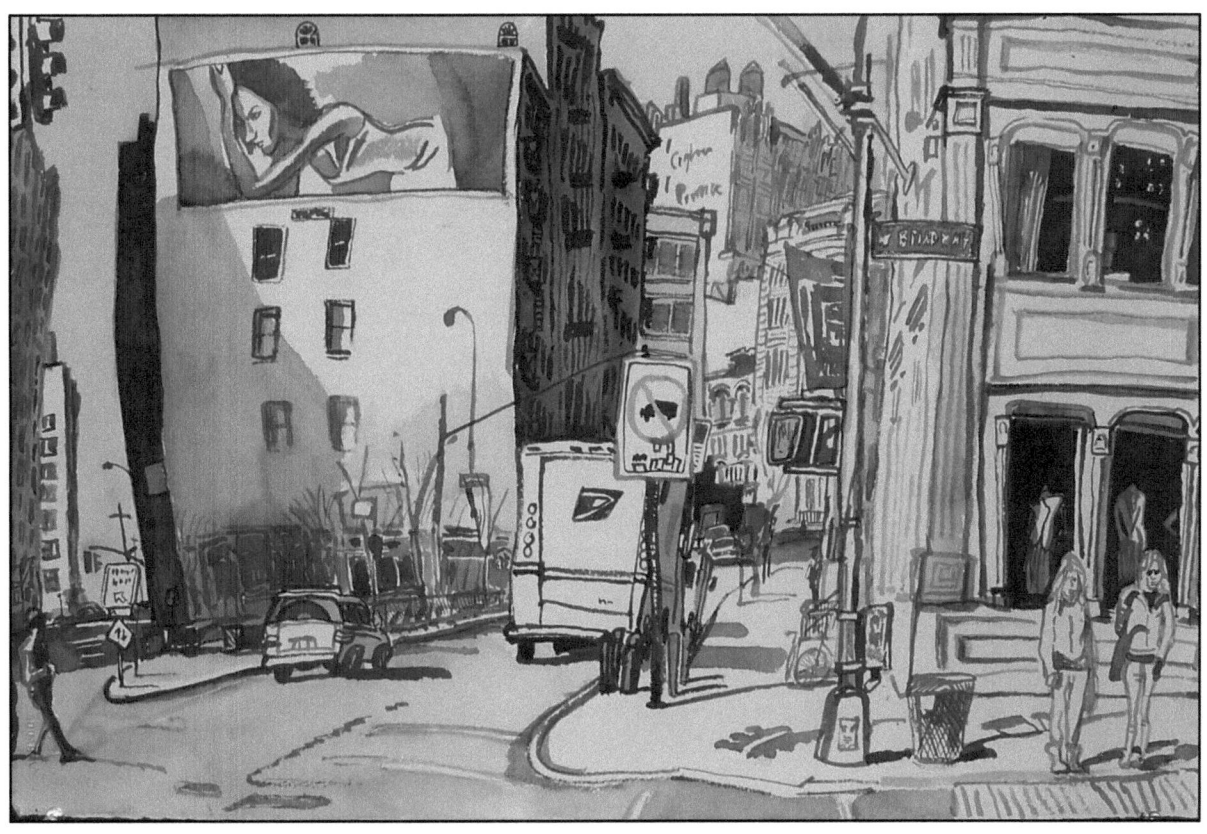

NYC 57th Street

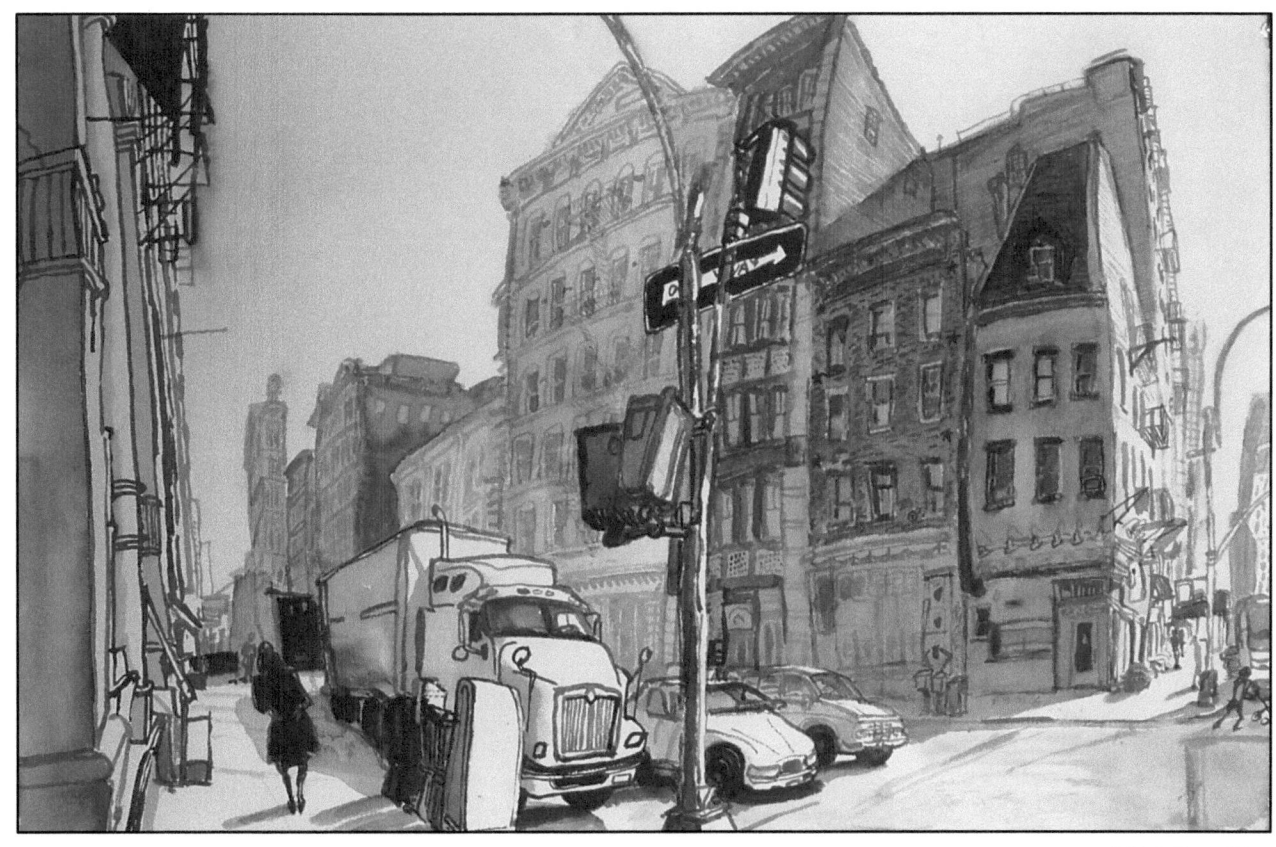

NYC One Way

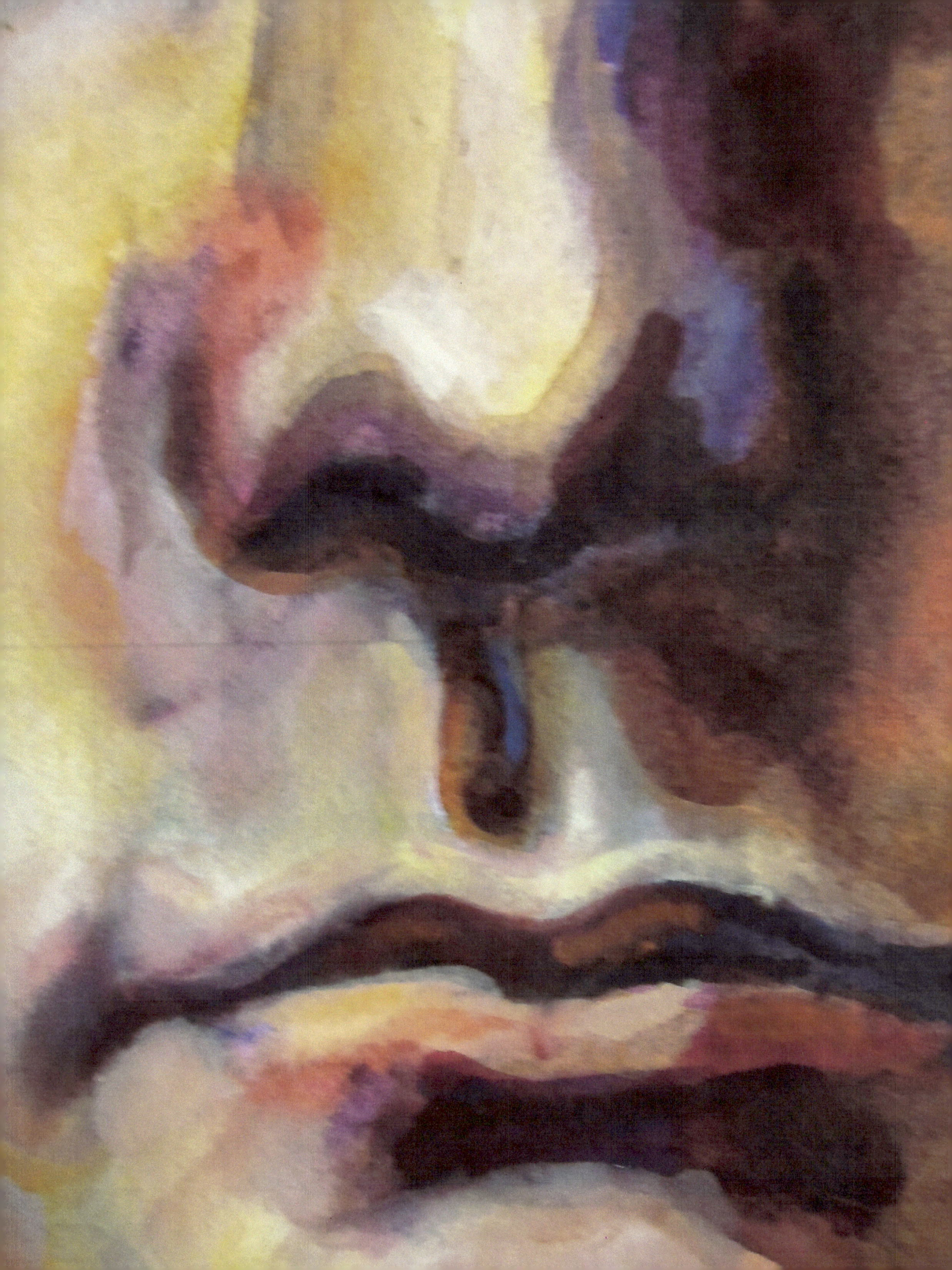

Value

*The word **value** as an art term and understanding means the dark and light of color. **This is a very important awareness that affects every aspect of making art.***

Value

The values are the *darks and lights* in a painting. They can be seen when you take a black and white photo of the painting. The painting will still look like the painting except the color will be gone. The photo will appear in white, black, and all the "values" of grey in between.

Value Scale

Values – darks and lights – can be organized in a range of steps from black to white. There are charts that classify 10 numbered steps from black to white. Photographers and artists sometimes use them. They are called *value scales*.

Some paint companies use these scales to give numbers to the value of the colors they make. The numbers correspond to how dark or light a color is. The scales list white as a 10 and black a zero. A light yellow color might be numbered 8.5. A dark purple might be a 1.7.

If the paint companies do this, they print the value number on the tube of paint.

When Color is Absent

Those old black and white family photos of Uncle Bob and Aunt Alice look like Uncle Bob and Aunt Alice. *Color is not necessary to create realism.*

Values form the **structure** of a picture. The structure is the recognizable part of the picture. Color just adds to the enjoyment of looking.

Photographers often choose to work in black and white because they want what they are presenting to be seen without the *emotional effects of color*. Occasionally movies are shot in black and white for the same reason. "Schindler's List" is an example. That movie, about an awful part of World War Two, is more effective and affecting without color. The newer movie "Nebraska" is another example of a movie shot to great and gritty effect in black and white.

The Importance of Value

Beginning painters usually hate hearing about value. They are struggling with drawing, color, and in watercolor painting, the water. They don't want to hear about one more thing.

Value and what it does in painting really can't be ignored. A good example of its use might be in how to paint a tree. The color green only helps a little when painting a tree. If you paint the tree using only one value of green, you might get something shaped like a tree but it will appear flat. Trees are not flat.

Say the sun is shining on the tree. The leaves on sunny side will appear lighter, so you need to use a light value of green. The other side of the tree is in shadow and will appear darker. It will need to be painted a darker value of green. These variations in light and dark are called *value changes*.

Greens can be made light or dark. When you see these different values, lights and darks, and reproduce them in the painting, the tree will begin to look full and round. The same will be true for the trunk of the tree and everything else in the painting.

*As a teacher I wander around the class saying, "If it's **dark,** make it **dark;** if it's **light,** make it **light.**" Value is that simple.*

Two Value Exercises

The most common exercise used to teach value is called a *value study.* The teacher sets up a full color still life and the students are asked to paint it using only one dark color, say black, and white. As they paint, they have to match the values of the colors they mix to the values of the colors they are looking at. A yellow color would become a light grey. A dark blue would be a dark grey, and so on.

This exercise is about seeing a full colored world not in color but in *darks and lights*. This is a very important skill for an artist.

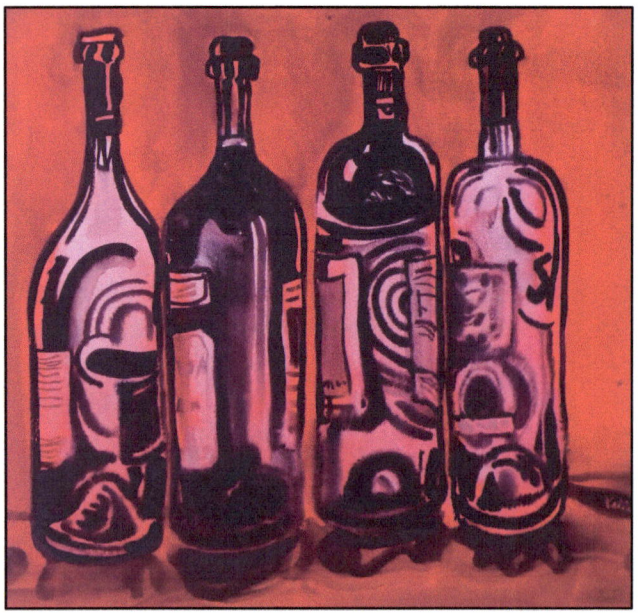

Wine Bottle Exercise

A good exercise in seeing values, one that I enjoy doing myself, is to paint wine bottles. Set the bottles up against a window or in front of a lamp to get some light through them. Then, using full color, paint the darks and lights as you see them. I like this because when you look at transparent glass objects, the darks and lights you see seem very random and extreme. You just have to *copy what you see;* your mind can't make it up. ***Don't pretend you know what is happening.***

If you are fairly accurate in reproducing the values you see, the painting will look like glass bottles with light coming thru them, very pretty. If you don't "push the values," making the darks really dark, and the lights light enough, the painting will look dull and lifeless. It is a challenging exercise. It requires careful seeing and an empty mind.

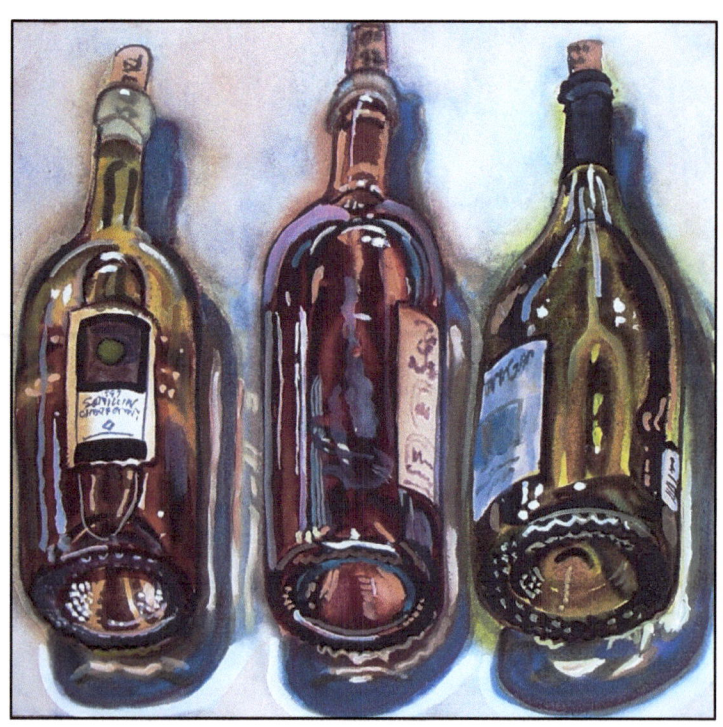

Artists often look for scenes with a large value range. A good range of darks and lights makes creating the illusion of three dimensions and portraying the effects of light easier.

Value Thoughts

Values matter more than color:
The use of color in a painting can be compelling, emotional and even musical. The use of value in a painting can be thought of as structural. It is how the artist creates form, the illusion of three-dimensions. *If you get the values right when painting a human face, you can paint it any color or colors that you want. It will still look like a human face.*

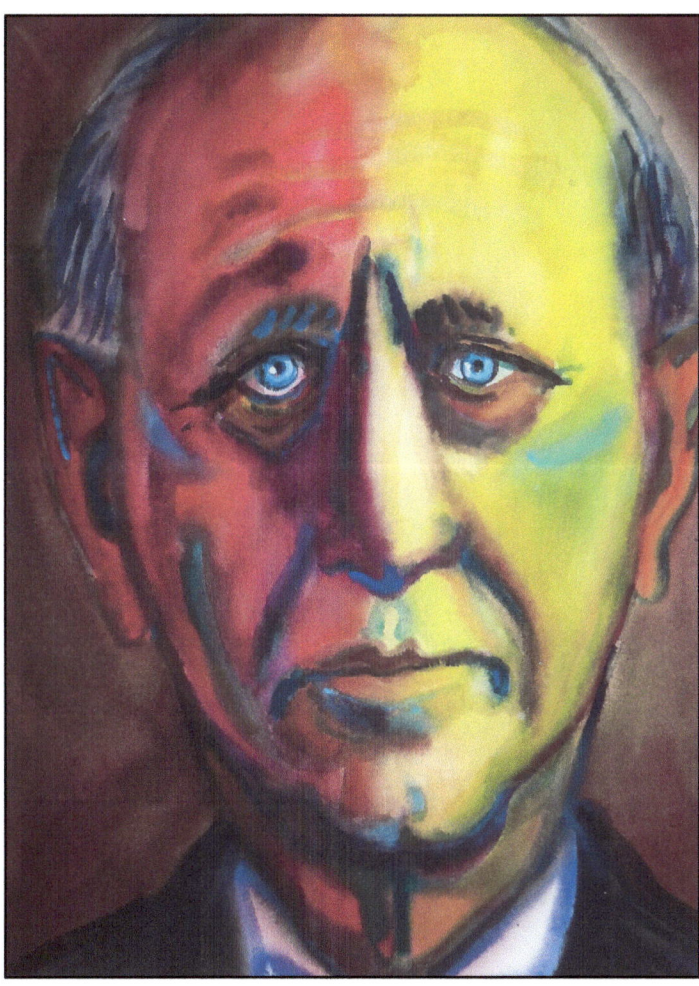

Colors and value:
The same named color can have different values. Take the color blue, for instance: a pair of new blue jeans that have not been stone washed is a darker value of blue than a pair of stone washed jeans, which are a lighter value of the same blue.

Different colors can have the same value. If you took a black and white photo of a red bell pepper and a green bell pepper sitting next to

each other, you would see they are close to the same value. They would each be about the same medium gray color in the photo. They would look alike.

Squinting:
When painting something and trying to get the values correct, it helps to *squint*. Squinting lessens the details and colors of a scene so you can see the areas of darks and lights.

Value and emotion:
Value can also play a large part in the emotional content of a painting. In life, on a sunny day, there are a large range of values. There are bright highlights and dark shadows. On an overcast day, the value range is less, mostly middle grays. There are no really bright lights or really dark darks. On a rainy day, the value range is even less. The amount of light on any given day can affect how we feel.

If you make a painting, whether realistic or abstract, with a *large value range,* bright lights and dark darks, it will feel like a sunny day. It will have *lots of energy*.

If you make a painting with a *small value range,* all light colors, all dark colors or all medium valued colors, the painting will feel like an overcast or rainy day, and it will feel quieter.

Value and form:
Painting correct values will create the illusion of three-dimensional form. Denying or ignoring values will flatten out a painting.

'Big for little' in value:
"Don't lose the big for the little." This is a saying of mine that has many uses in painting. It helps those that want to paint well understand the use of values.

If we consider painting a night scene, this time as a value exercise, we will see that there are many *little* value changes in the scene. Those small changes are the *little*. They need to be painted but they are not the most important thing that is happening.

The *big* is that it's night time and everything in the painting needs to be mostly dark, with dark values. If you don't get the *big* correct, the painting will not look like night time.

Value and a sense of light: The painter Rockwell Kent was very good at keeping his values, the big and the little, where they belonged. In one of his landscape paintings there is a herd of sheep. The painting has late afternoon light. Some of the herd are in sunlight, and some are in a shadow cast by a hill. The sheep and everything else in that shadow are painted darker and with a closer value range than the things still in the light. Even though all the sheep are white, the white sheep in the shadow appear, and are painted, darker than the white sheep in sunlight.

Kent knew how to use value correctly. The sheep painting is filled with lovely, visually understandable late afternoon light because of it.

Correct values can fill a landscape painting with sunlight. A recognizable sense of light in a painting adds enjoyment for the people who view it. They will feel the warmth and understand it in their bodies.
Scenes depicting late afternoon light, or darkness, can also evoke feelings of pleasure and connection in the viewer.

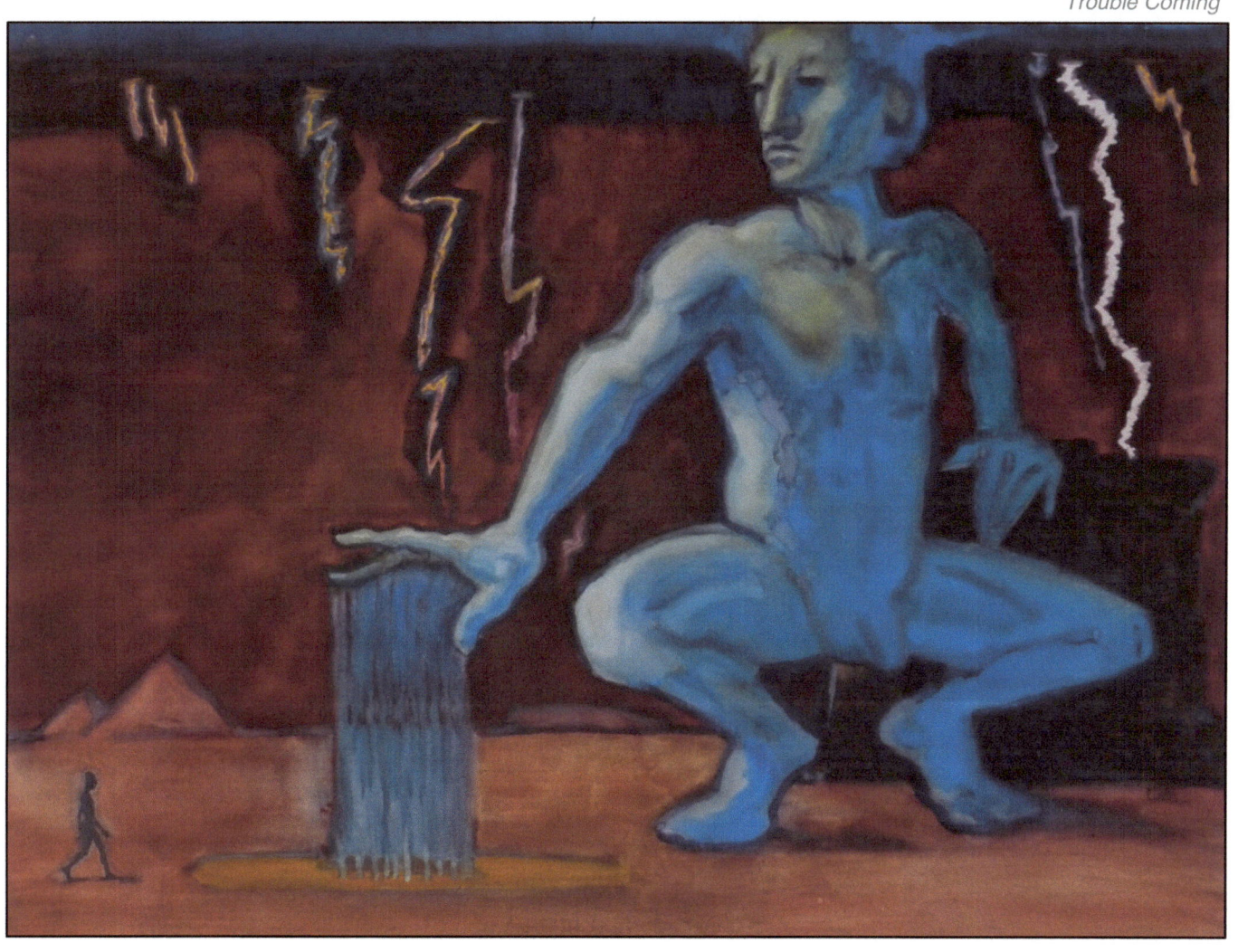

When I paint, I spend most of my time looking at what's dark and what's light, value. My drawing skills are pretty good so I don't worry much about that. Color is the other major consideration. If you paint what is dark with dark colors, and what is light with light colors or washes, you can be creative about color. The structure of the painting, value, will hold the image. The emotional part of the painting, the colors, warm, cool, subdued, garish, etc., becomes open to exploration.

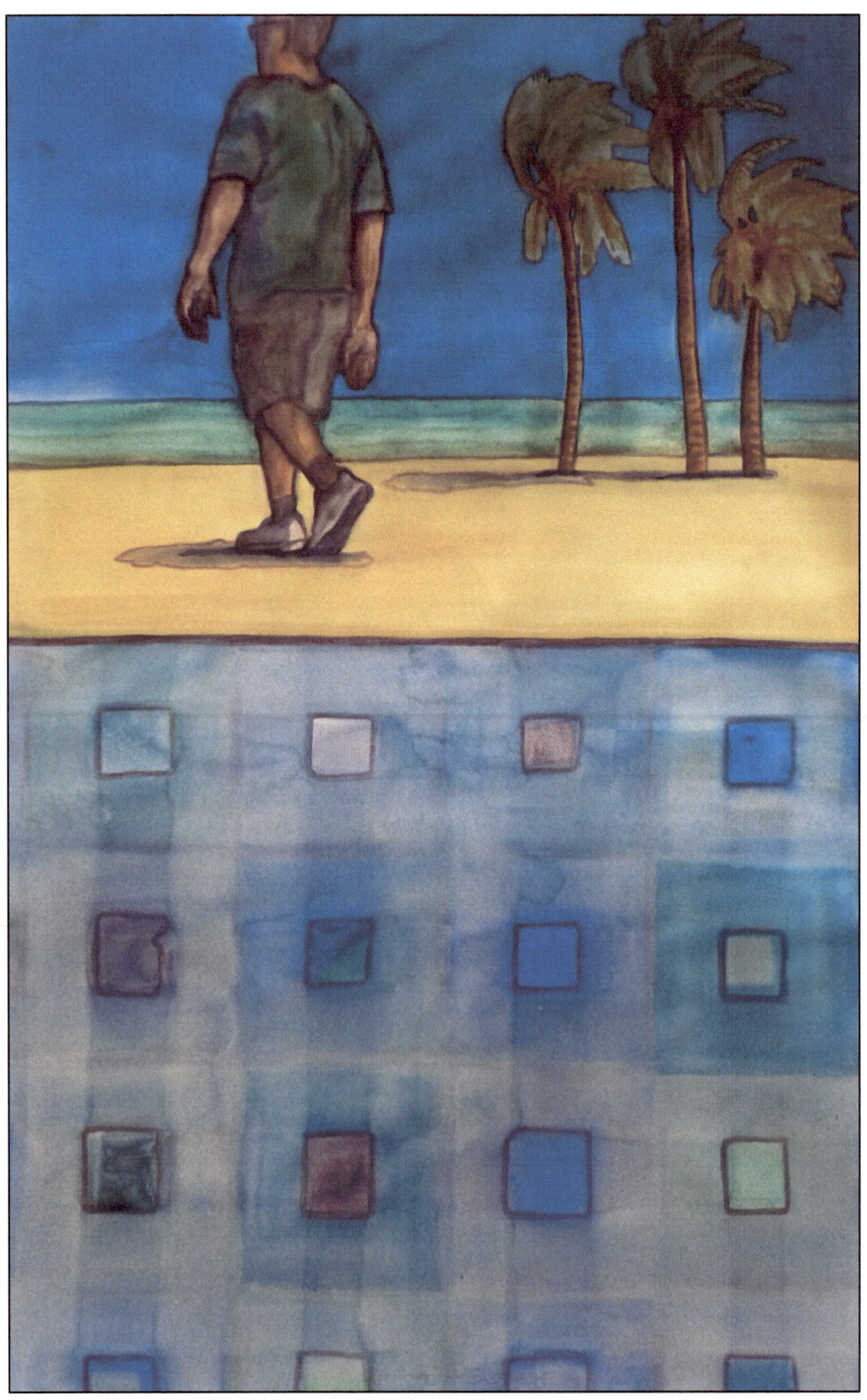

Philosophy

This section of the book covers varied thoughts on painting and art that are not part of the physical act of painting.

What is a Painting?

I started to paint seriously at age 53, after spending the previous 30 years making pottery. I did bring some good skills to the new interest. I had gone to art school and later had taught many university art classes. I could draw. I knew the mechanics of color. I could create or deny the illusion of three dimension. I had a fair understanding of "value," the darks and lights of painting. These are skills that a person making paintings needs to have. What I didn't know was, *what is a painting?* What are these things we look at and admire?

When I started to make paintings, I also poured through art books. I didn't take notes. I just absorbed what the paintings looked like. Here is what I came to understand.

Each painting is a planned limited event: Each presents a visual idea. The idea might be clear and easily understood, or obscure and mysterious. It can be repetitious, chaotic, simple or complex, and so on. Paintings are limited by their size and edges.

Paintings are not random: Paintings are designed. They make sense in a *visual* way. They are not unlike an essay, a poem, or piece of music.

Paintings pursue something: Some paintings are political. Some are purely emotional. Some are about color, form, or ideas. Some are realistic, others are not. Some are serious, some lighthearted. In all paintings, the painter is pursuing something and desiring that that "something" has value.

Skill and mystery: Painting is not only skill and control. Painting is a combination of the artist's skill, the ability to *control what's happening,* and the artist "allowing" mystery, flow, or life into the painting, *the uncontrolled.* Good skills and some mystery are in all great art. Let me give an example.

Van Gogh is not famous because he painted flowers. A lot of people have painted flowers much more skillfully than Van Gogh ever did.

Van Gogh's art had only a little to do with his choice of subject matter. Although not a particularly happy person, *Life* poured through Vincent and into everything he painted or drew. There was no way that he could keep it out. It is like a heartbeat in his work. People who know his art can see and feel that and they love him for it.

Art Museums

In cities large and small, impressive buildings called museums are built solely to house artworks. What is that about? What is in "art" that it deserves such respect? There must be something in the process and results that resonate with enough people so that this adoration and expense makes sense.

These are interesting questions that I'm not capable of fully answering. I may have hinted at it in the above paragraph about Van Gogh and in other parts of this book. Maybe it's something else. They are good questions to think about.

Talent and Tools

In discussions about art, it is often said that this person who paints, or that one, is very talented. I am never sure exactly what that means. How can talent really be judged? There are as many ways to create a painting as there are painters. Every interested person who paints brings their own uniqueness to their work. Every viewer responds to the work from his or her own individual perspective. Evaluation of an artist's talent is a very subjective undertaking.

Less subjective is an understanding of the essential personal tools that an artist needs in order to excel at making art. The tools might include the following:

Interest: This also might be called talent. A strong interest in making art will make things happen. A mild interest can build into a strong interest as skills are built. Art, like any human endeavor, gets more interesting, and then even compelling, as you get more skilled at it.

Discipline, doggedness, determination, diligence: These "d" words are what get things done. Some people are good at these. *Some need to get good at these.* In order to develop artistic skills, you need discipline. *The ability to work independently is critical.*

Creativity: What do I paint next and next and next? No one calls the artist up and gives out assignments. No help comes in the mail. What do you paint?

The person who wants to paint needs to be able to figure out what to paint, again and again and again. This takes creativity. Creativity might be described, in part, as the ability to keep yourself interested and your audience intrigued.

Creativity is different than cleverness. Clever things are often fun, but usually shallow and short lived. Creativity is deeper.

The ability to earn a living: How does one do art without starving to death? A personal situation has to be created that provides a way to exist. That situation must also allow time for enough painting to happen so the interest doesn't die. Actors classically wait on tables between acting jobs.

I started out making and selling pottery. I then taught art classes part time at a university. I taught years and years of classes but never took the security of a full-time position. Security was secondary to the desire to make art. Security can be a problem when making art work.

Once, a wealthy man told me I was lucky not to be rich. He wanted to do artwork but felt that having money took away the pressure to put in the time and effort. That might be true. Having money might also allow time to get a lot done.

Many people are able to start art later in life, when things quiet down a little. As stated, I started painting at age 53.

With diligence and effort, one may be able to start selling paintings. Selling paintings begins to support the making of paintings.

Having a place to paint: Having a studio or a good place to work does not make you a good painter, but not having one makes doing anything more difficult. I have had students who have had to paint at the kitchen table in a very small house with six other family members around. That would be hard.

Watercoloring does not need a big studio. If possible, create a private area just for you and your painting. Pin up your paintings on the wall so you can keep track of what you're doing. Make yourself a space that honors the process you've taken on.

Other tools:

· The need for self expression and the feeling that one has something worth offering can help in getting things done.

· It is useful to have the ability to set and meet personal goals.

· A person can use his or her ego and the

desire to prove something as a way to put in the effort. A strong ego might also help deal with the inevitable comments and happenings, both good and bad, that come with doing artwork. (It also might not.)

· The ability to market yourself and your work can be quite useful. Making money from what you do can be very stimulating.

*At the beginning of many painting classes, I would write on the teaching board in big letters, **"Paint anyway."** The students who had struggled knew what that meant.*

Some Thoughts on Art Classes

What you achieve in art ultimately comes from yourself.

Most art teachers do their best to convey what they know. Some are good at teaching; some are not. Being a good painter doesn't necessarily make one a good teacher.

Students of art need to understand that if they really do want to get good, *it is up to them.*
Teachers can teach what can be taught. They can inspire, and require hours of practice. The student needs to take what they find useful from the teaching and incorporate it into their own thinking and artwork. *How a student ends up painting is most likely going to be very different from how the teacher paints.*

If something said in an art class rings a bell or even hurts a little, it is important to pay attention. These moments can be useful to an interested student. They don't happen often.

A Story

When I started teaching college art I taught a lot of Basic Design classes (an introduction to the mechanics that go into making artworks). I was required to follow a book written by a professor in the art department of that university. Some of what was in the book made good sense to me as a young teacher. I taught that.

The author broke down doing art work into parts so that it could be better taught and understood. College teachers do this all the time with almost all topics. I've done it in this book. Breaking topics like art into parts usually works well to explain the parts, but often doesn't help explain the whole.

The Ladies Docent (museum guide) group at the local museum asked me to teach them about design so that they could better explain the museum's paintings to the visitors.

I spent about six hours with the group in a classroom. We ended the class by going into the museum where I was going to show them how all this design information worked in the paintings. I looked at the paintings and went quiet. What I was teaching was not readily there in the paintings.

I was not painting at the time. Had I been painting, I would have known more.

The *parts* of making art, I discovered, especially as I began painting, exist but they don't completely explain the *whole* of art.

The parts don't explain the whole because there is more involved. *There is an area of painting that is very personal and deep. That area doesn't have parts or rules.*

Understanding the blood, muscles, bones, and organs of a human body does not adequately explain a living person. It is similar with painting.

Teaching Less

I find that I teach less and less as I get older. Yes, I teach mechanical things like blue recedes, red advances. But I do not teach composition and what art looks like. These are special, individual things. It is up to each artist to figure out these for themselves. Teaching less can be hard on students who are used to being led.

I don't try to dictate results. If an art teacher allows teenage boys, for instance, to choose their own subject matter, the results will likely include monsters and super-heroes. A lot of teachers don't like that, but monsters and super-heroes are workable subjects. The results that students get are their own, and should be their own, for better or worse.

Painting for the Class

Often, when teaching a watercolor class, I will bring paper and paints to class and paint along with the students. The students can watch if they wish. I have found that this is one of the most valuable teaching tools that I have. The students gain a great deal watching me struggle with the painting process using this lively medium.

A Few Final Words

Art vs. Illustration

I had an older student who loved illustrations and the painters who did them. He would argue that the illustrators were better than a lot of painters who were considered great artists. It is an interesting thought. In many cases, the skill level of illustrators is extremely high. Many illustrations are very well done. Is this level of skill *art*?

Some illustrations certainly are art. Generally, though, the approach and hoped for outcome are different for the artist and the illustrator.

Let me use words by Walt Whitman, the American poet, as an example of an artist's work. He wrote the poetic line, "A lilac by the dooryard bloomed." We will call that *art*.

An *illustration*, using words, of the same idea might be, "A lilac bush grew by the door of the house and it was in bloom."

The first takes your breath away. The second tells the story of the scene. Close, but different.

Old Fashioned

These thoughts, and in fact this entire book on how to approach art, may seem old fashioned to young artists. Many young artists, especially in big cities, work on evolving into or being part of "the next big thing" in art. That is fine and probably just right. I was young a short while ago.

Later on, these cutting-edge artists may find that, as this old song line by Herman Hupfeld says, "*The fundamental things apply as time goes by.*"

The fundamental things don't change. They don't get old.

Cutting-edge, or more familiar forms of artwork, are in essence all the same. That essence is the inexpressible combined with the utter humanness of the process.

The important things last.

"Watercolors are the first and the last things an artist does"

Willem De Kooning

Charles Burchfield   Frida Kahlo   Georgia O'keeffe
Willem De Kooning

70

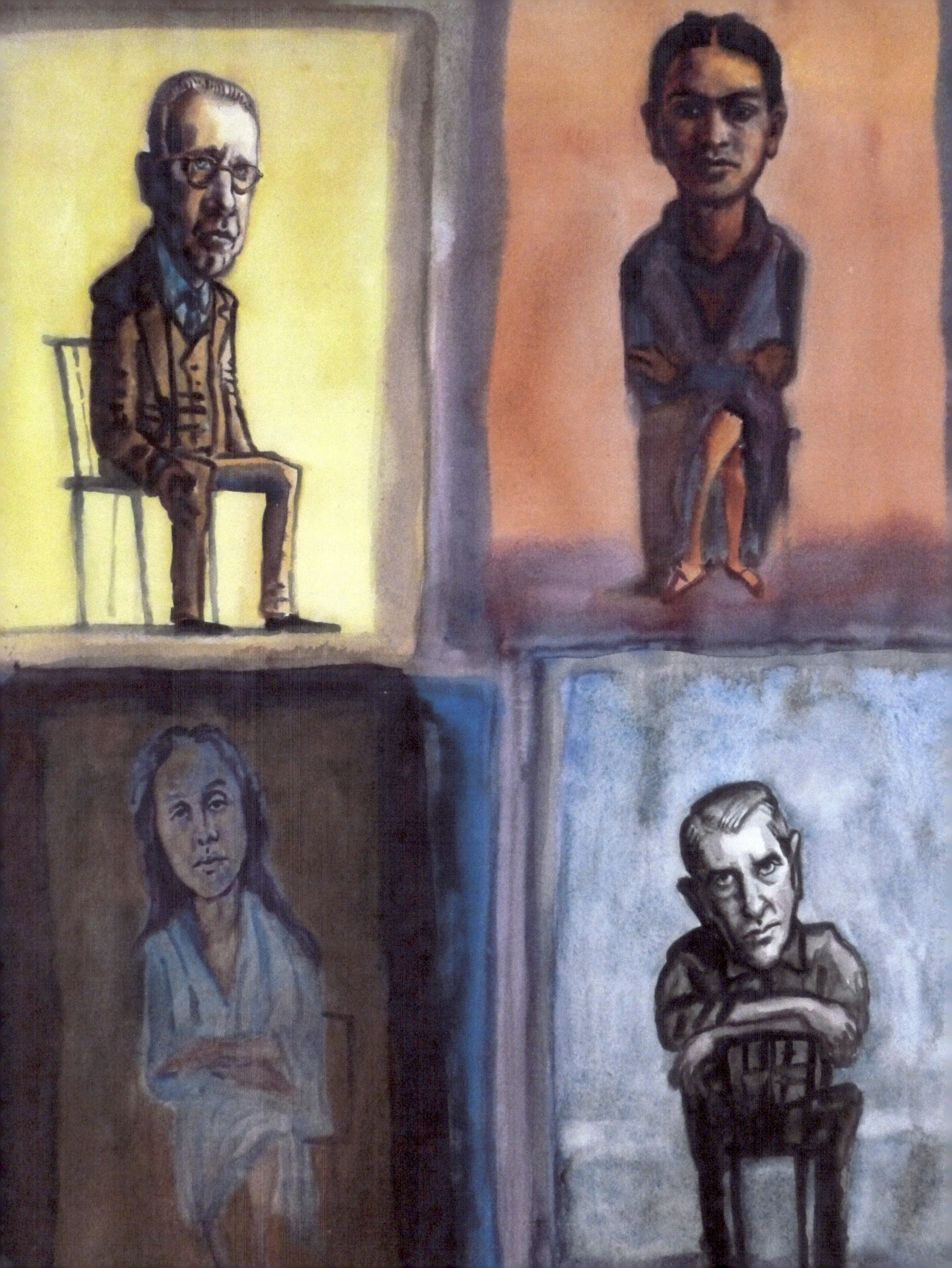

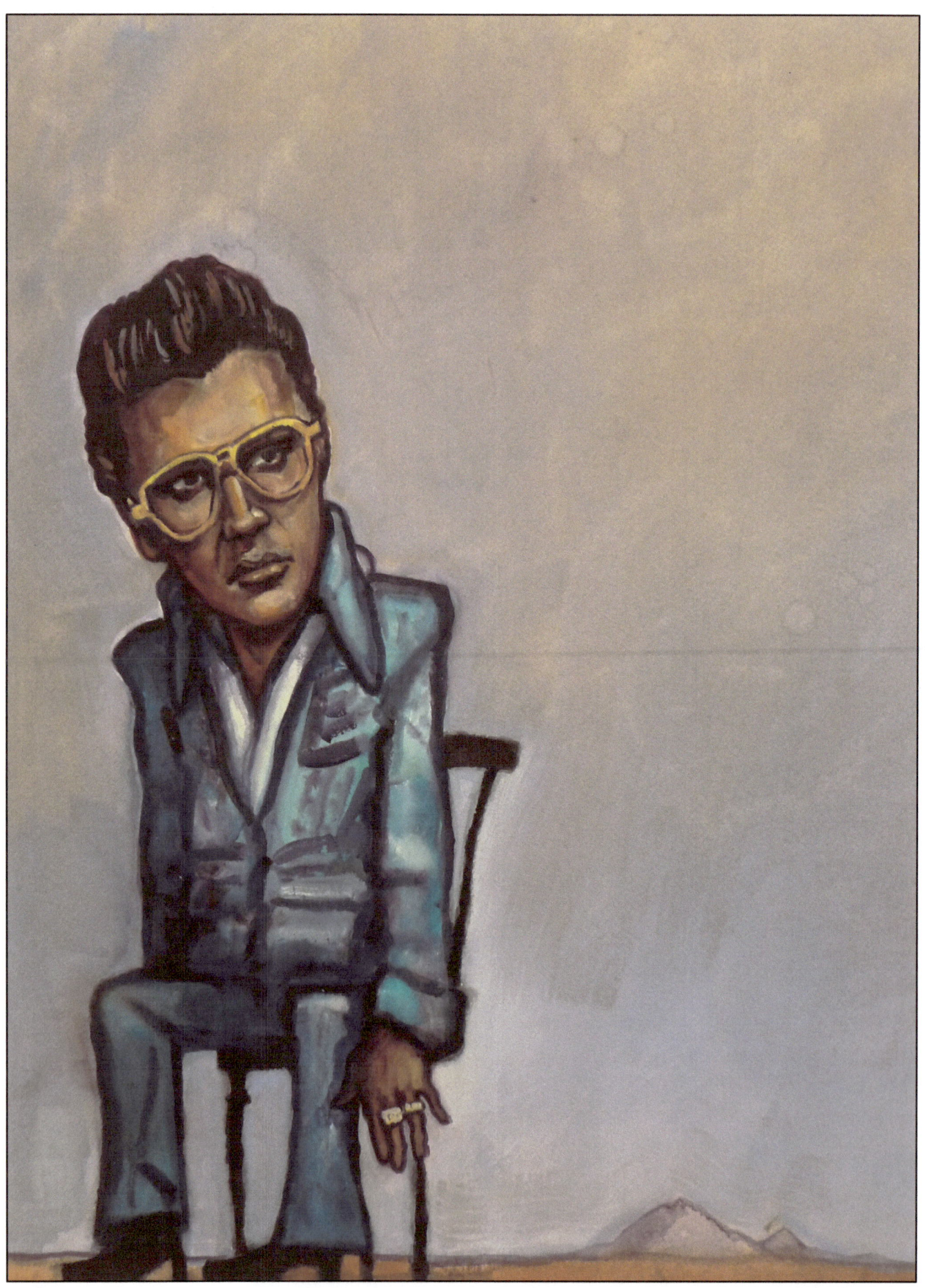

Galleries and Selling

When you first start painting, you can just paint. You don't need to add the pressure of trying to sell what you do. If selling artwork is part of your plan, give yourself time to learn and get good at making the work before you pursue selling it.

Selling Artwork

My paintings are not particularly good sellers. They are quite personal, mostly about people, and not very decorative. None of these attributes are particularly advantageous for selling. I have sold a lot of paintings, though. Here's what I can offer about selling artwork.

Body of work: You need to do a lot of work, creating what is called a "body of work." That means *a lot of paintings*. You need to do enough paintings to get very good at painting.

Galleries will want to see number of paintings, not just a couple of good ones. They want to know that you are serious and doing the work.

Signature style: If you do enough work, you will get to painting *how you paint*. This is, as has been said, called a "signature style."

When you paint like *you* paint, your paintings begin to have value. Galleries do look for that distinctive "personality" in your work.

'Take It or Leave It:'   Once you get to the point that what you are doing is *your* work, you might develop a "take it or leave it" attitude. Some people will like what you do, some won't. While it can be difficult when people do not like your work, you will feel okay about this. These are *your* paintings now, and you can't paint any other way.

Finding a gallery: When you are ready to begin to show your work to galleries, you need to find a gallery that you like that carries work somewhat like yours. Make an appointment to show the gallery owners your work and see what happens. It is helpful to bring along a CD of photos of your paintings that you can leave at the gallery, if they wish.

There are articles and books available on how to approach galleries. The business of galleries is to represent artists and sell art. Remember they represent artists, not just paintings.

It's not easy for most artists to approach galleries. The galleries know this and are usually kind. Galleries need artists.

Ted Gets a Gallery

I have had representation in seven different galleries. I'll talk about the process but first, a story.

An artist friend of mine had an one-person show at a well-known gallery in Portland, Maine. It was a great show with quality work. There were 20 to 25 pieces in it. He sold most of them. He sold around $22,000 worth of work. I thought that was great. Then I thought some more.

The gallery took 50% of the proceeds. That left $11,000 for the artist. He had to buy the materials, do the work, frame the pieces (never cheap), heat the studio, transport the work to the gallery, and so on. It was a successful showing, but there really wasn't that much money in it.

After giving myself three years to learn to paint, I wanted to show some work. I lived on the coast of Maine. That is a good area to sell art. I had a good reputation in that area as an art teacher. A student of mine worked at a gallery. I started there. I made an appointment and took a pile of unframed work to show. The gallery owner liked it and agreed to let me show there. There was no contract. It was fun. I enjoyed the gallery people. I sold well there for two years, and then the gallery closed. I learned, galleries come and go. It's a tough business.

At the same time I was in the above gallery, I called one of the best galleries in Portland and asked if I could send slides (no CDs then). They said yes. Most galleries do want to see work. It is the product that they sell. I sent a sleeve of slides. They liked them. With that gallery I signed a year contract. I was represented by them for seven years until my wife and I moved out to New Mexico. It was difficult to arrange to drop off and pick up framed paintings from 2,500 miles away, so I let the contract go.

Over the years, before the New Mexico move, I worked with five other galleries. Some closed. Some changed owners. I sold poorly at another, so she kicked me out. One gallery representation has worked out well for myself and the gallery. I remain represented by that gallery to this day.

More Thoughts on Galleries and Selling Art

Pricing your work: Pricing artwork is never easy. It is very subjective.

• The gallery might give assistance and guidance. They are in the business of knowing what paintings are worth or a least what they want to sell them for.

• Watercolors generally sell for less than oils.

• It is much easier to raise your prices than to lower them. People who have bought your work at one show don't want to see similar work selling for less at the next show.

• Good luck. Just do your best.

Framing: Framing watercolors is expensive. They need to be put behind glass for protection. They are normally framed with a matt, which makes the final product bigger. Bigger is more expensive to frame.

The artist is responsible for the cost of the framing.

You can do the framing yourself, but it is not easy and must be well done. I did my own framing for years, for better or worse. One gallery I showed at had its own framing department. It was not unusual for someone who purchased one of my paintings to have it taken out of my frame and then have the gallery frame it.

One-artist and group shows:
Galleries usually have some form of art show each month. The artists represented by the gallery will often get a show of their own every year or two. The gallery also may have a show featuring several artists at once.

In my experience, if you are represented by a gallery, the gallery will keep at least one or two of your pieces of work showing at all times and other pieces available.

Other avenues to sell: You can show your work at juried or non juried shows, restaurants, banks, town halls and so on. Wherever your work is shown, it can be for sale.

Artists can be poor sales people: Few artists are good business people and they often find it a challenge to market their work. They have a different approach to life. If you are good at business, you are most likely in business, rather than painting. Of course, there are exceptions to this - people who are good artists and good marketers.

Web site and/or Facebook page: You will need an internet presence. It is the business card of today. I have sold only one painting through my site alone, but it is visited frequently by people interested in my work.

Decorative or not: Artwork is normally bought to hang on walls in private homes. People have to live with it. Artwork with a decorative quality often sells well. Let me explain what I mean by *decorative*.

Work with a decorative quality is quiet. It steps back from intensity. When you look at it there is a distance. It doesn't grab you. It can be very beautiful. Matisse's work has this quality. Landscapes often have this quieter nature.

Artwork that is more emotive can be hard to live with. That usually makes it harder to sell.

Subject matter: The subject matter of my paintings varies a great deal. I paint what makes sense to me at the time. Here are several stories on this issue:

• For a period of time I painted horses. I took them to a gallery I was in and was told that they already had an artist who painted horses. They didn't want another. I thought that horses are a pretty big subject with lots of possibilities, but I didn't run the gallery.

• The gallery in Portland, Maine where I showed regularly has a holiday show every year. They show about eight small paintings by each represented artist. The first year I showed there, I did a group of smallish plein-air paintings of Maine scenes. They all sold. The next year, for the same holiday show, I did ballet scenes. I really liked them. They were important to me and to the paintings I would do later. The owner of the gallery told me they wouldn't sell. I thought about Christmas and The Nutcracker Suite Ballet, and I was sure that they would. They didn't sell at all.

These were good lessons. They didn't change what I chose to paint, but I learned something about art and money and galleries.

Getting turned down: Getting turned down from shows or galleries happens all the time. It is difficult. It is the price artists have to pay for having the courage to bring their work to the public. It's also okay. It is important to get used to it, and not let it stop you.

Famous living artists: There are artists with big names who sell their art for very high prices. They are usually represented in the big cities by well known galleries.

Famous local artists: In every smaller city or town, there are always a few local artists who gain a reputation and sell well. They often have a recognizable product that is very well done, attractive, and sought after. Their work often has a connection to where they live. They usually make a living with their art.

Popularity: Being a good selling popular artist is great. If there is a downside to being popular, it might be that it could limit what you paint. If one type of painting you make sells well, you might find yourself doing more of those. If you became well known for selling lighthouse paintings, the people buying your paintings will want lighthouses. You may find yourself painting a lot of lighthouses.

A Painting, "Lincoln"

Let me take you through the making of a painting, in this case one of Lincoln. There are many stages depicted here of the process of the painting. I was attracted to painting Lincoln after reading a book about him.

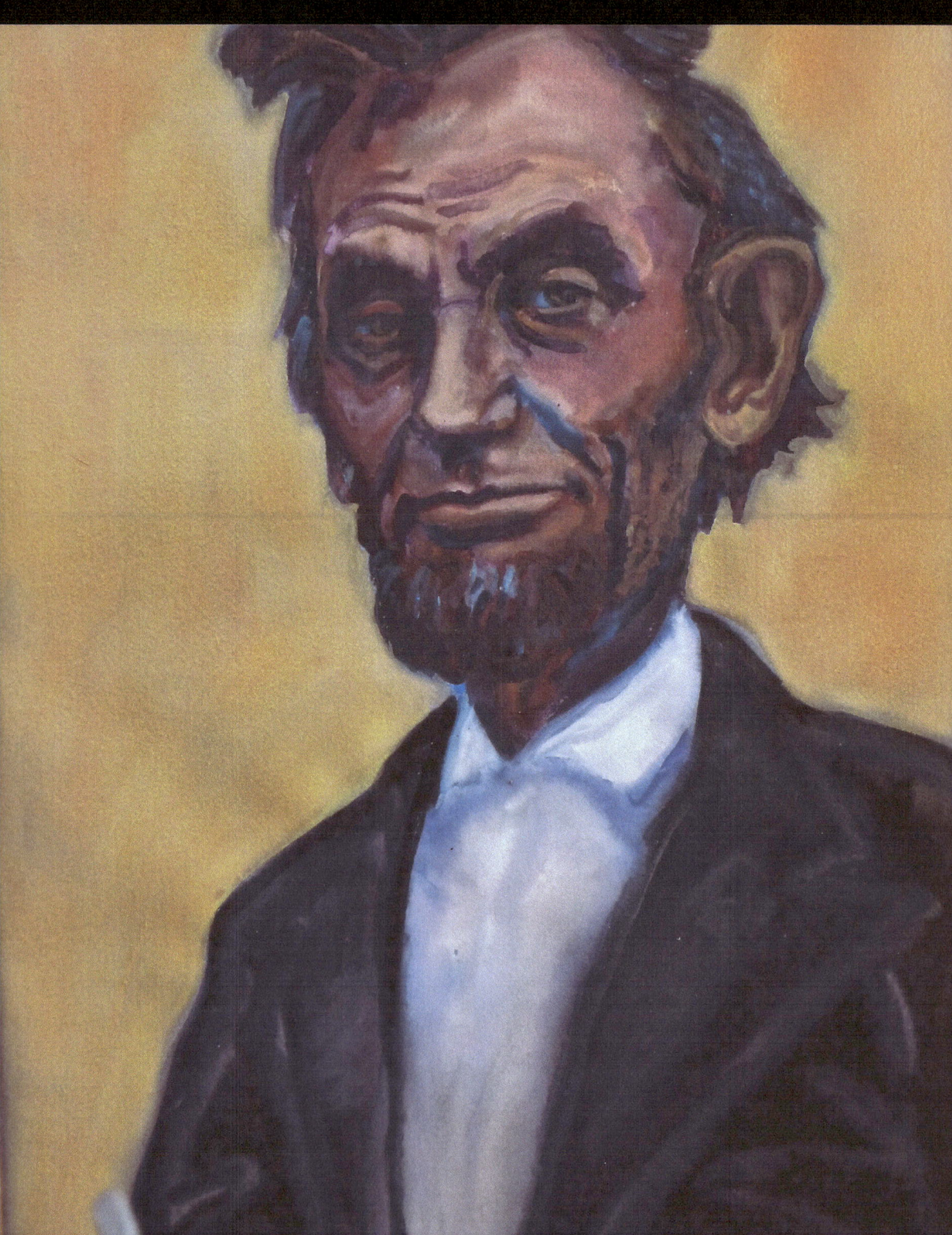

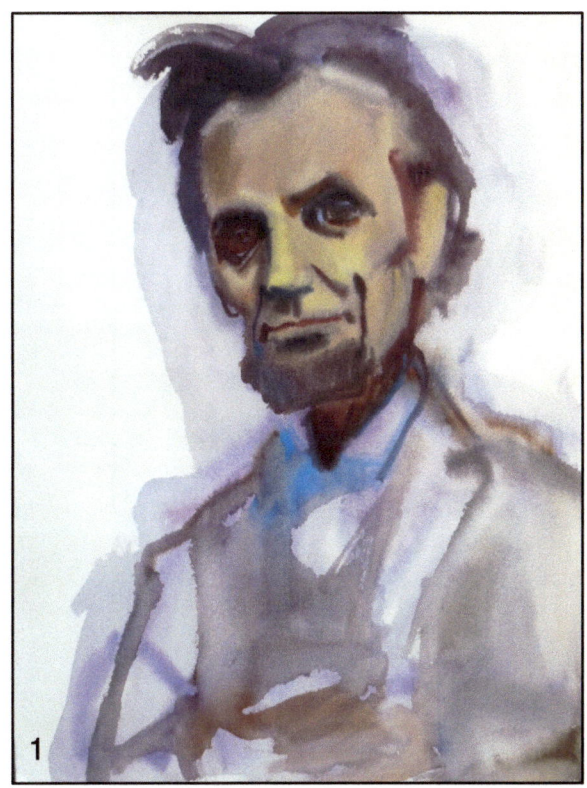

1

The painting begins: The paper has been thoroughly wet using a 2" wash brush. The preliminary drawing is done with a round paint brush and paint. (I start with manganese violet because it has very little staining power.) I begin making marks, drawing, not worrying about right or wrong, just getting something on the paper to look at. Then I proceed using whatever colors feel right. The wet paper keeps things moving and a little out of control. It's important to not get stopped here by thinking too much. Just paint. Get started.

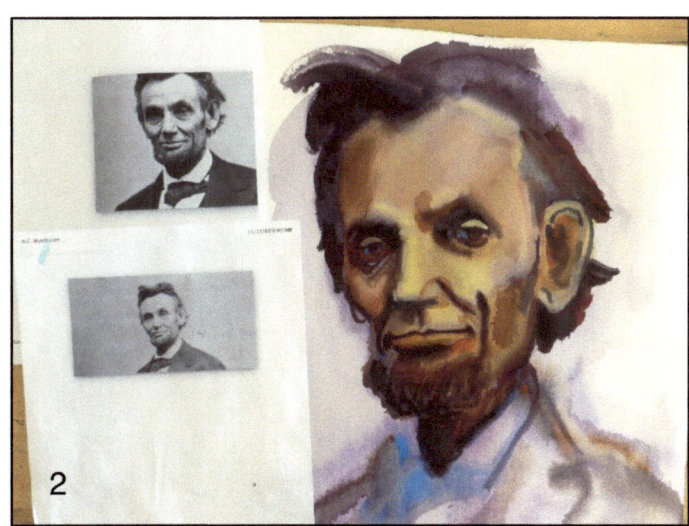

2

I am working from a couple of old photos of Lincoln. There are not many photos of him. I chose these photos because his eyes appear tired and his hair is a mess.
I have added some color in the face here. The jaw is too small.

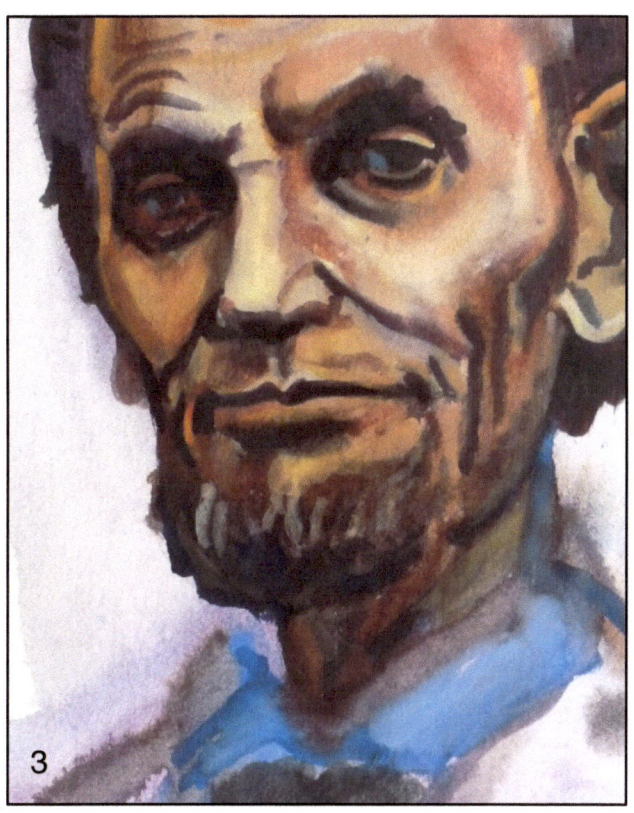

3

The painting proceeds.

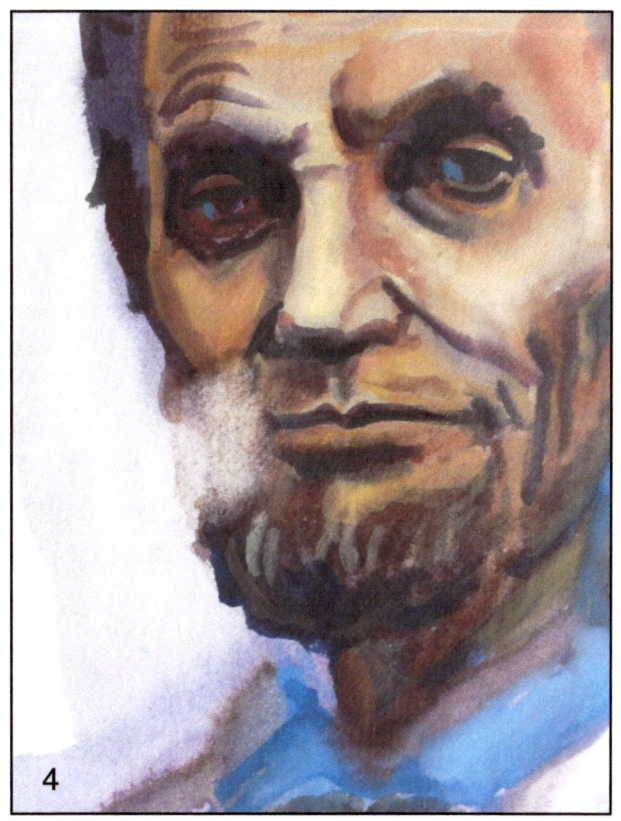

4

Watercolors are workable: If something is wrong, change it. Here I have *lifted* an area of paint that I didn't like. I used a wet paint brush to loosen the paint, and then mopped it off the paper with a damp brush.

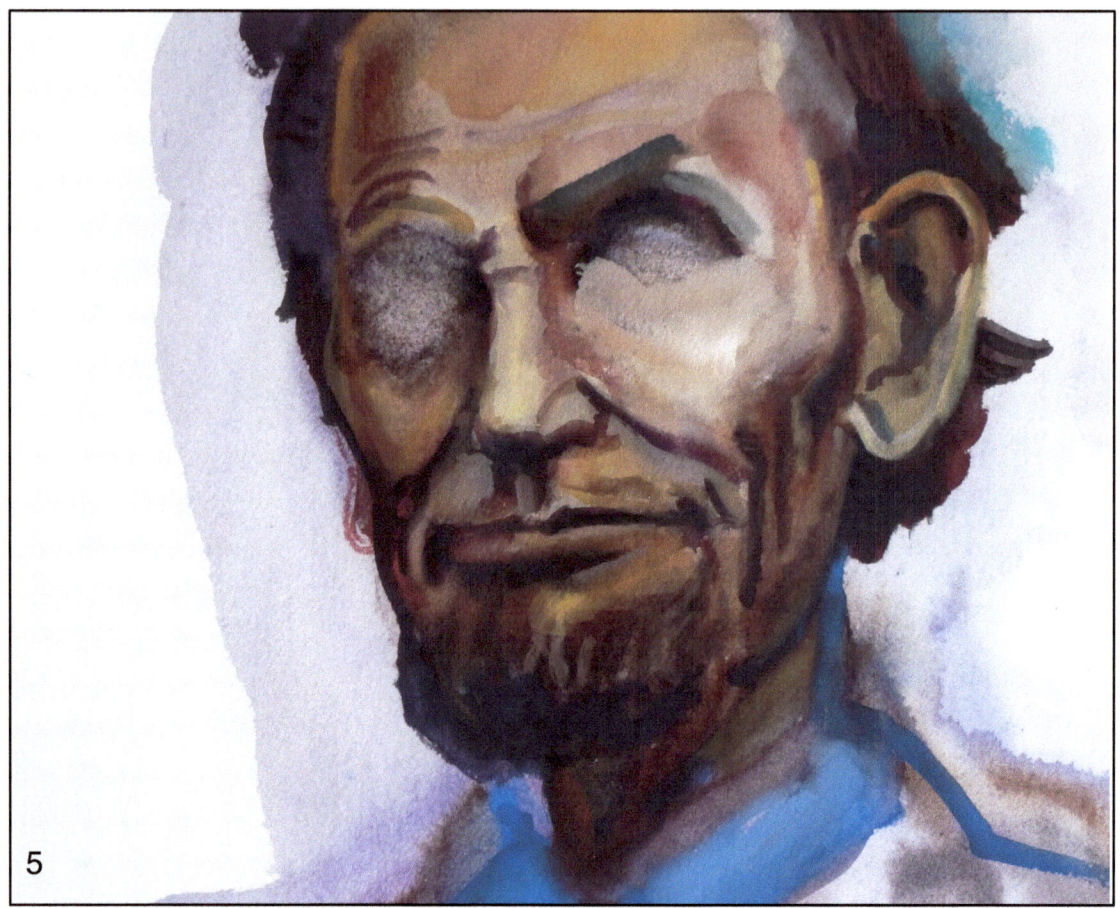

I'm not liking what's going on in the painting: Things are feeling wrong. I don't like how I am painting. It's too fussy and I am not using enough paint. My frustration is building. I want the painting to be more than just correct. I want "something" to happen. I don't know what that "something" is. It has to do with relinquishing, I think, *allowing* rather than *forcing*.

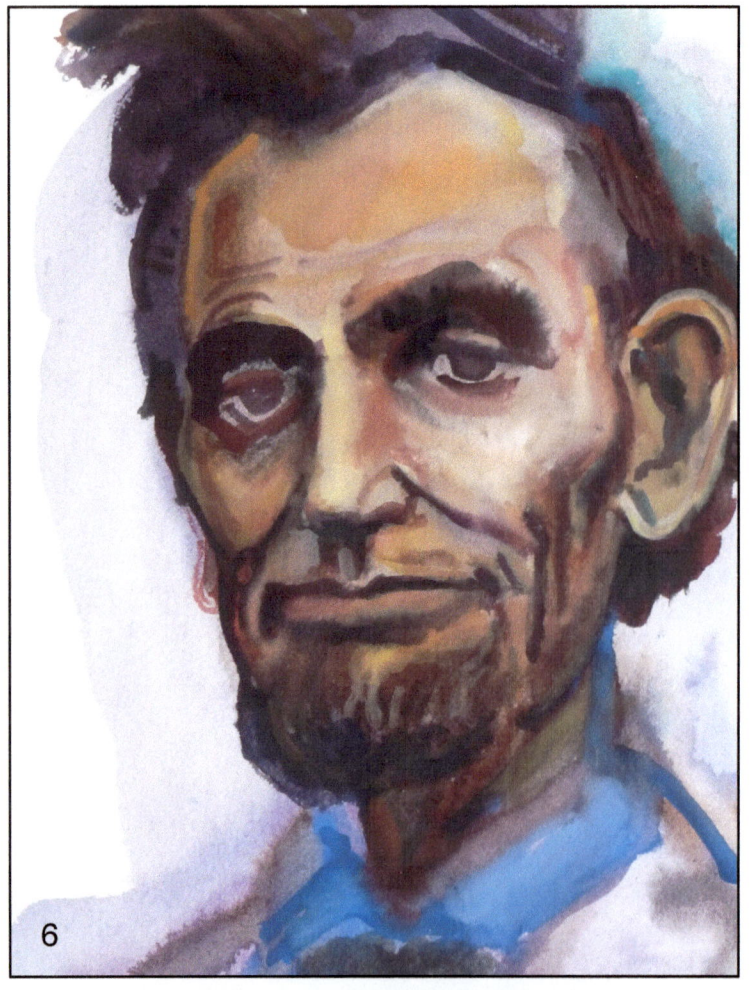

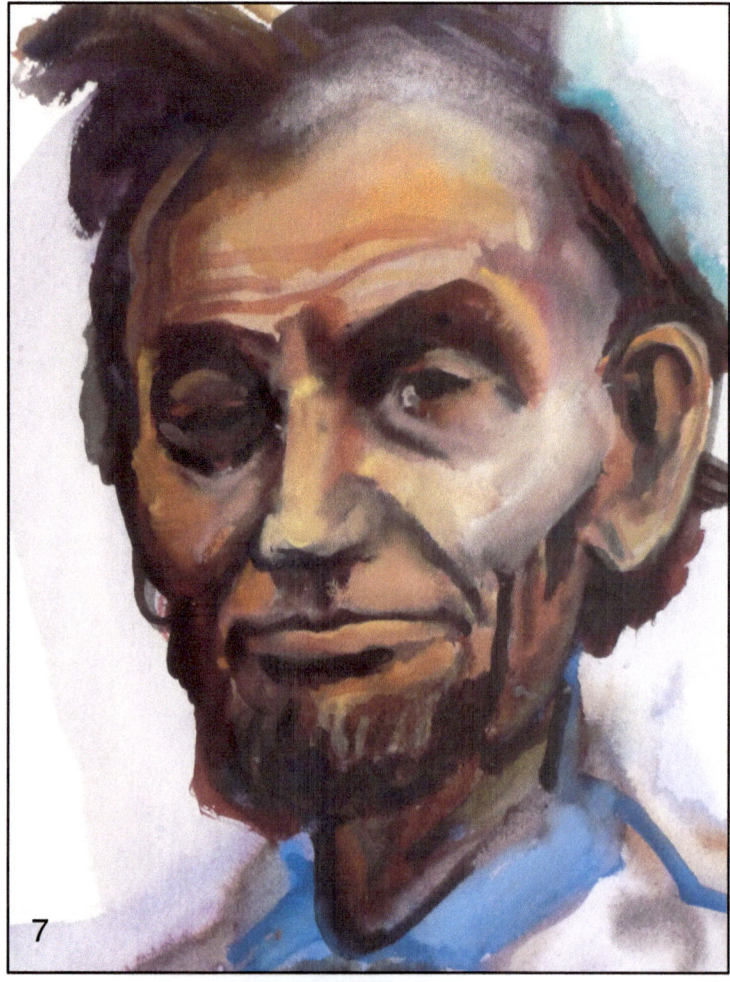

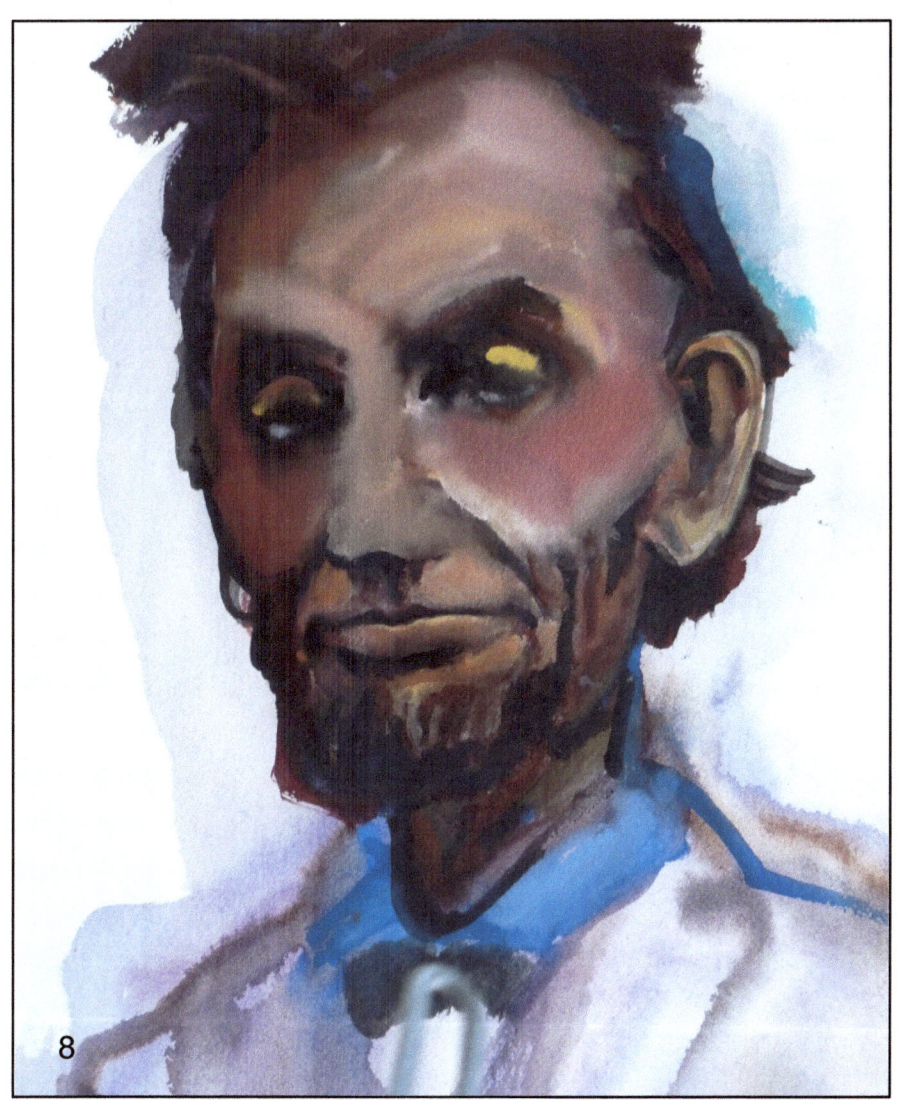

A big change: I wetted large parts of the face and got some paint on the paper. It's a mess but it makes me happy. From here the painting can proceed freshly. This type of big change seems to happen in most paintings I do. It is a *letting go moment*. It is a decision that comes from the body. It feels good. It can be trusted.

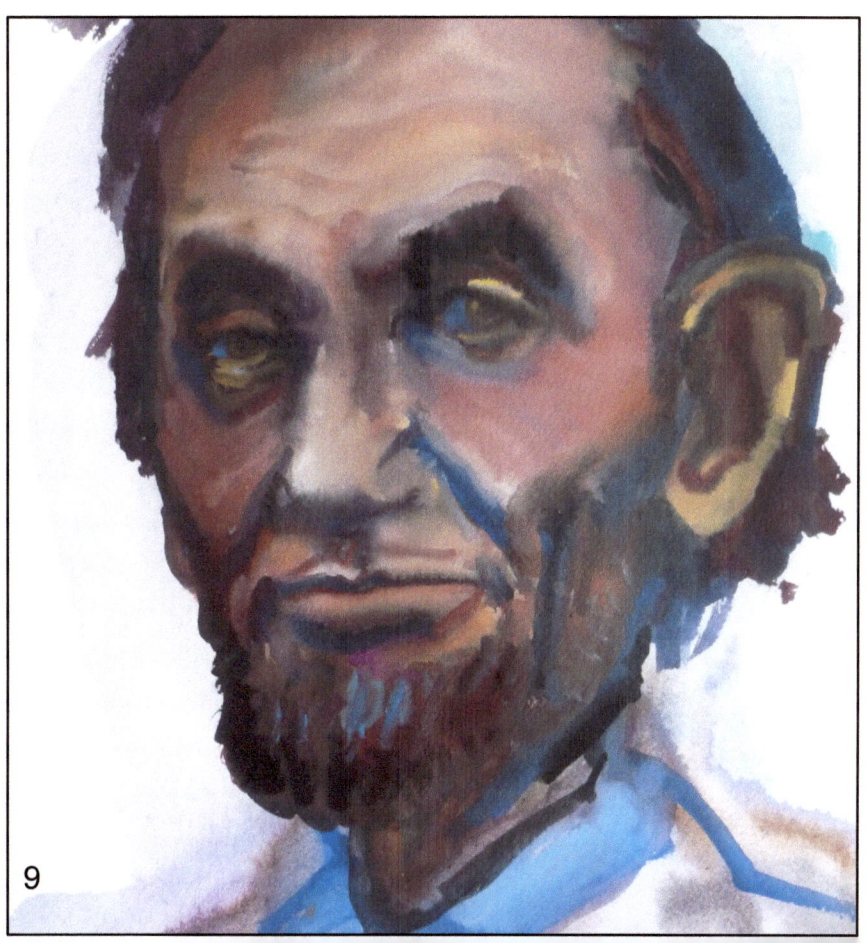

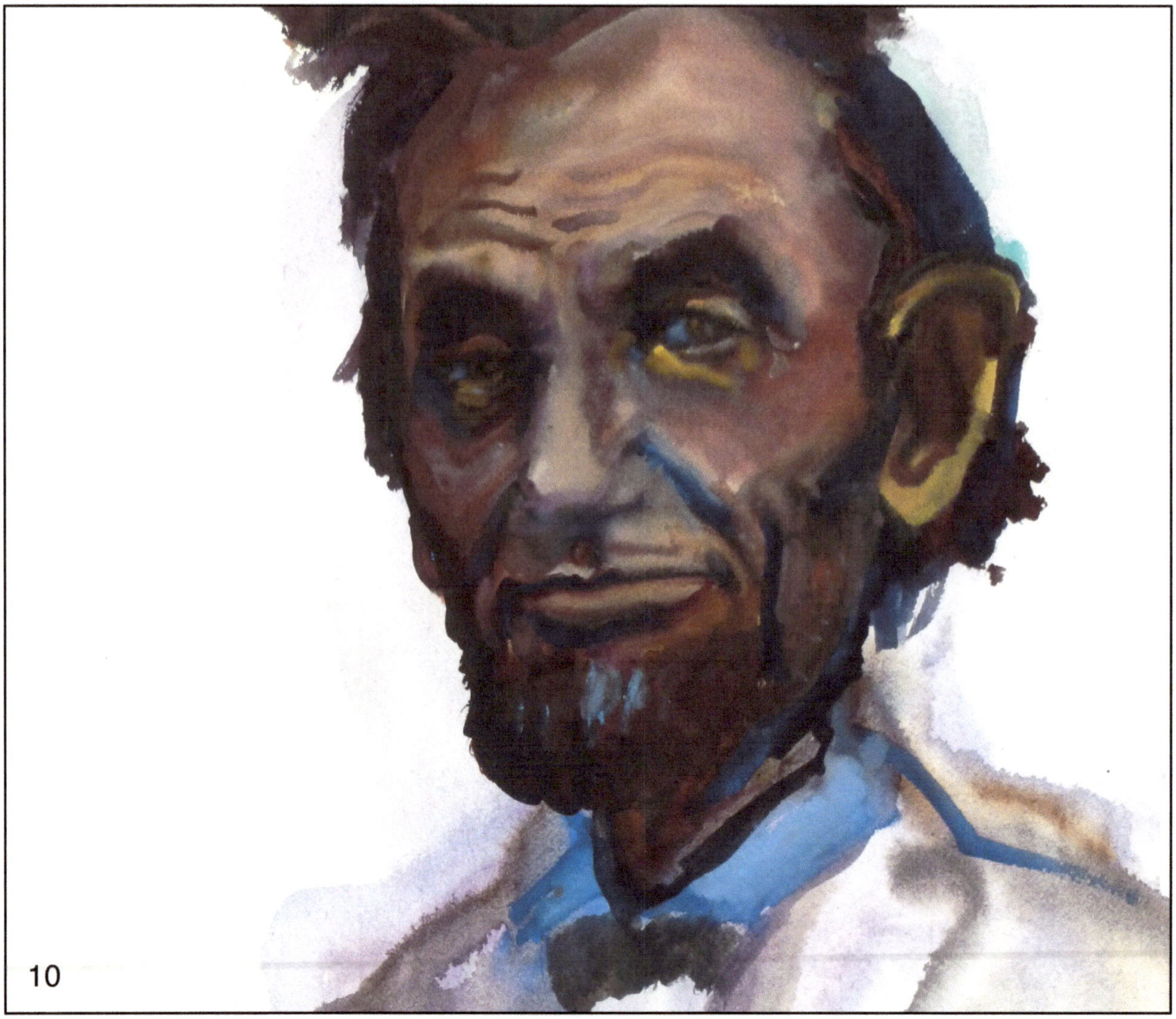

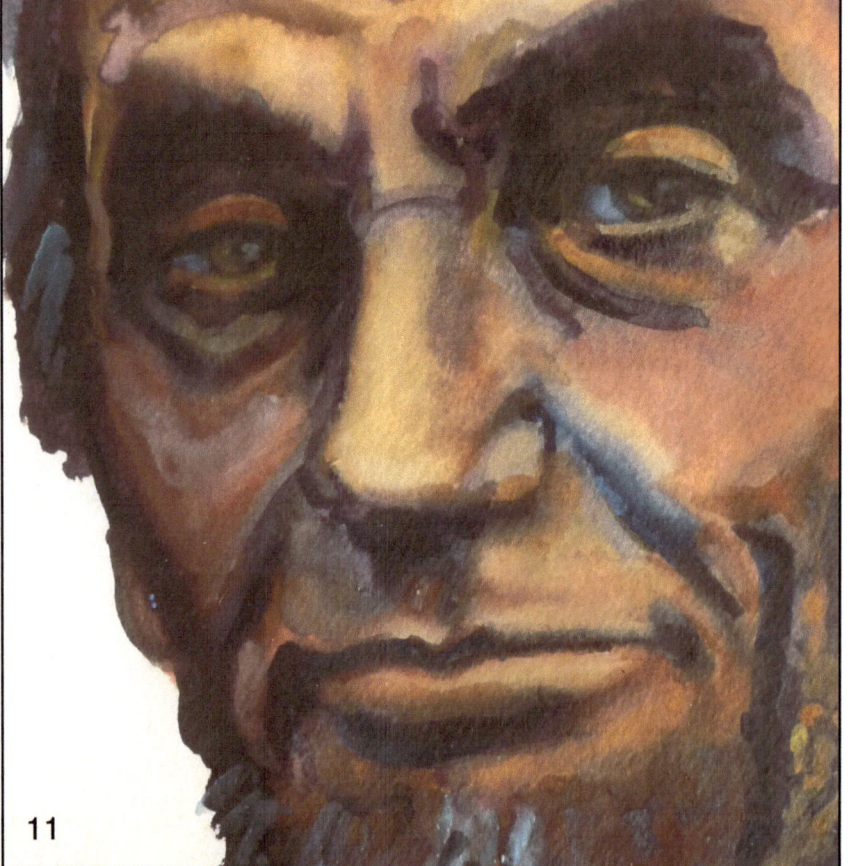

10

The painting proceeds. Now it is feeling good. Getting more physical, losing control, has allowed my own compassion to enter the painting. I think this shows in Lincoln's face.

I remove the tie to allow Lincoln to be less trapped in time.

Having worked on this painting for some time now, I know what Lincoln looks like. The marks I make can be bolder because I know where they belong.

At this point, the photo that this painting came from is no longer part of the painting. The painting has become more human, more humane, more compassionate.

11

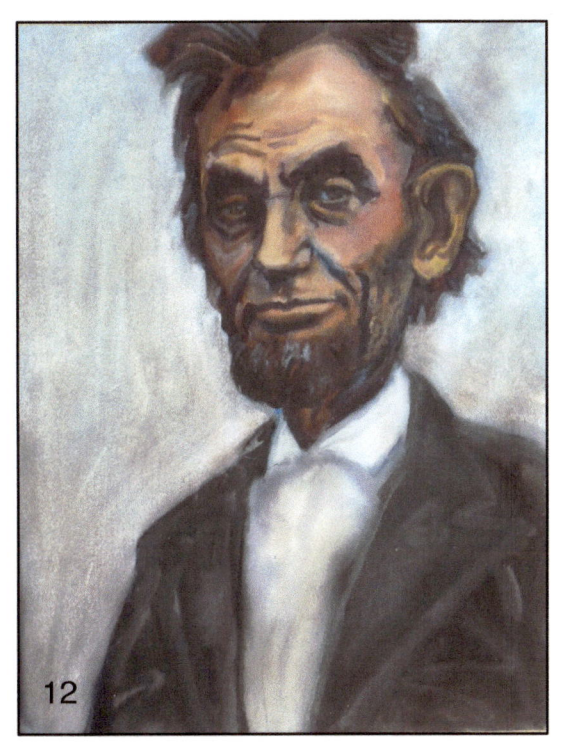

12

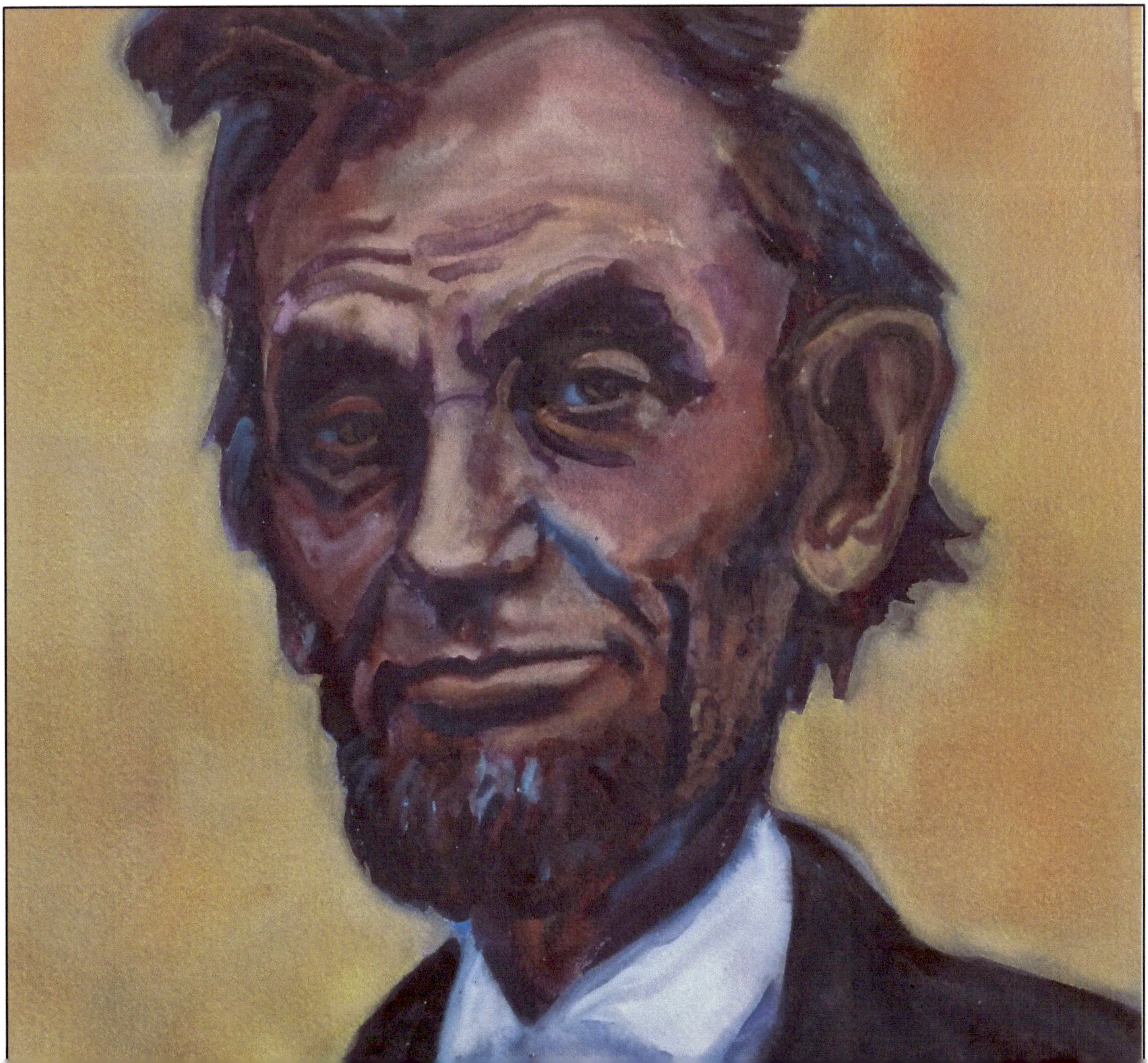

How to Do 1,000 Paintings and What it Means to Do So.

How Do You Do It?

*   Decide to do it and don't be deterred. It has got to make sense to you on a deep enough level to keep going.

*   Develop a way to get some work done every day. Create a space to do it in.

*   When you experience emotional issues, move through them. When you have judgmental thoughts, don't believe them. Don't let these things stop you. They are just part of being human. They will always be there. Paint anyway.

*   Don't work on making "art." Paint just what you want to paint. Do your own work. If you do enough work, it just might become part of "art."

*   When you get something that works, follow it for a number of paintings. You will know when the energy from the idea is gone. Learn to do this. Good paintings often take a number of paintings to develop. It is the artist's work.

*   Paint something even when you haven't a thought in your head. Paint outdoors, paint a still life, a self portrait... something. Work abstractly. Put color on paper to see what happens. Don't worry about great "ideas."

*   Paintings are paintings. They don't have to be masterpieces. Some might have value, but most won't. I went to a large Van Gogh show years ago. A lot of his paintings didn't seem like great works. They appeared somewhat uninteresting and repetitive. I still love Van Gogh.

*   Painting leads to more painting.

*   Don't count on your interest to always be strong. You are working to achieve something. Do the work. The interest might wax and wane.

*   When you take breaks from the studio, figure out ways to get started again. The ways can be clumsy. Get something going.

*   One hundred paintings a year is not hard to do with watercolors. Finish one every three or four days, and in 10 years, you'll have done 1,000 paintings.

*   Don't worry about selling them or what to do with them. That will happen by itself in time. Pile them up. Watercolors don't take a lot of space to store.

*   If you need to make money, and most people do, make it in a way that allows you to keep painting. I taught art classes three days a week.

* Life's needs can overwhelm art ambitions. Figure it out, or wait until later in life when things quiet down.

What Does It Mean?

* It means you have a chance to get good, maybe very good, at painting. You just might surprise yourself.

* People who paint wonder if they are artists. Do 1,000 paintings and you can call yourself an artist. You have done the work.

1,000 paintings is enough for a number of things to happen:

* You will learn to paint like yourself. You will develop a signature style.

* Your work will have value. Galleries will likely be interested.

* You will have worked through many mental problems that stop many people who want to paint.

* You can teach painting if you want. You will have much to offer.

* You can write a book.

The world of art is an intriguing and vital part of being human. It is an ongoing wave of energy. You have become part of it.

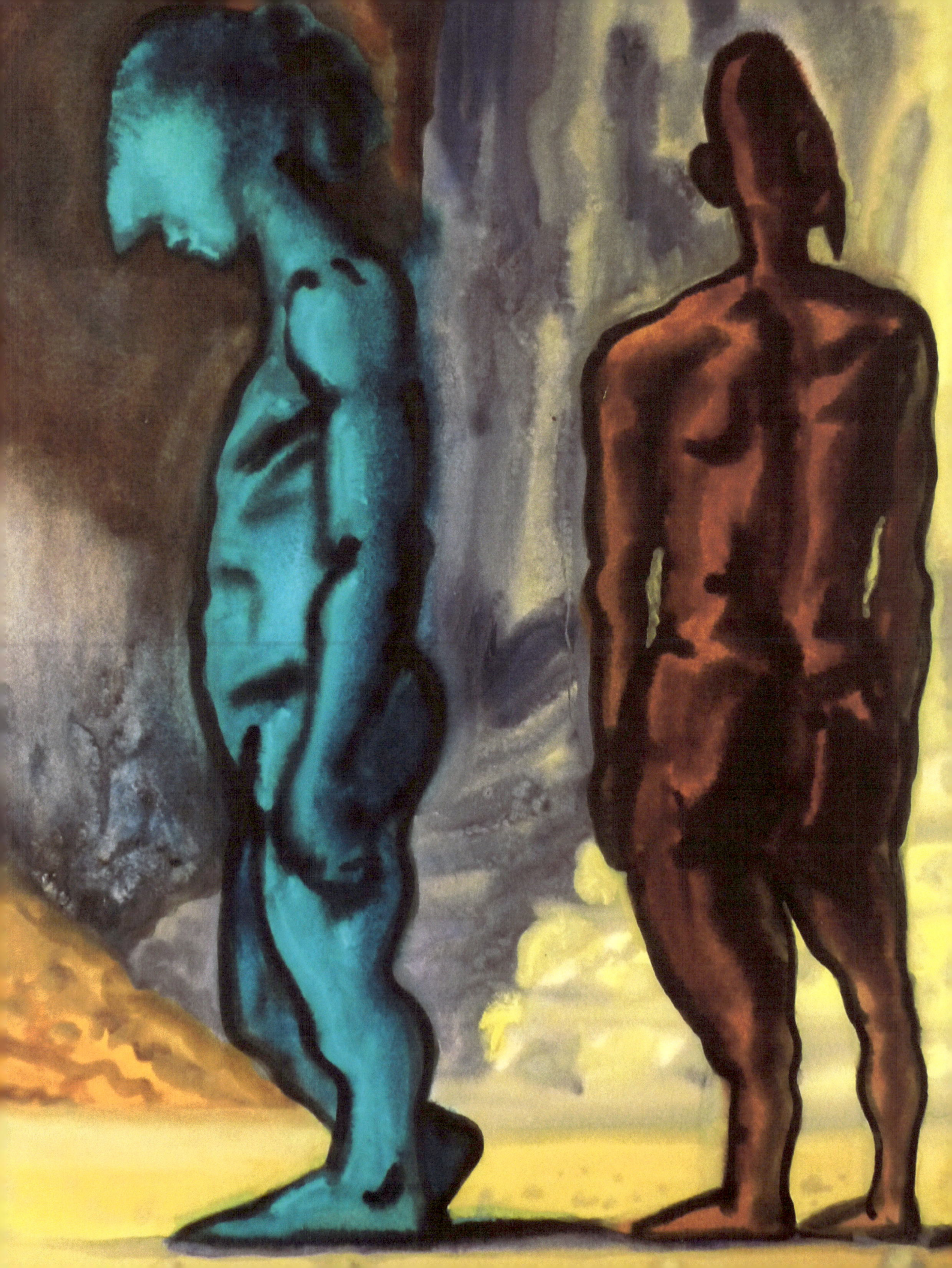

The gallery is divided into two large sections - Maine and The West. The Maine paintings are earlier work. Under these two main headings the paintings are divided into topics. These topics are areas of interest I pursued in paintings for a while or still work on. A few paintings are shown from each of these pursuits. All the paintings in this book are watercolors done by myself.

The Gallery

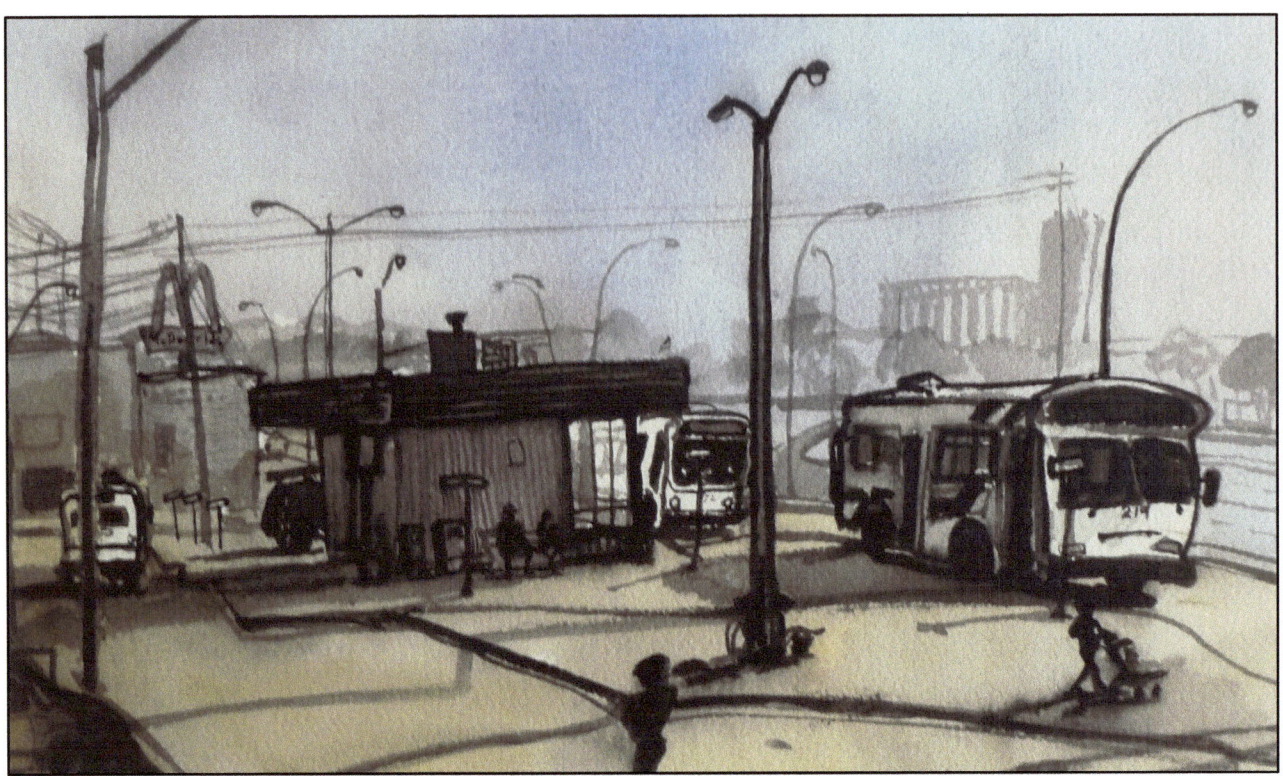

Bus Stop   11" x 14"

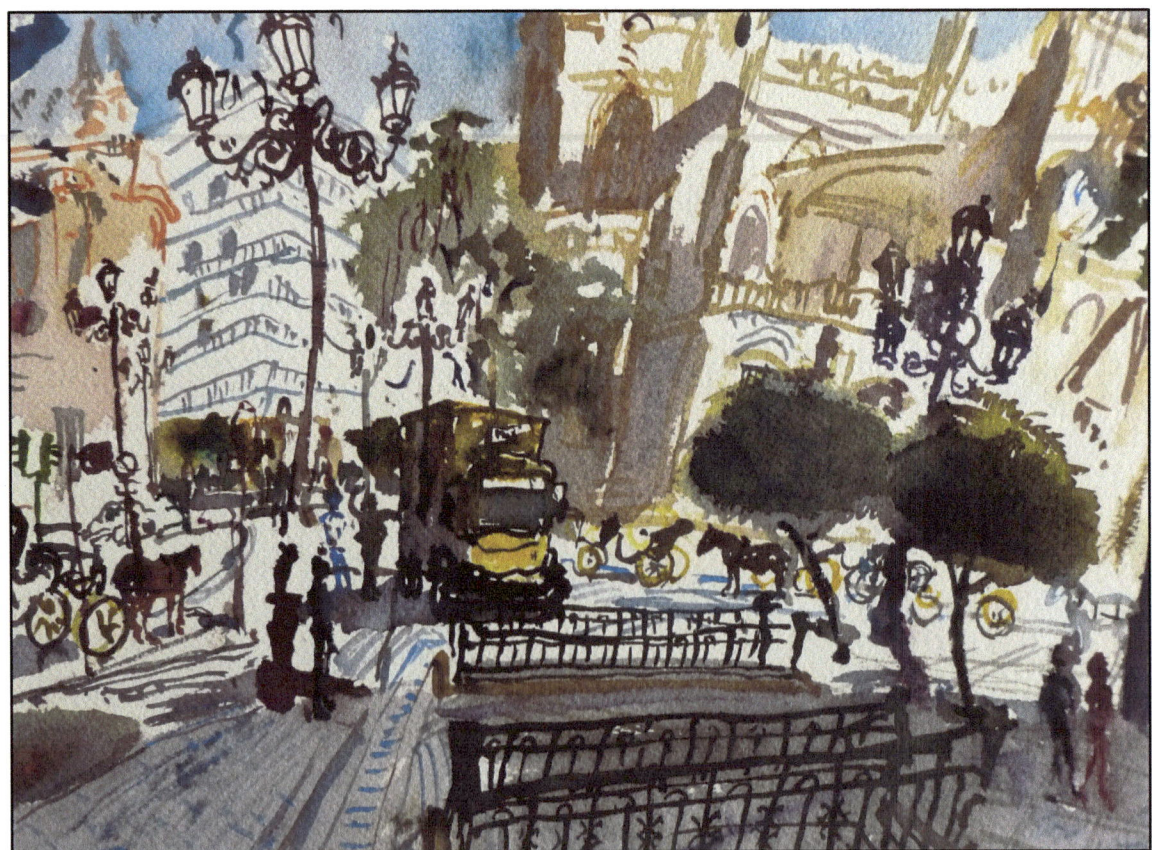

Seville Spain   11" x 14"

Plein air travel painting

I started using watercolors while traveling. I made
small plein air pictures during our trip. When I got
home and looked at them I realized this medium fit
my skills very well. I loved how they looked.

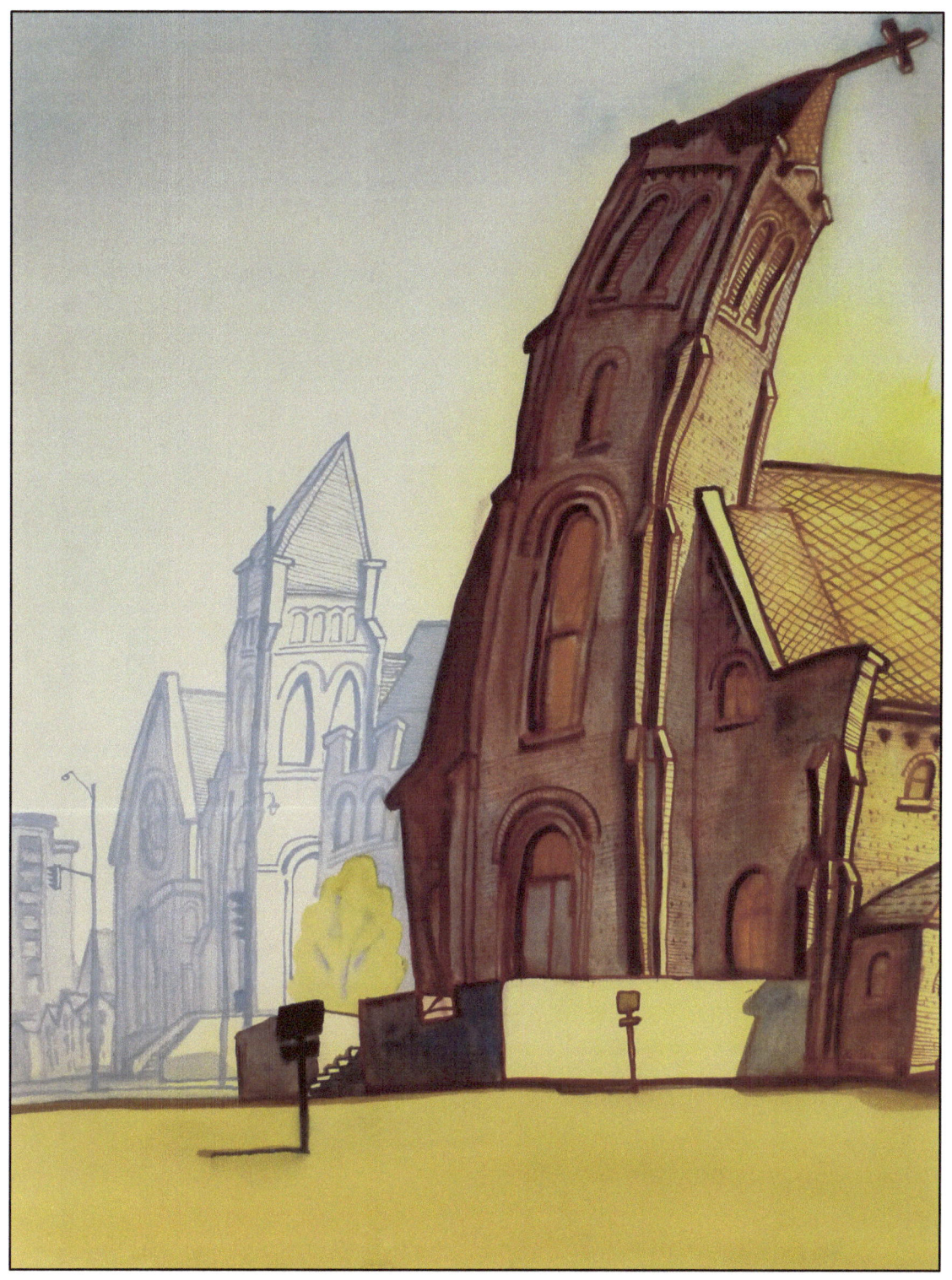

This painting came from a small plein-air work. As I was painting it, the steeple didn't fit, so I bent it into the corner of the paper. When I got back to the studio I thought that the bent steeple was an interesting image, so I made this large painting of it. I was learning that there aren't really any rules. That made painting more fun.

Release your responsibility to the scene you are painting. Artists are not cameras. This may involve allowing the position and or size of objects to change. Relaxing compositional "rules" allows the painting to become more personal.

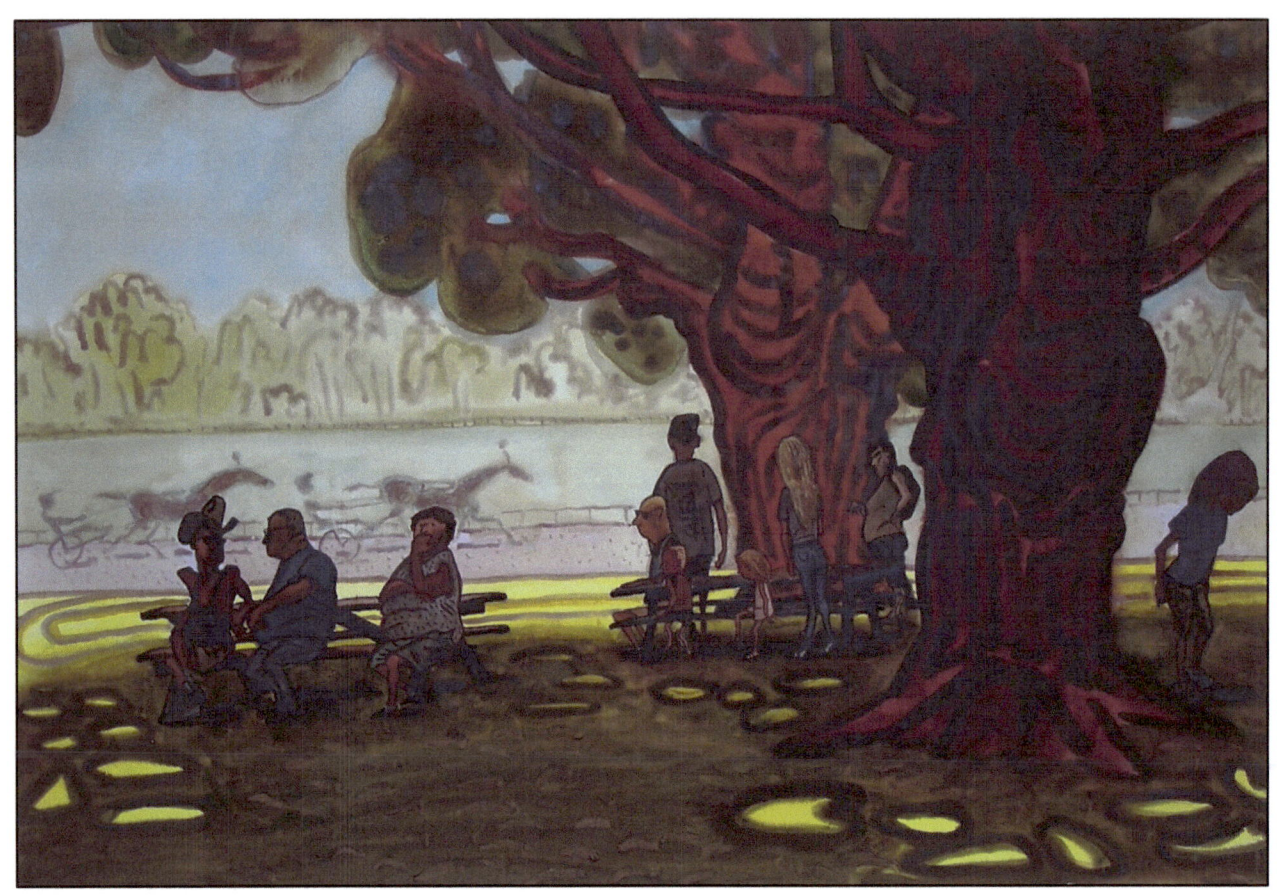

Union Fair Horse Racing 27" x 34"

Maine

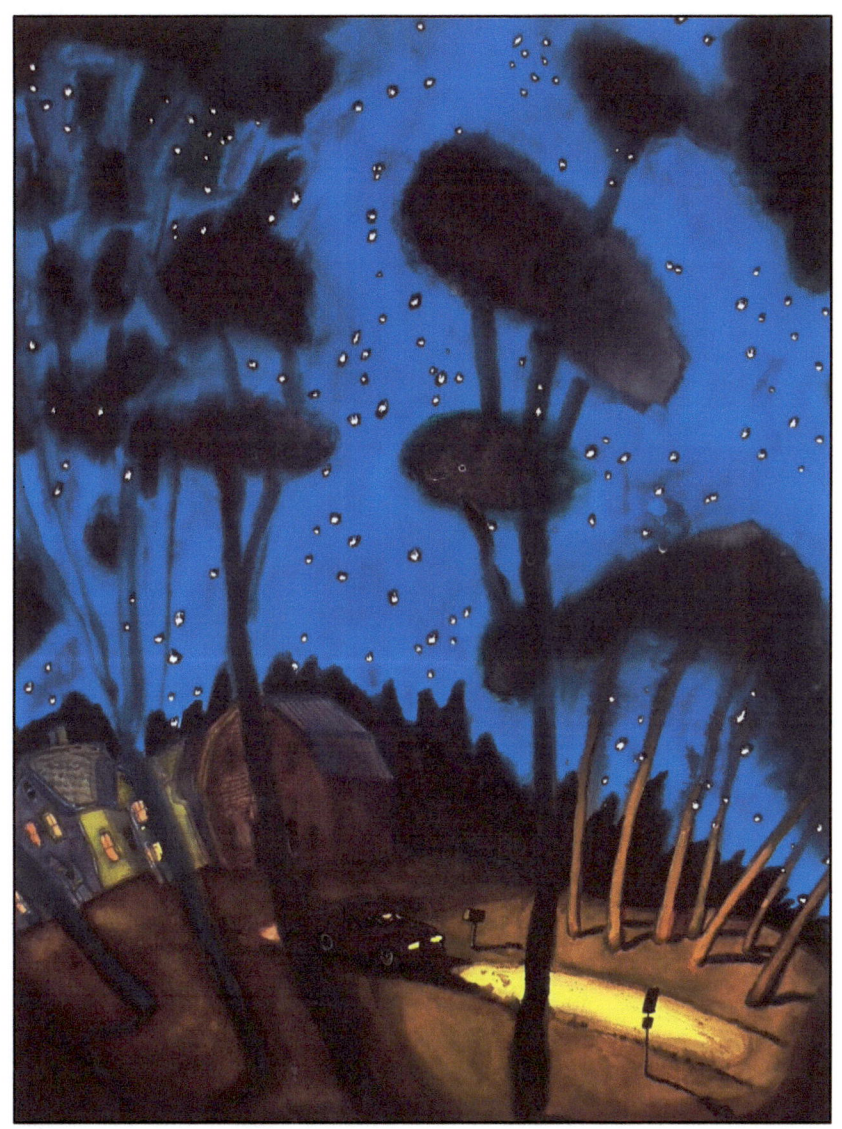

Night Message   22" x 30"

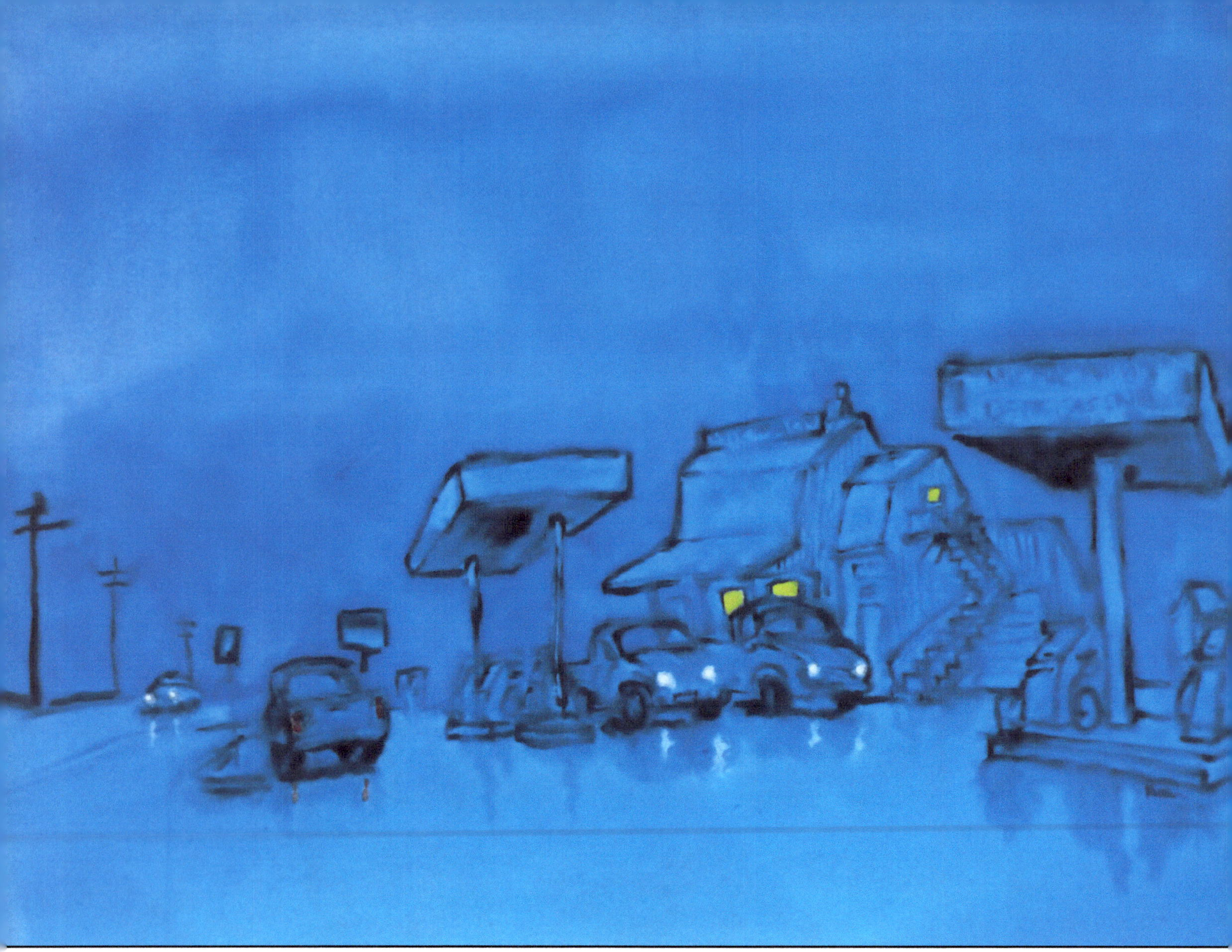

Gas Station In Blue   28" x 36"

King of Port Clyde   22" x 30"

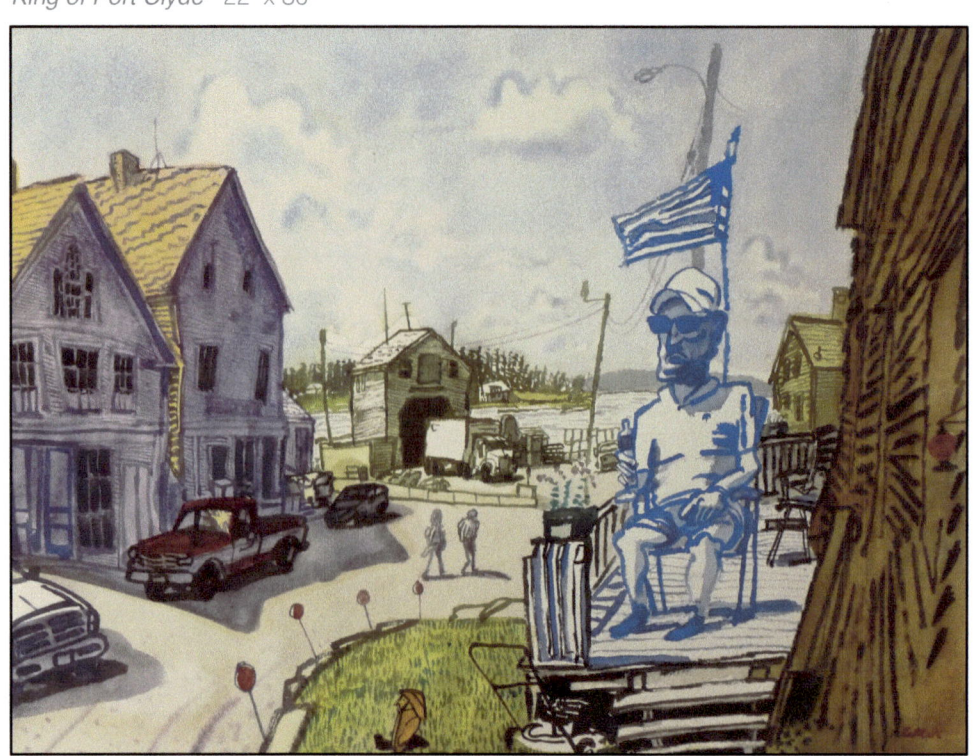

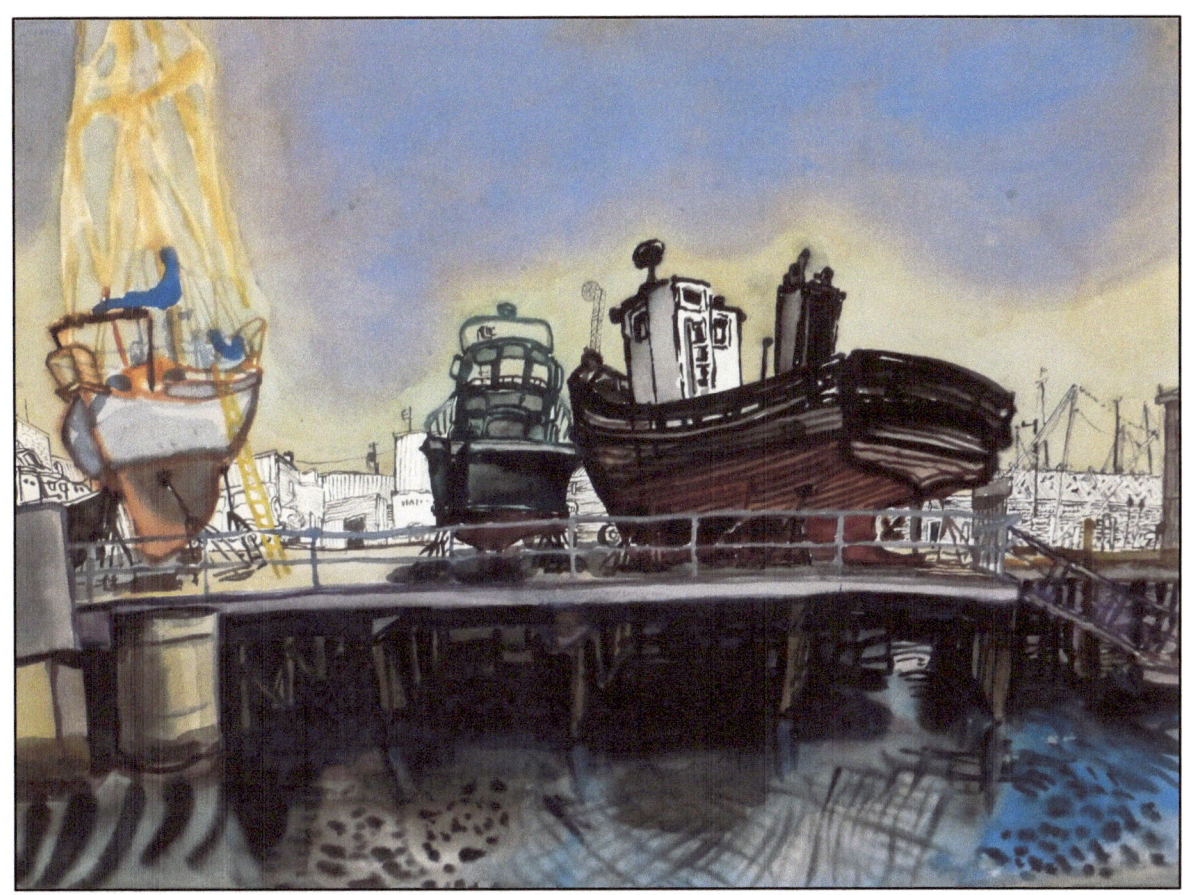

Rockland Harbor   22" x 30"

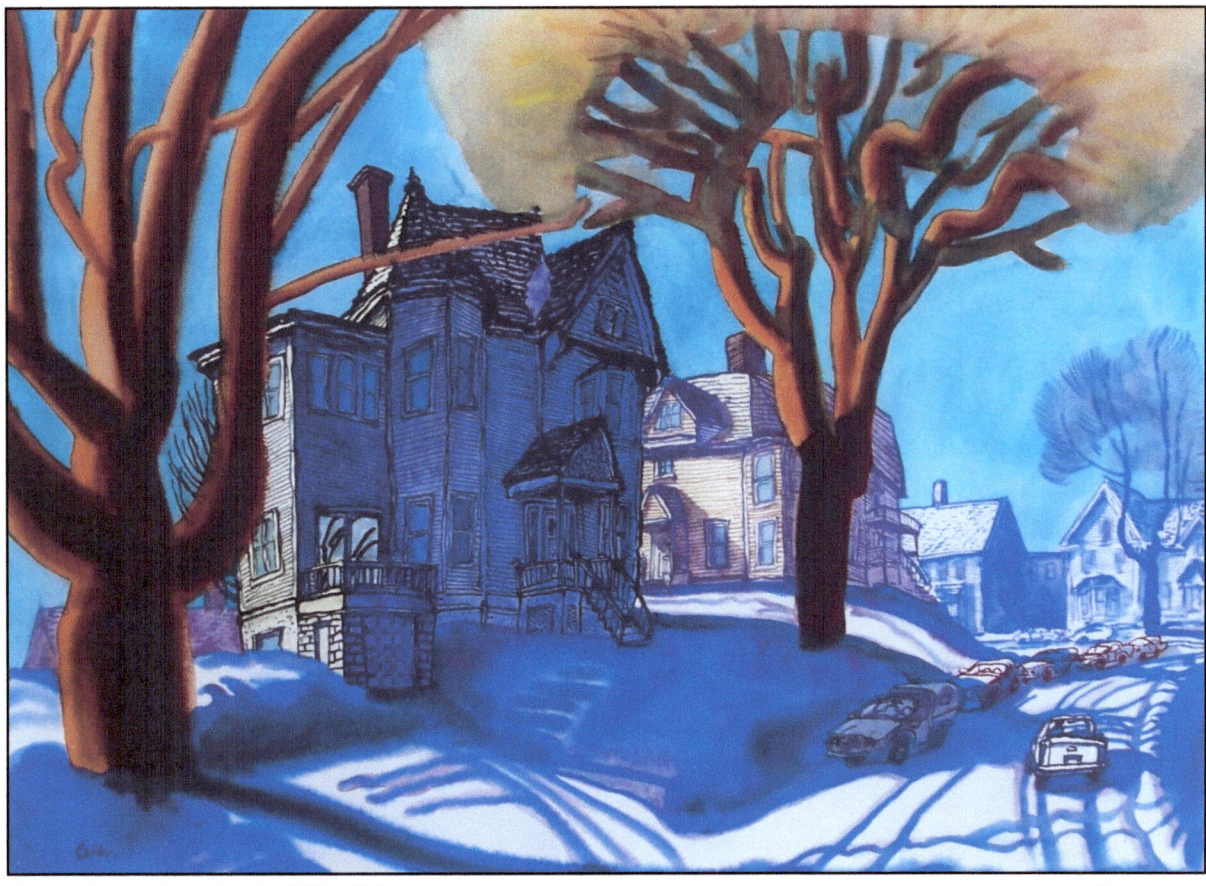

Street Scene, Rockland   22" x 30"

caddys

Inspiration does happen but it doesn't happen everyday. You may have to wait for it. In the meanwhile, keep painting. Picasso said, "Inspiration exists, but it has to find us working."

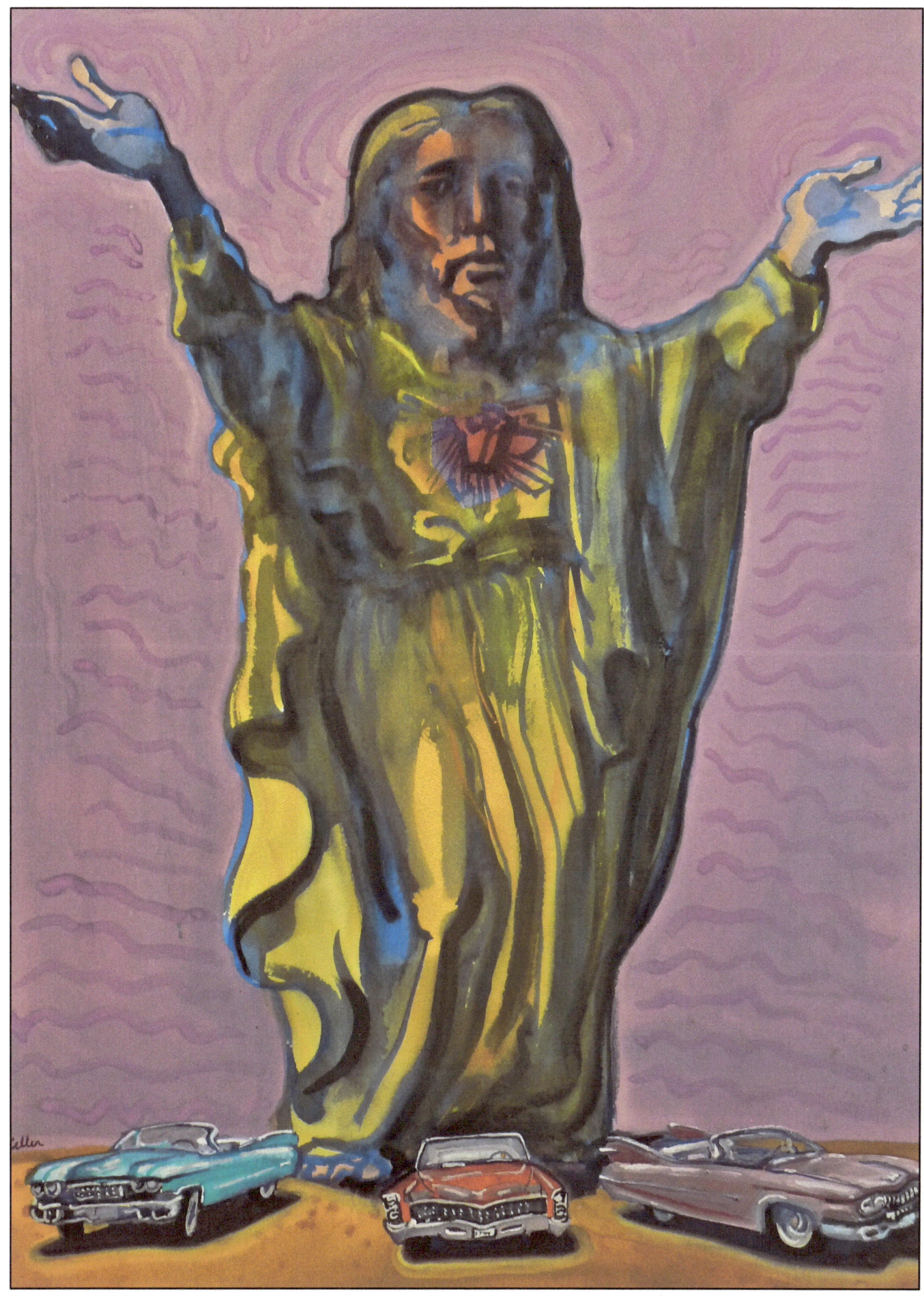

Belfast Angels #1 22" x 30"

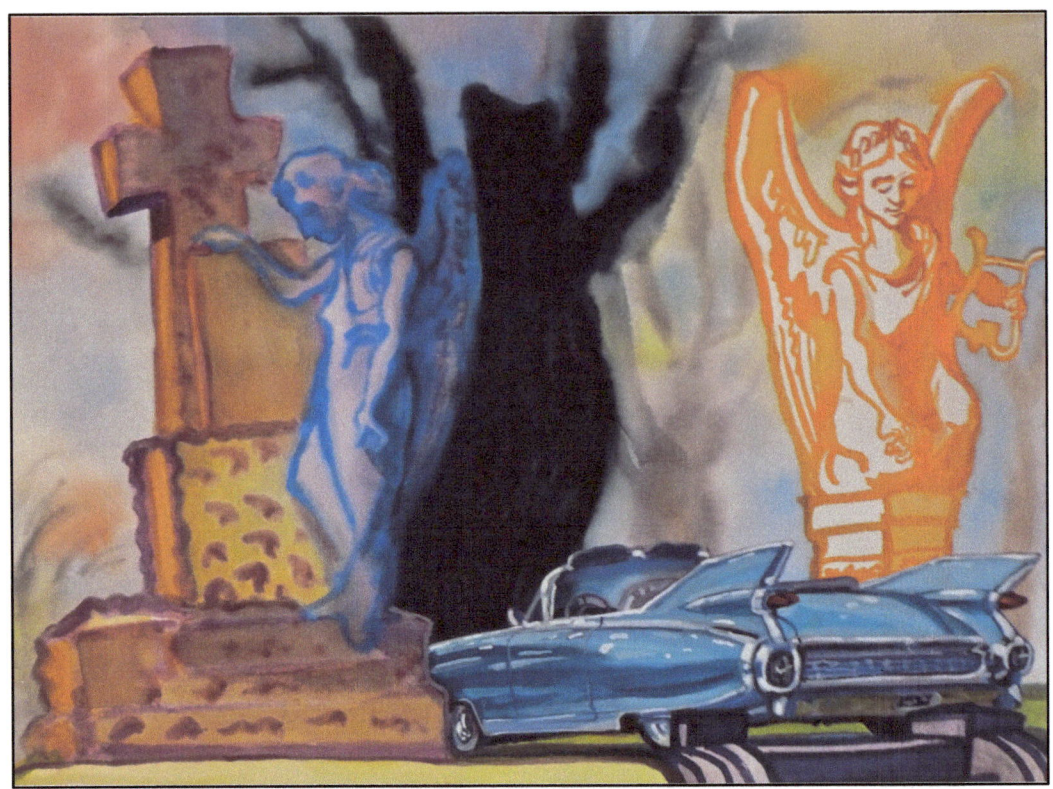

The image of Cadillacs came to me one morning. I considered it inspiration
for better or worse. The result tickles me and I feel has some depth.

Belfast Angels #2 22" x 30"
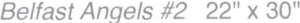

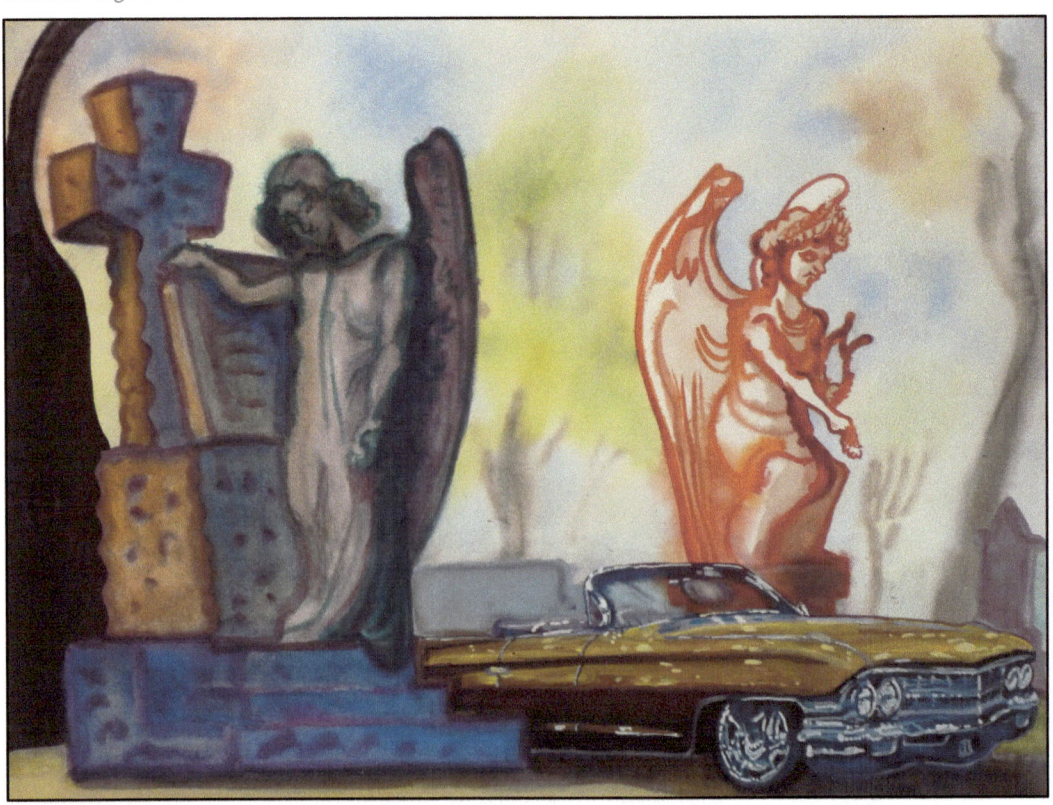

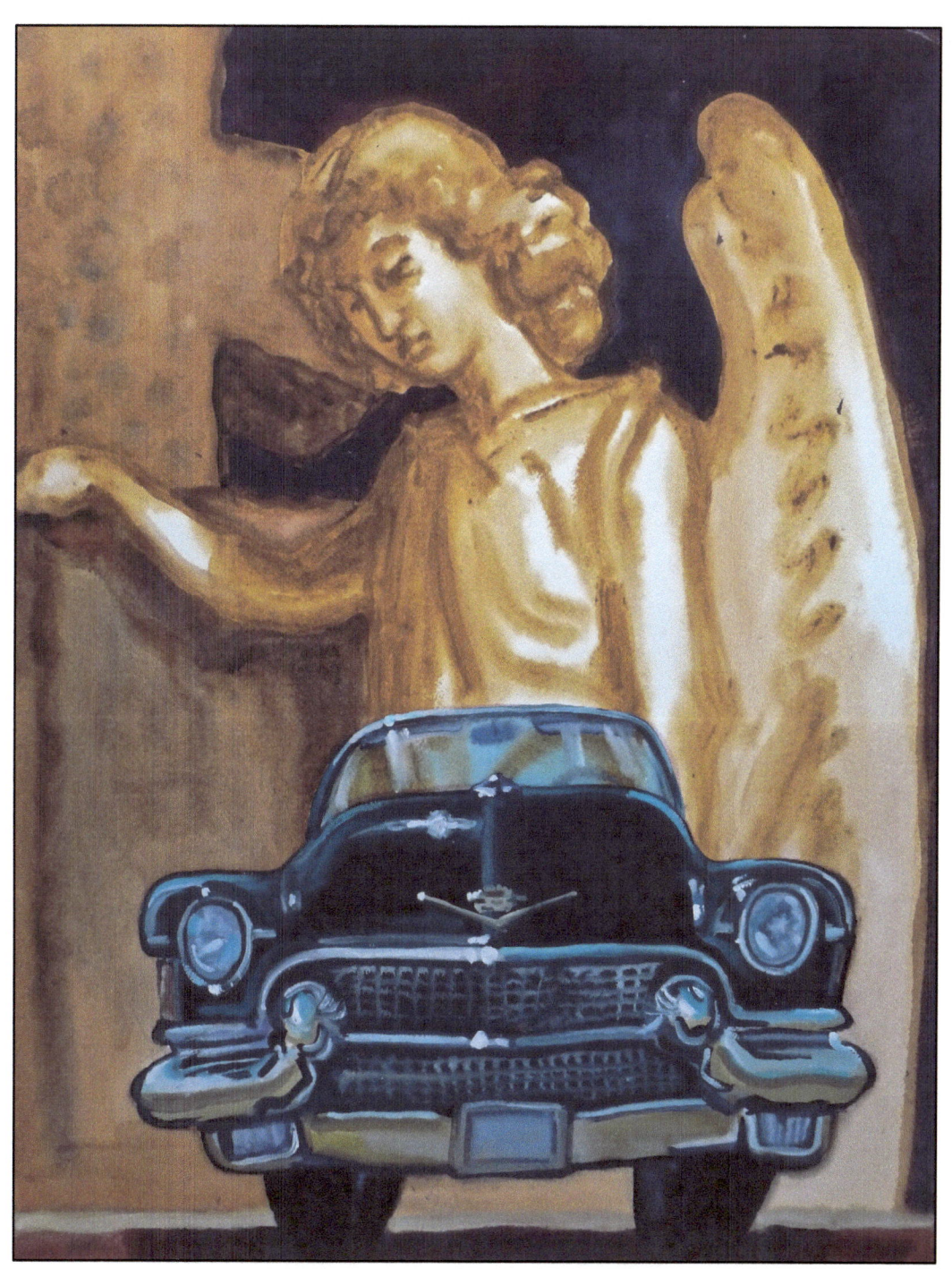

'59 Caddy   18" x 24"

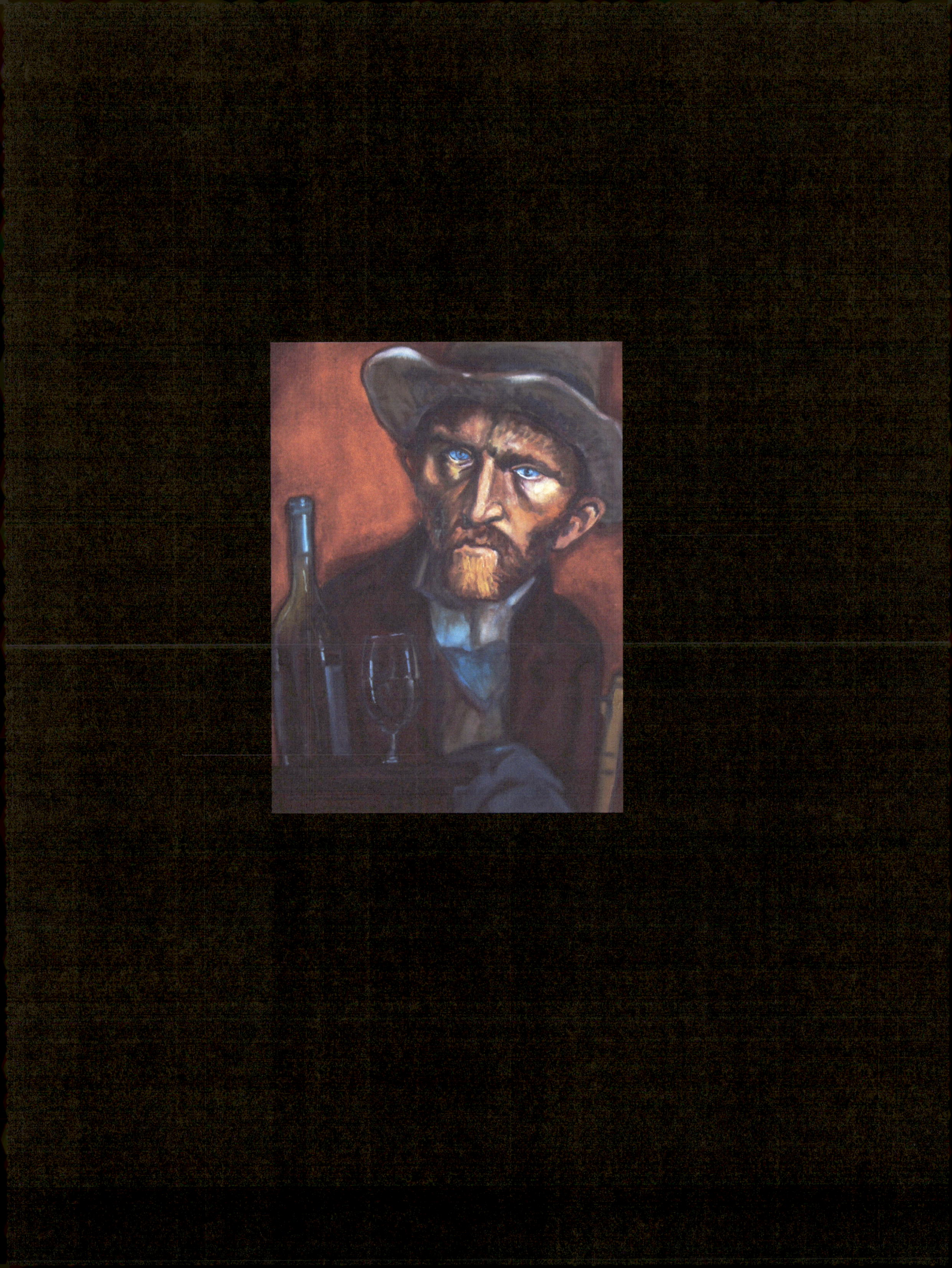

dead artists

Alice Neel

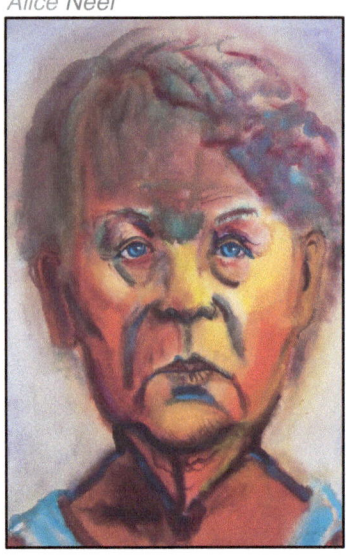

Gauguin

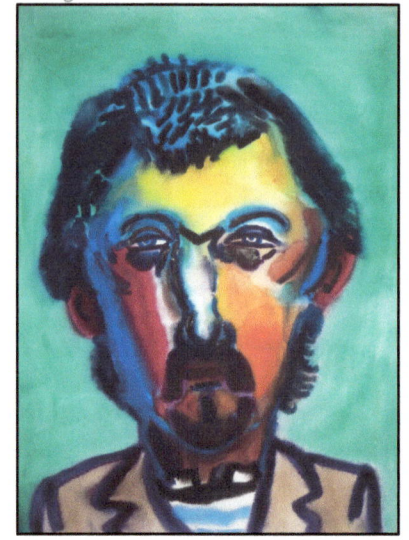

Giacometti

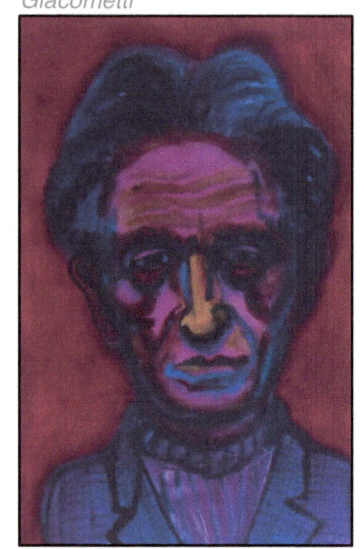

Warhol

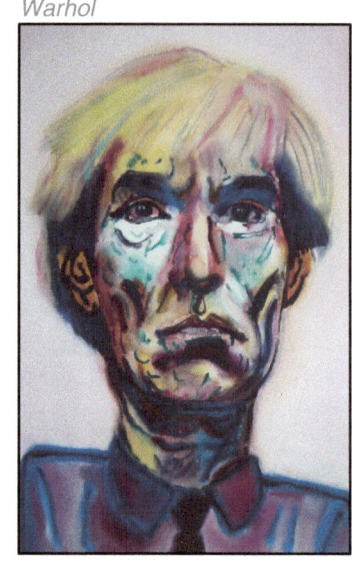

Marsden Hartley

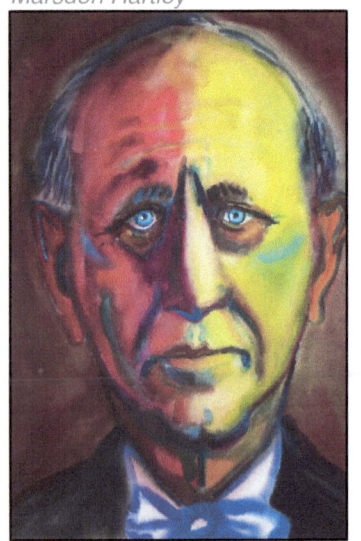

Modigliani

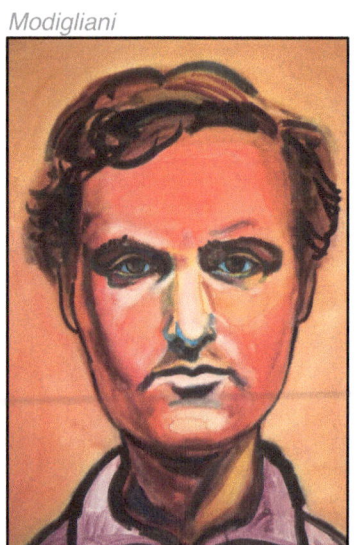

Ted, not dead yet

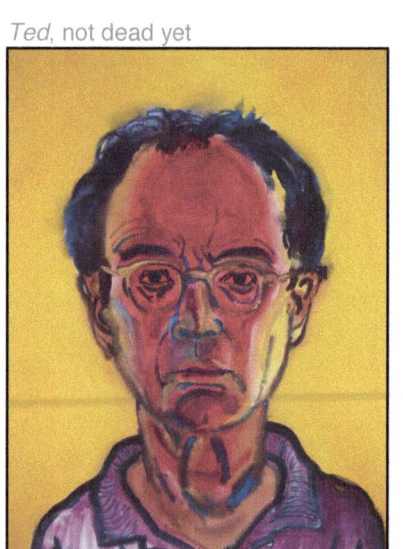

Matisse

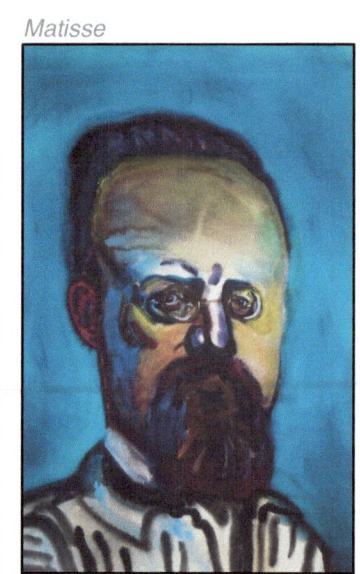

Van Gogh

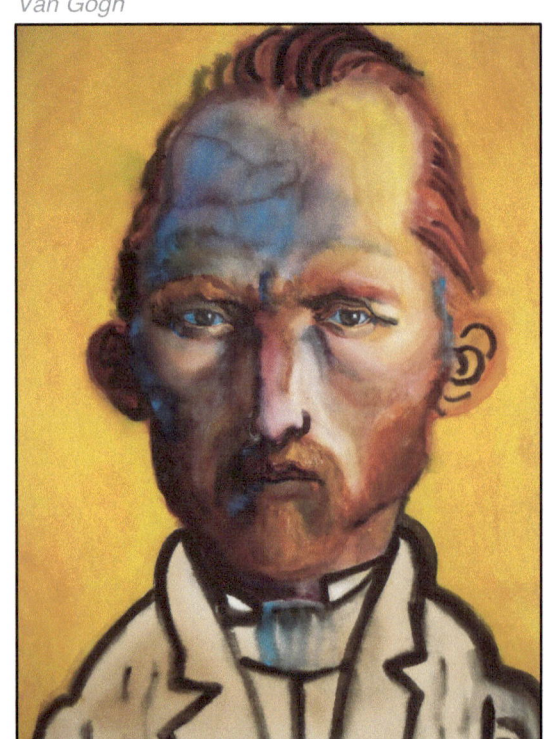

Morris Louis

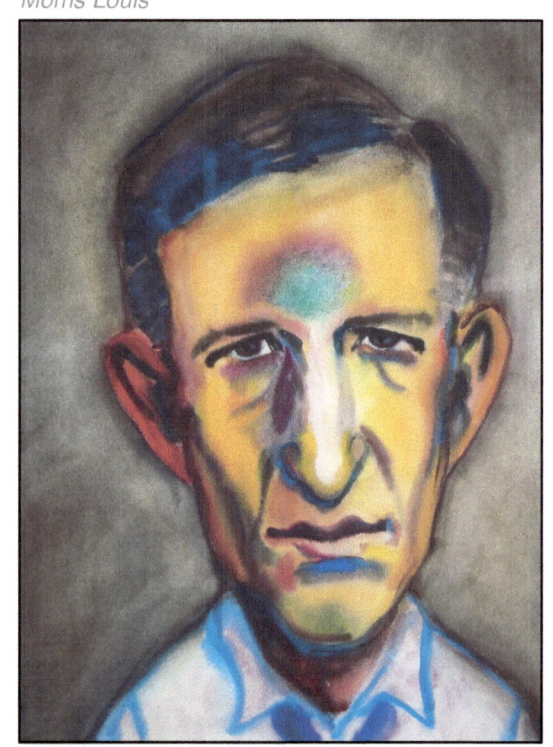

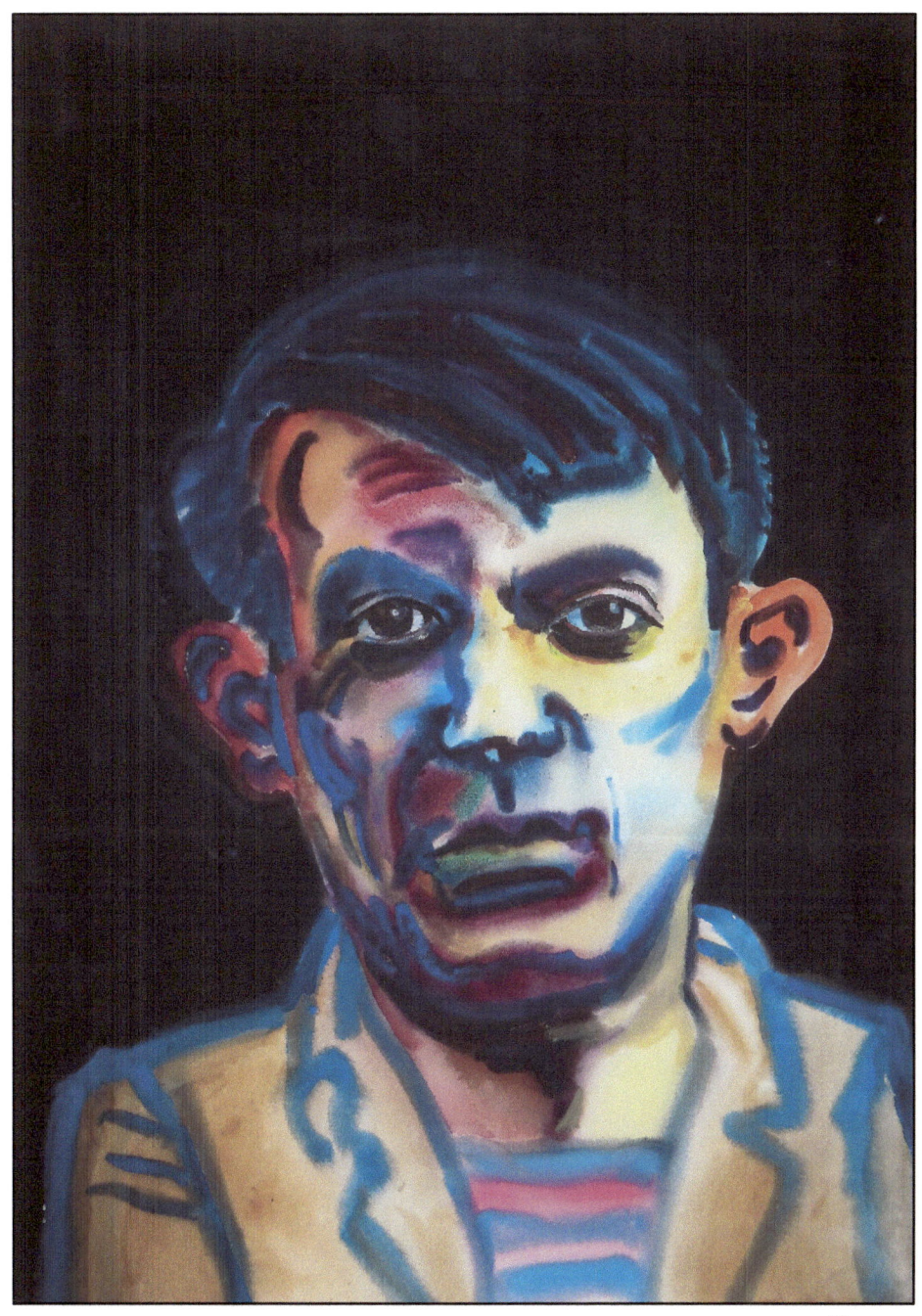

Picasso

I wanted a large project as part of my painting work. The "dead artists" paintings have become that. I have done many of them and still continue to pursue this idea. When you get something started that interests you, don't be afraid to follow it from painting to painting.

Young Frida 18"x24"

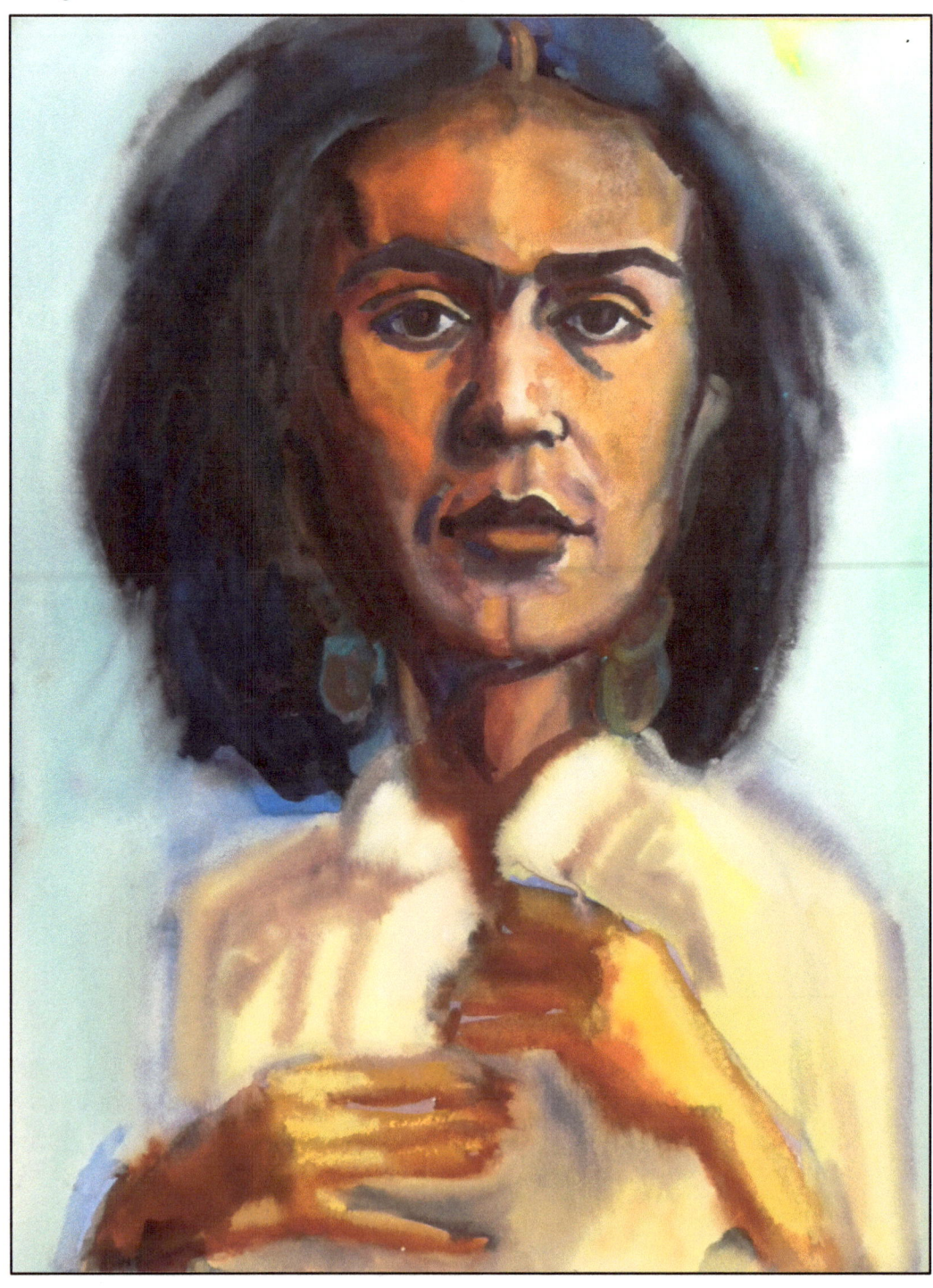

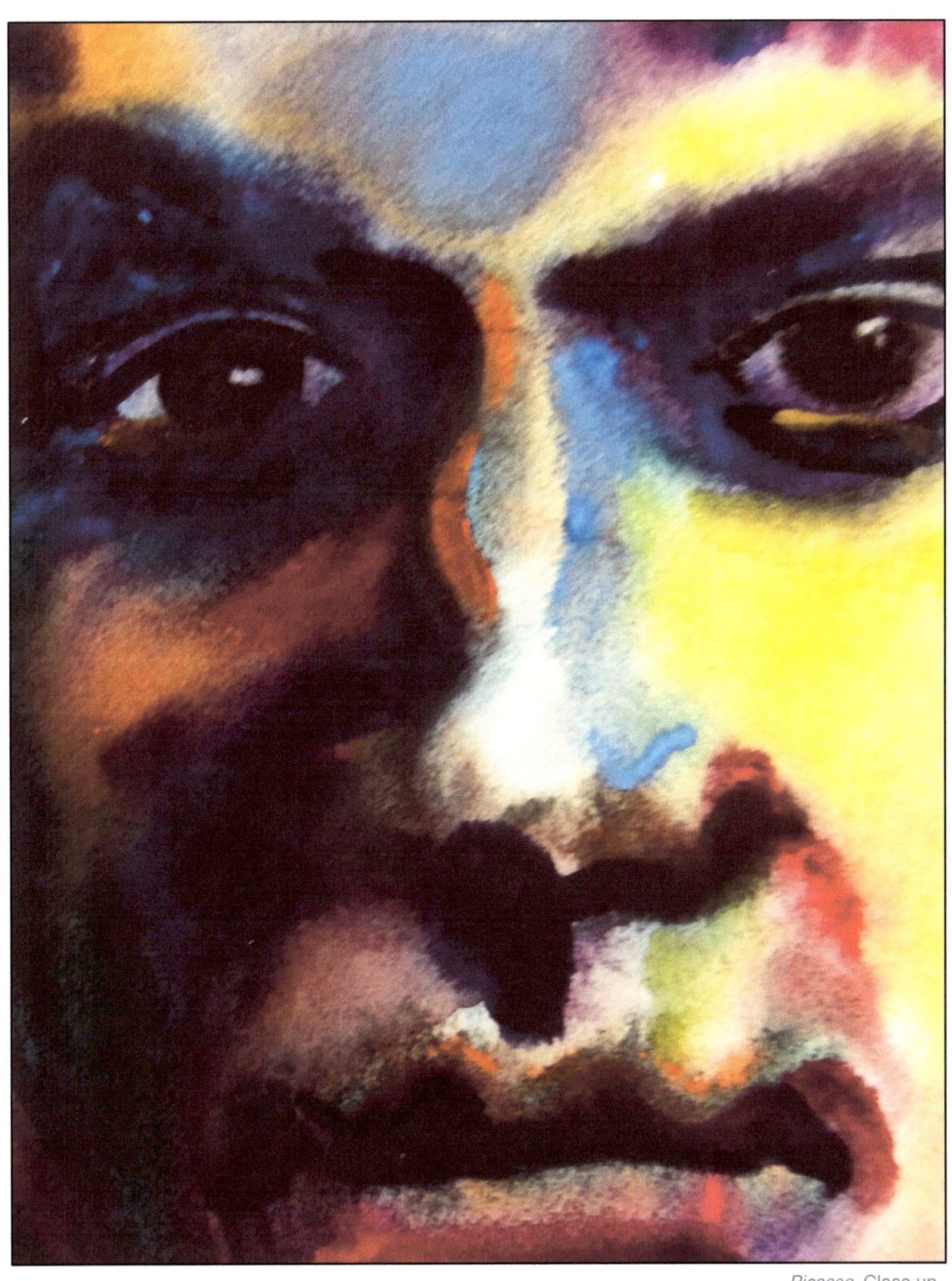

Picasso, Close up

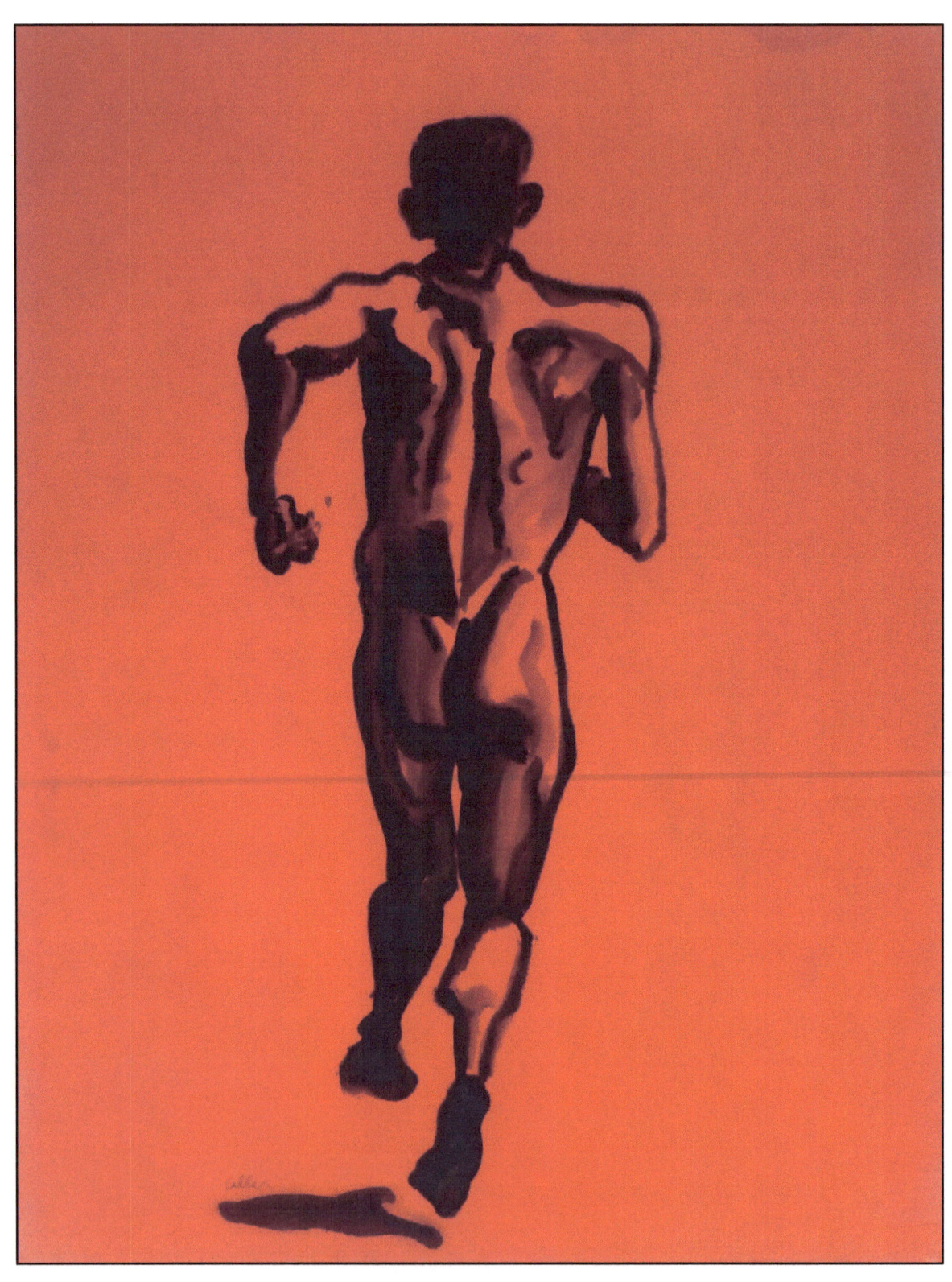

red men

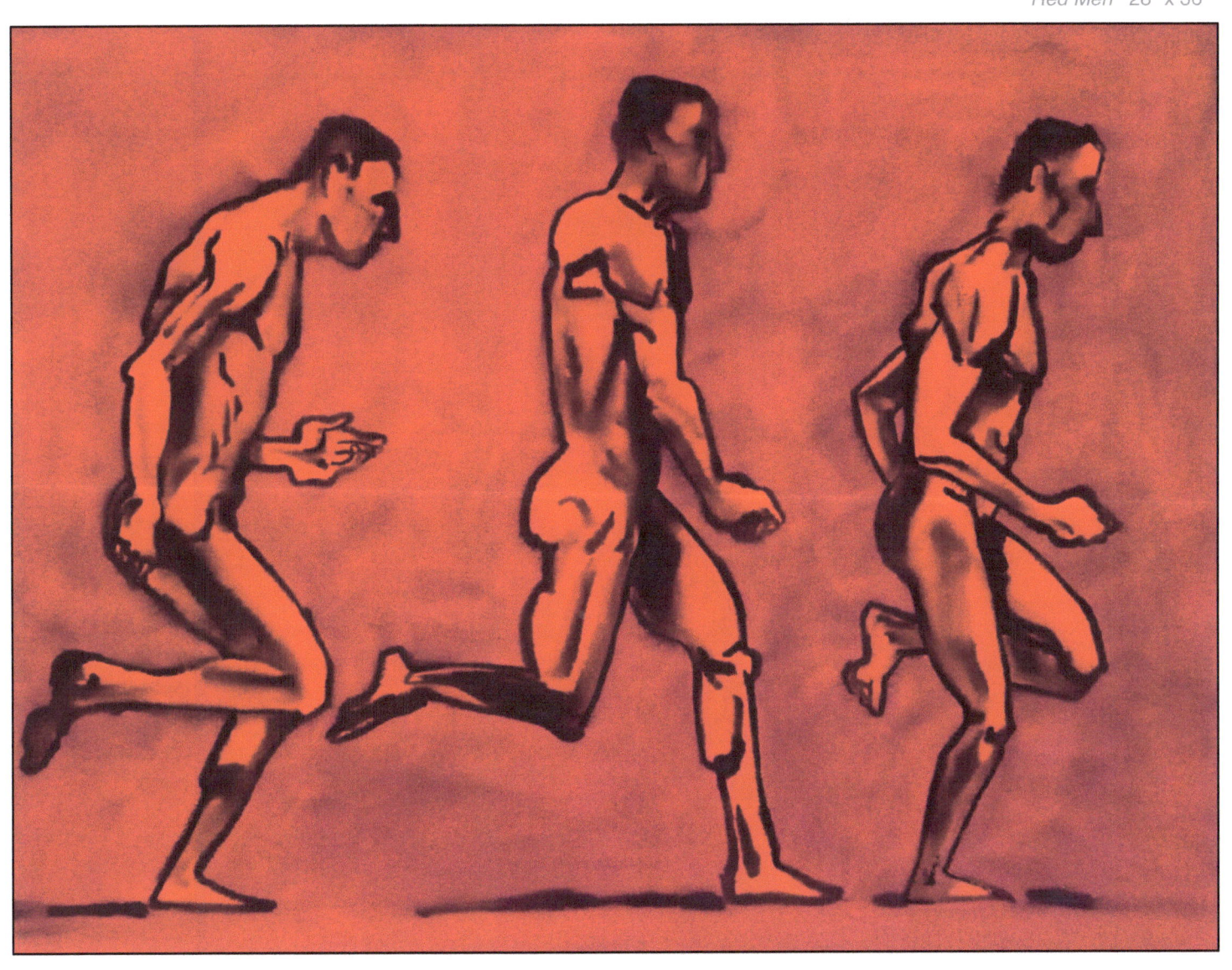

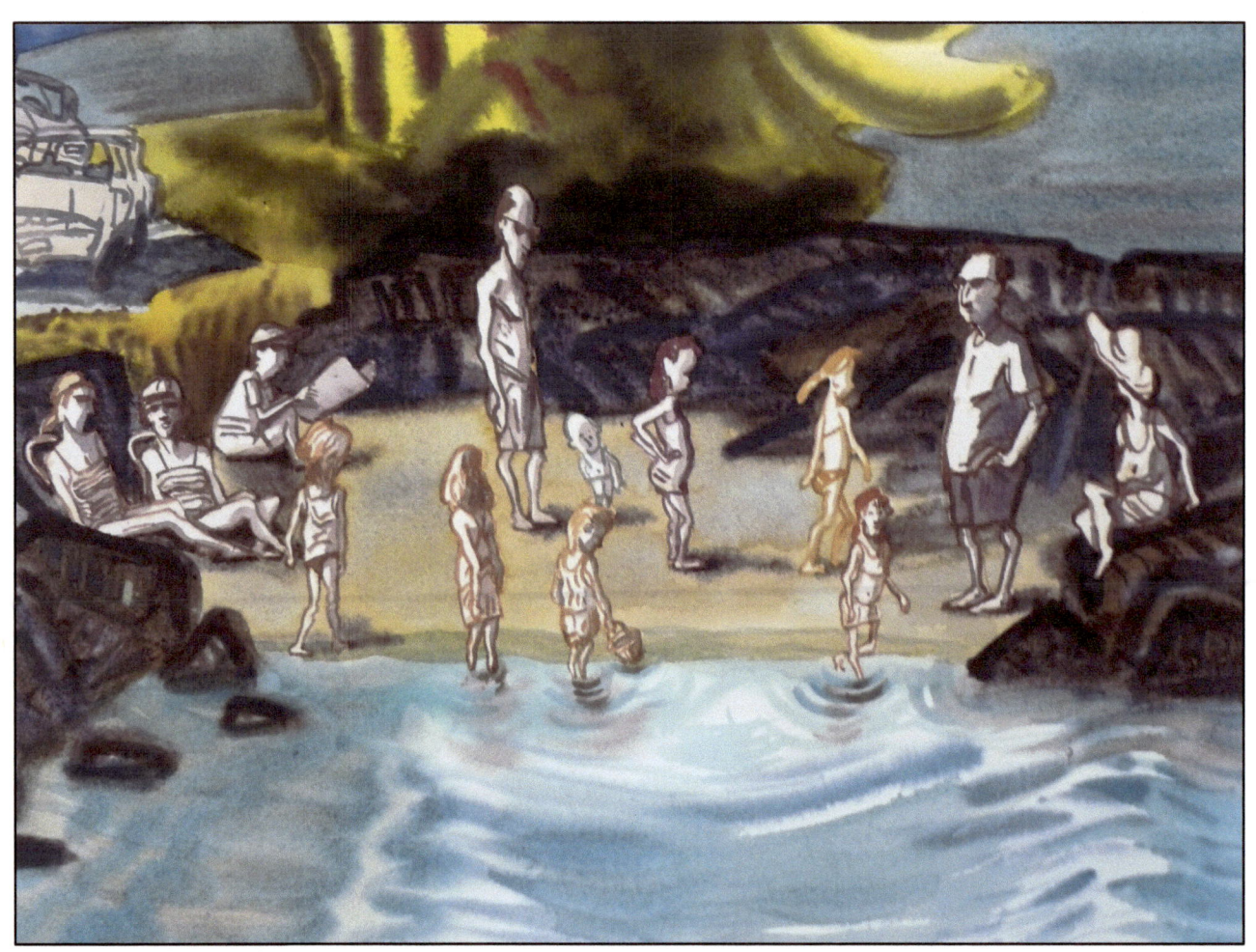

Port Clyde Beach, close up
22" x 30"

genre
paintings of ordinary life

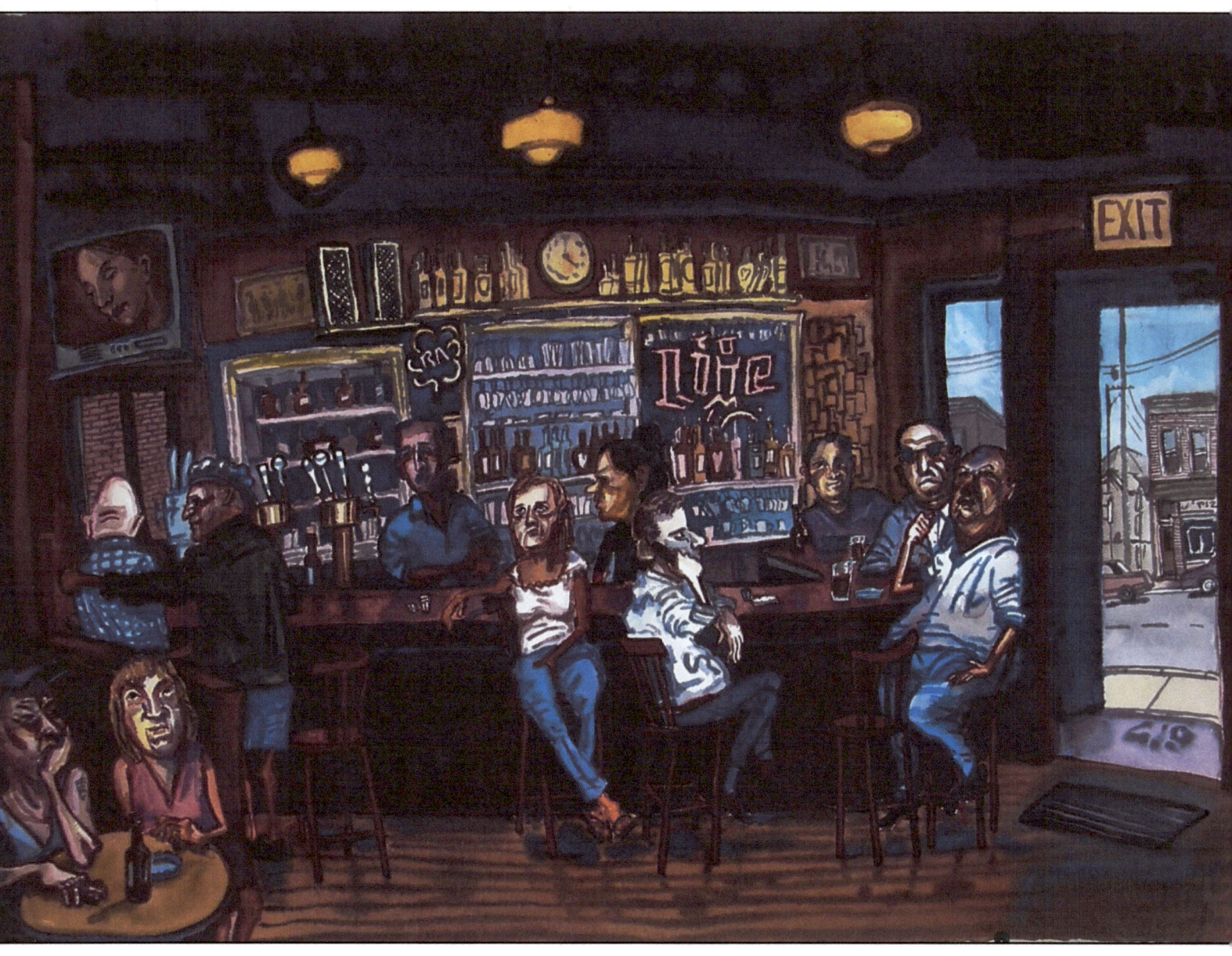

The Hall 28" x 36"

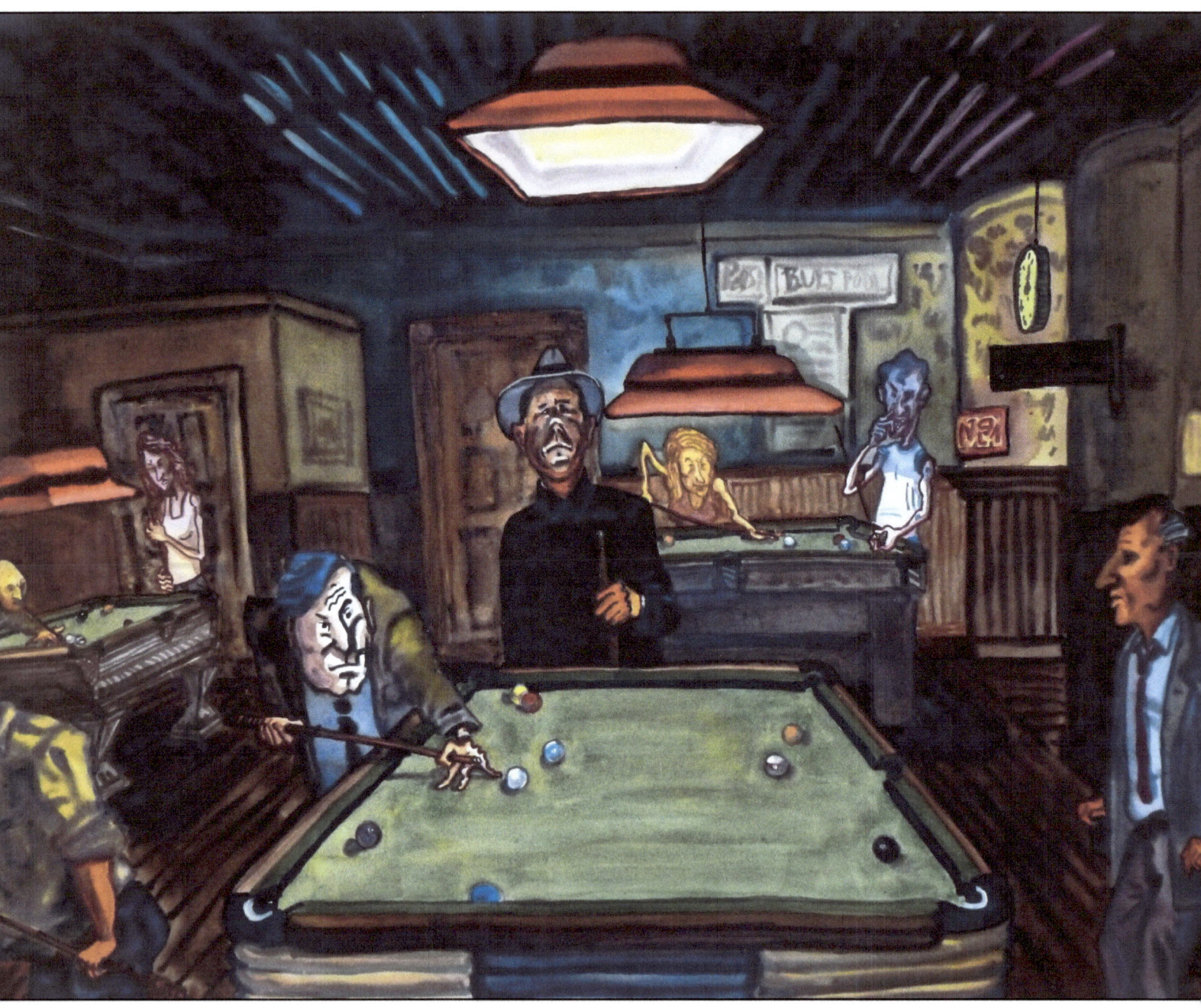

I often will do a painting that I feel has value more than one time. There are two versions of every painting shown in this "genre" section. The bottom Stephen King painting on the right was done in 2005. The painting above it was done about six years later.

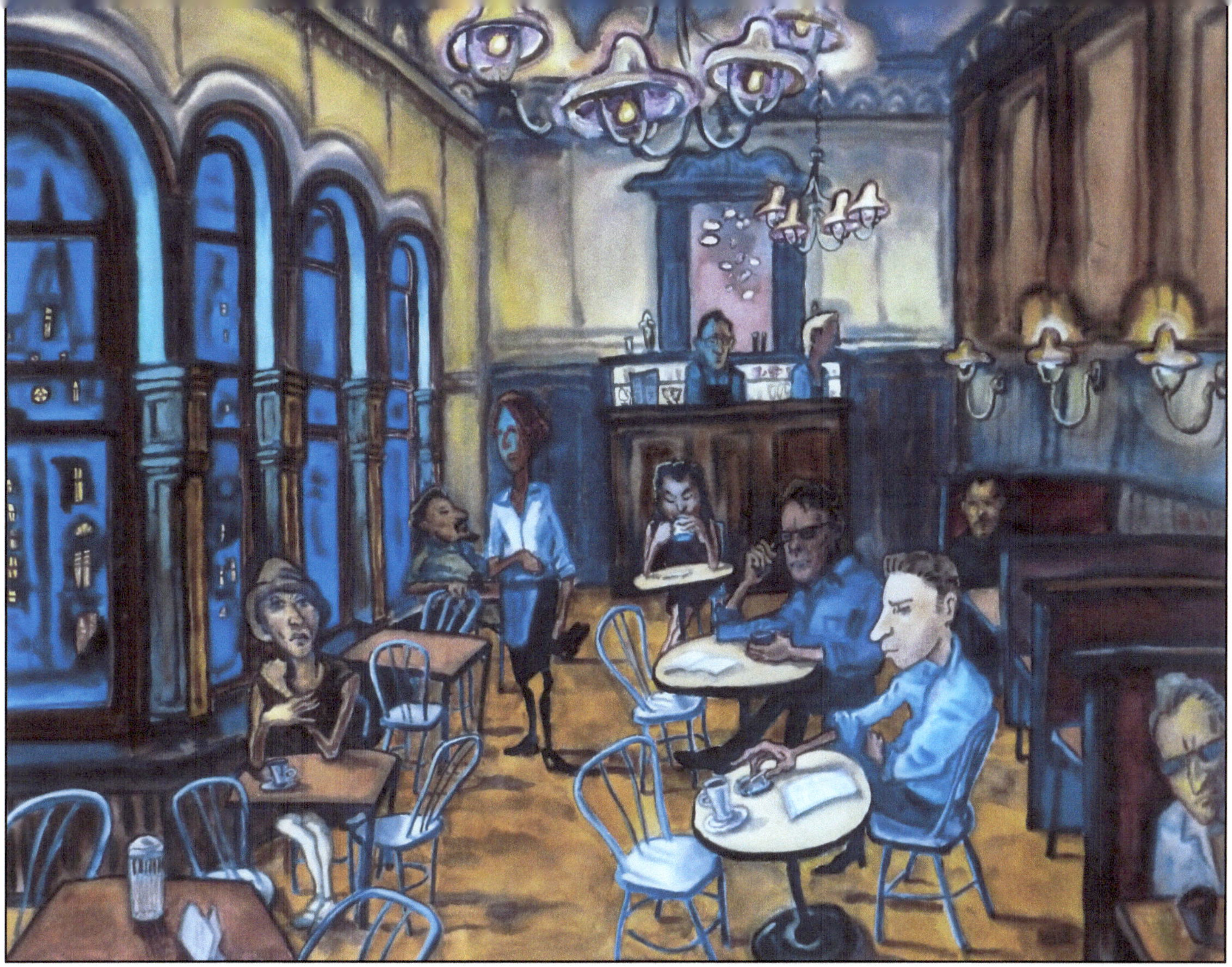

Steven King Gets an Idea #1 (22" x 30" below) and *#2* (28" x 36" above)

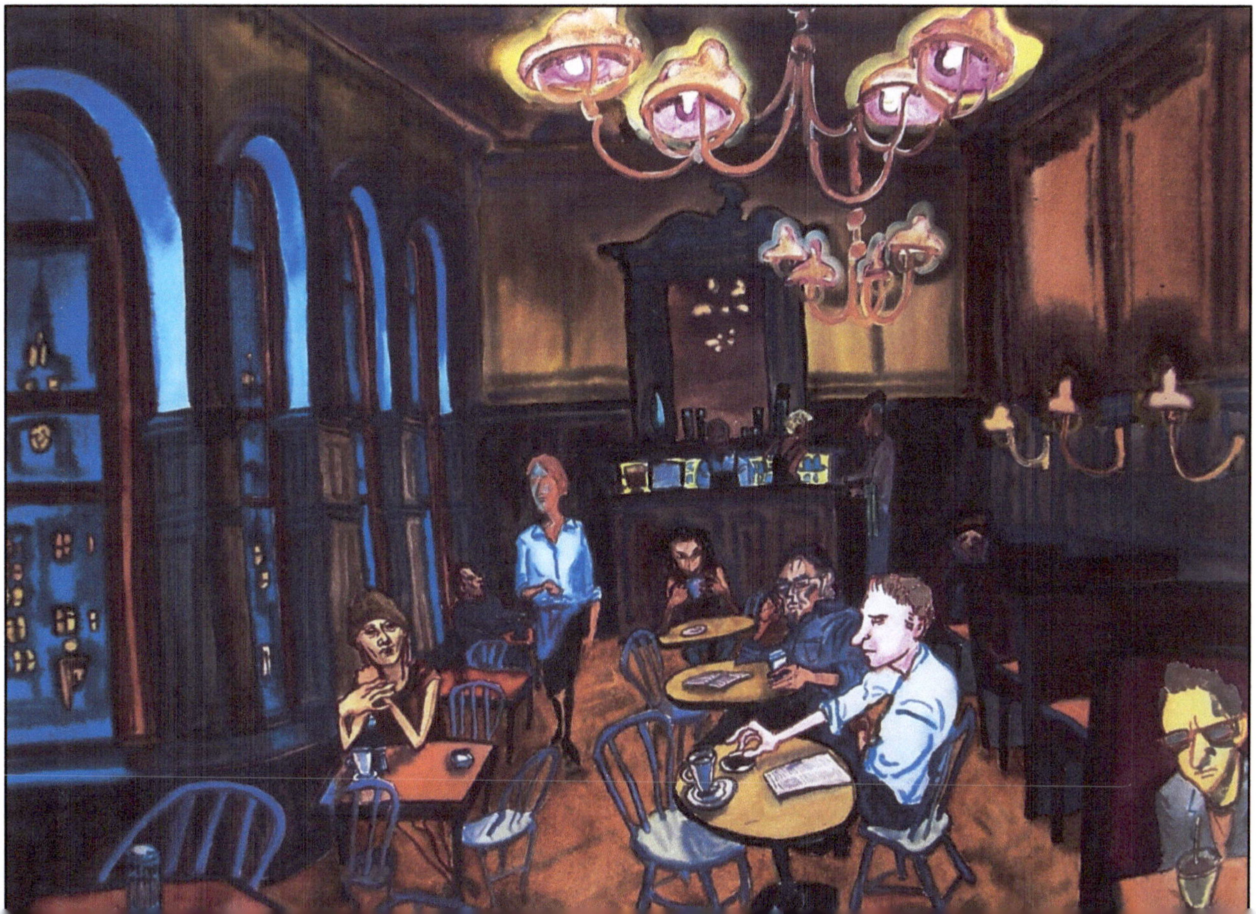

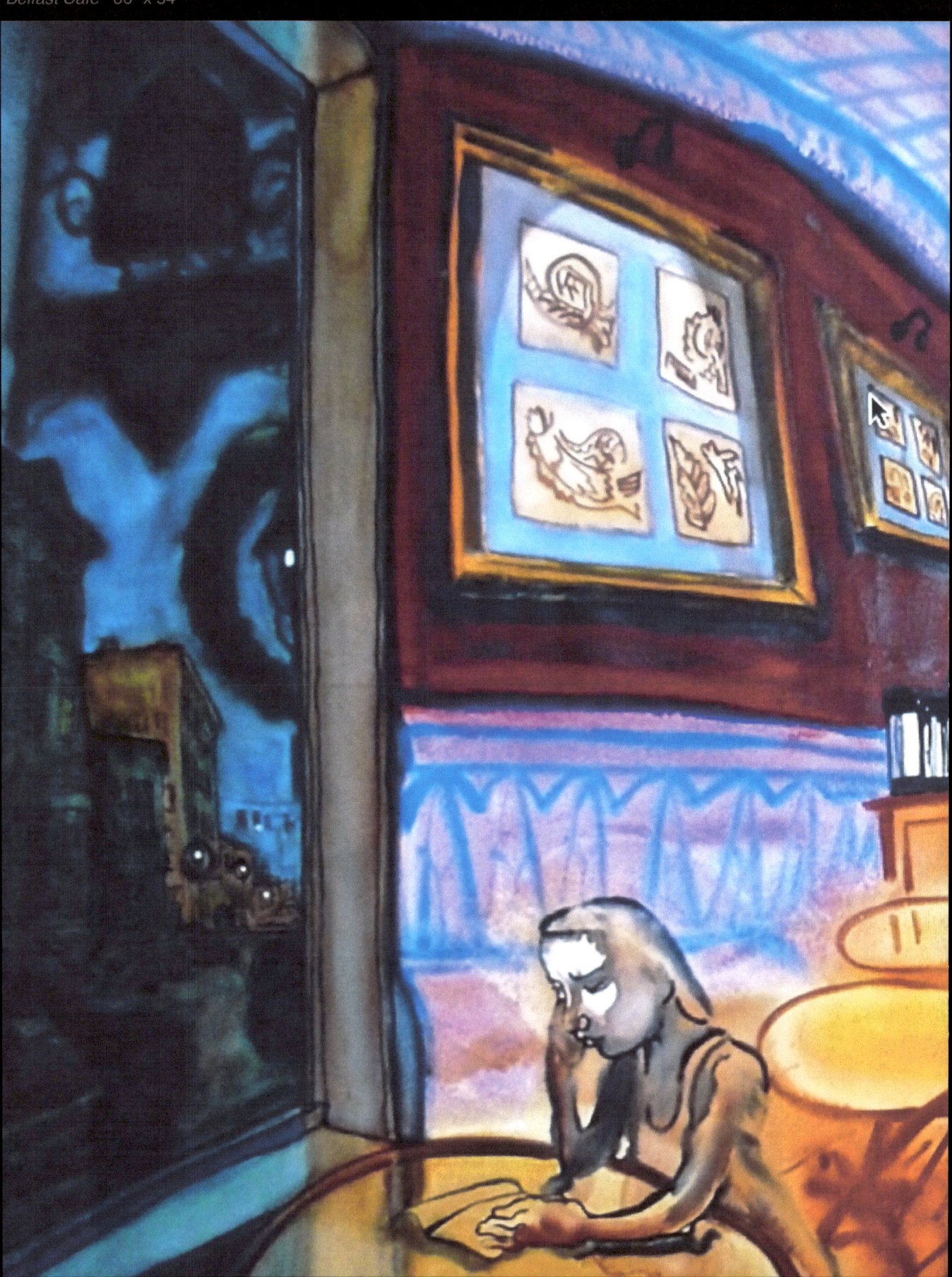

Belfast Cafe 36" x 54"

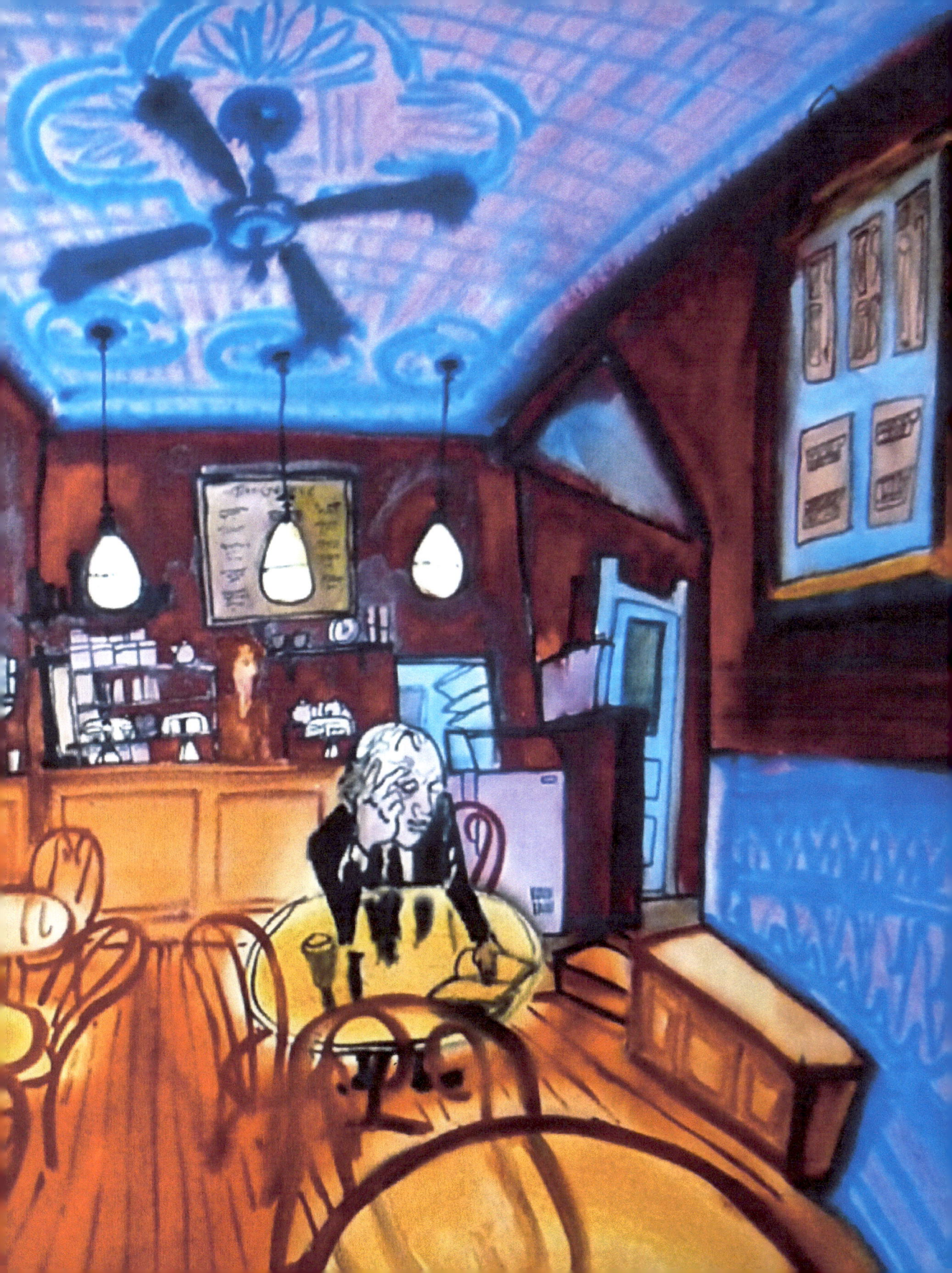

Untitled 22" x 30"

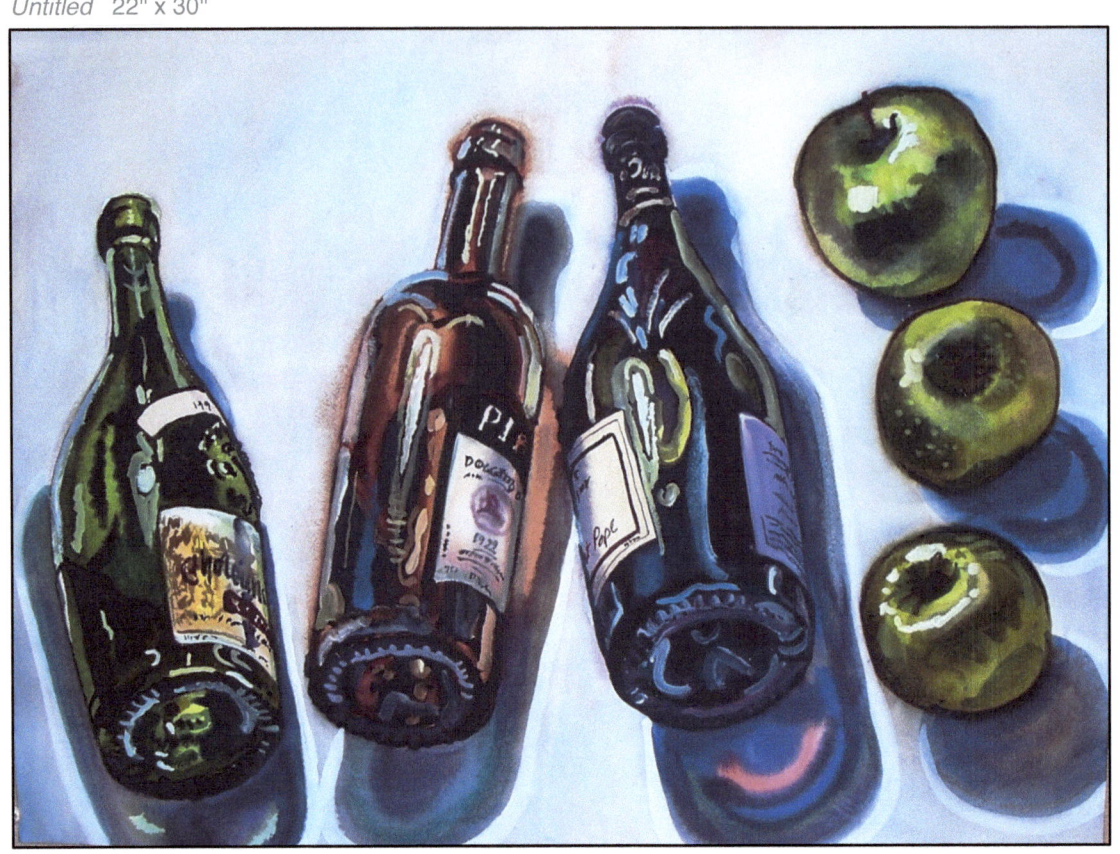

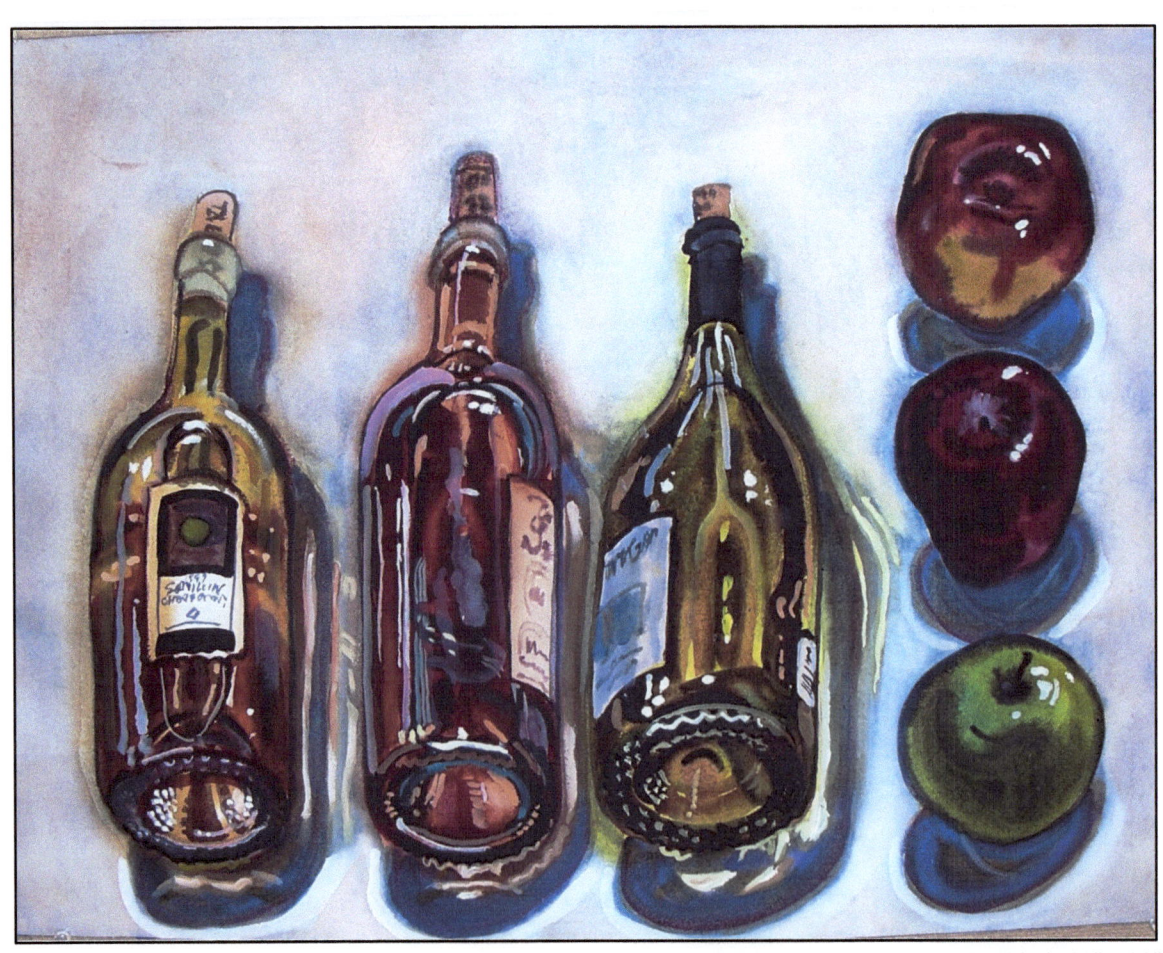

Untitled 22" x 30"

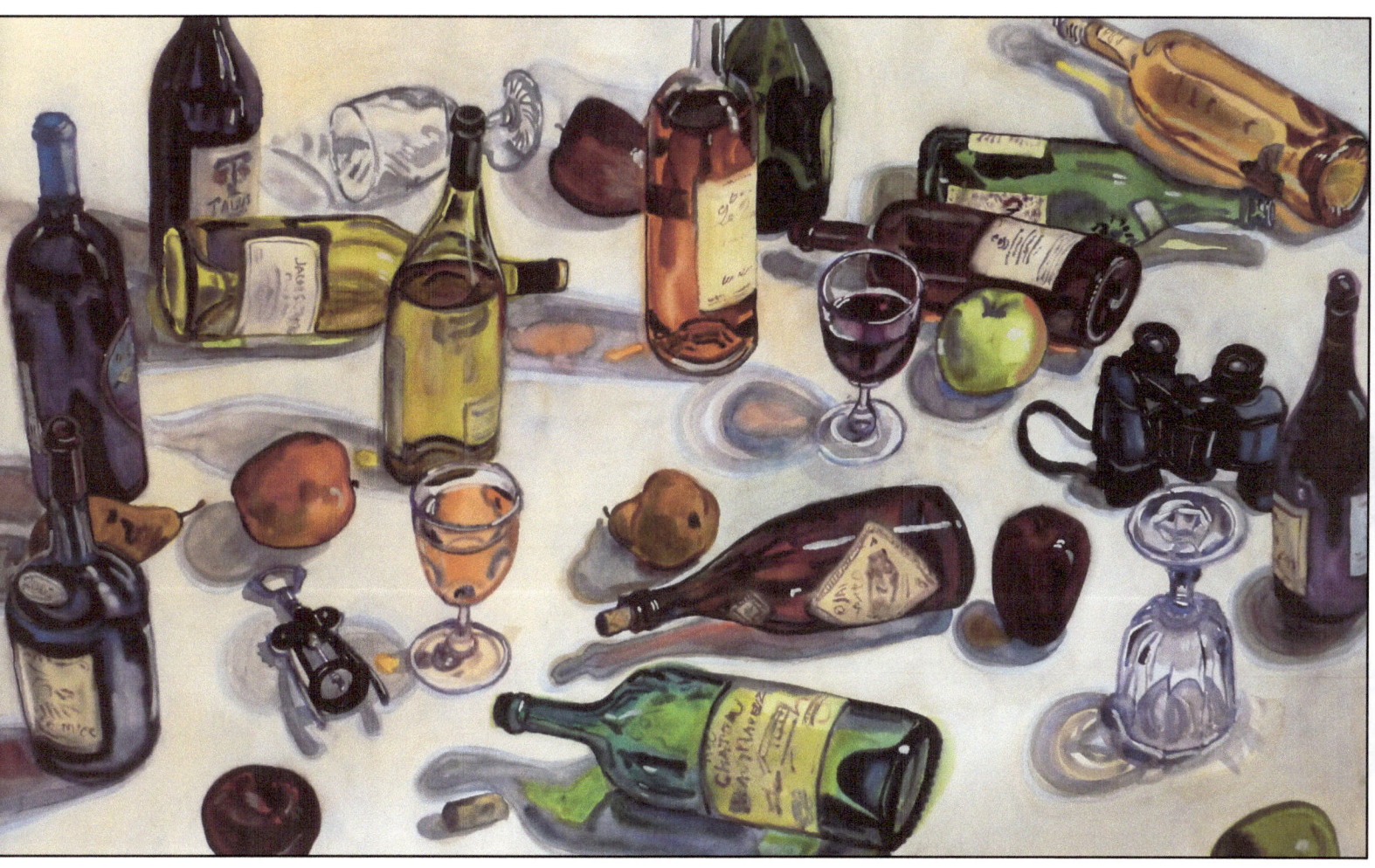

still lifes

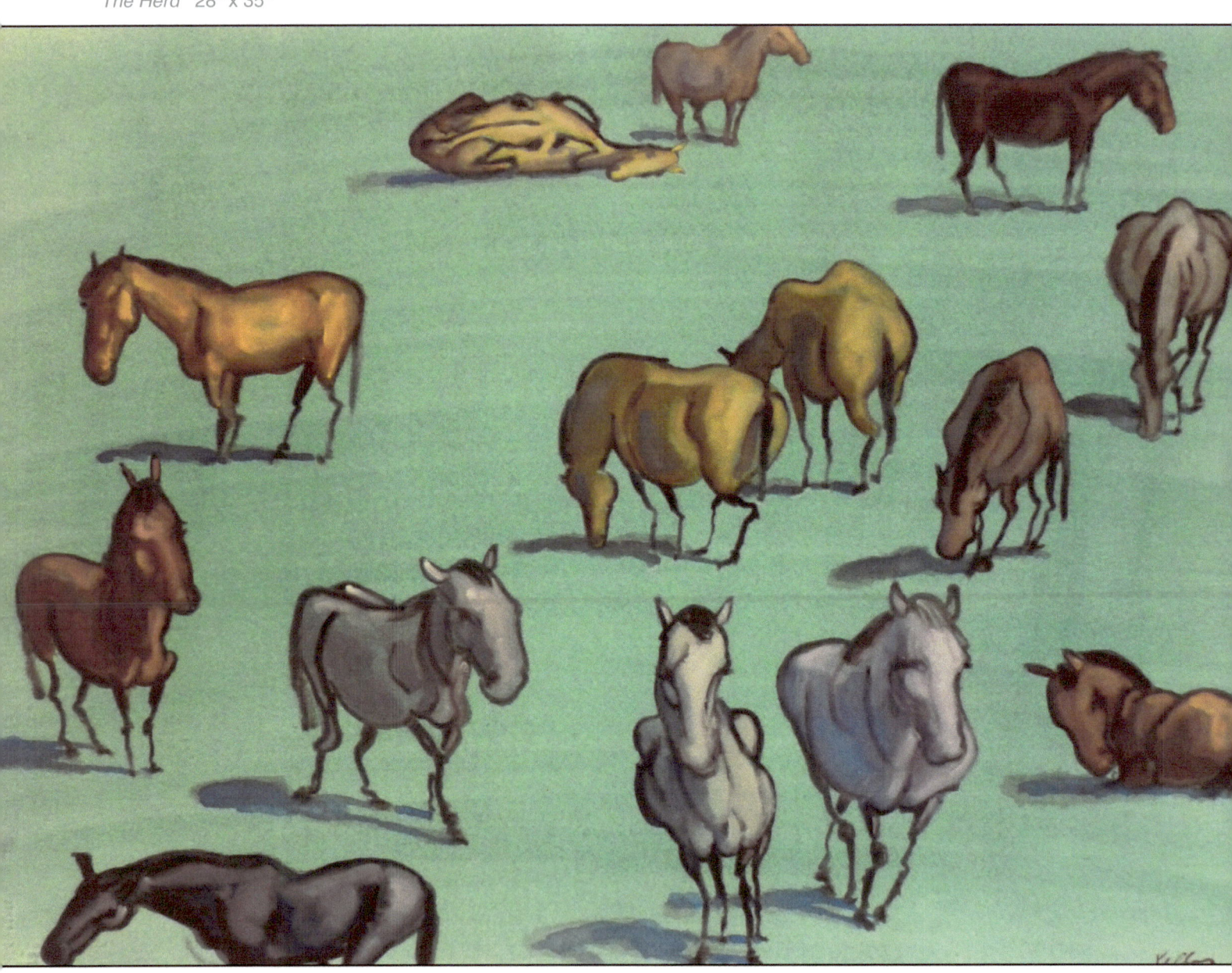

horses

Work Horses - each painting is 18" x 24"

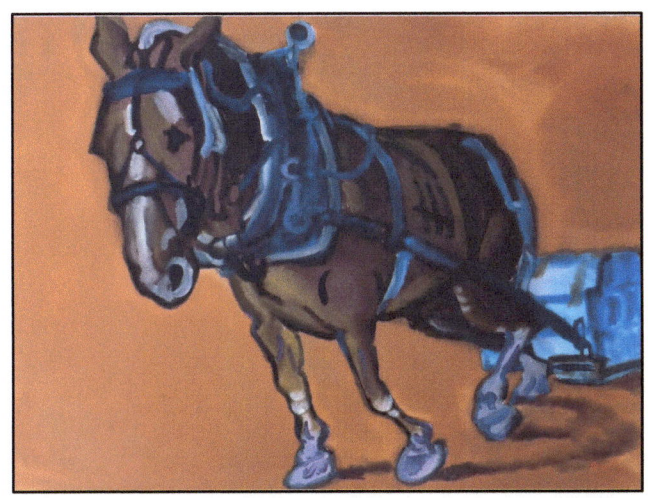
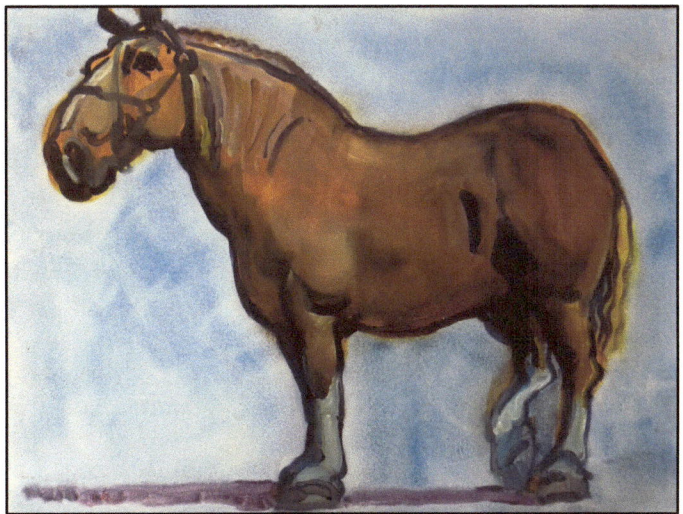

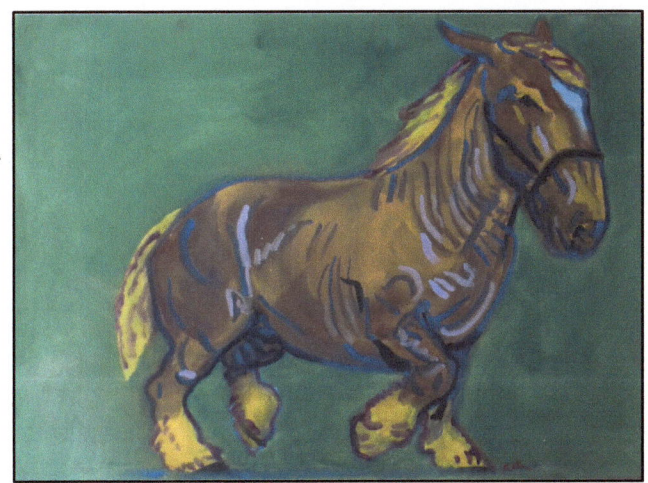
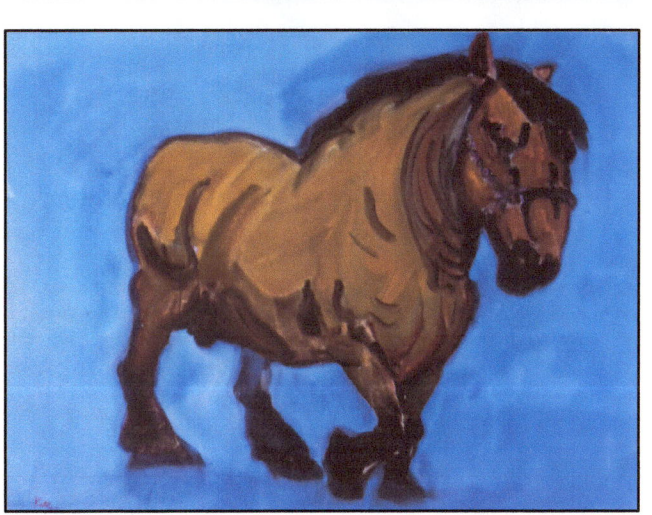

Large Work Horse 28" x 36"

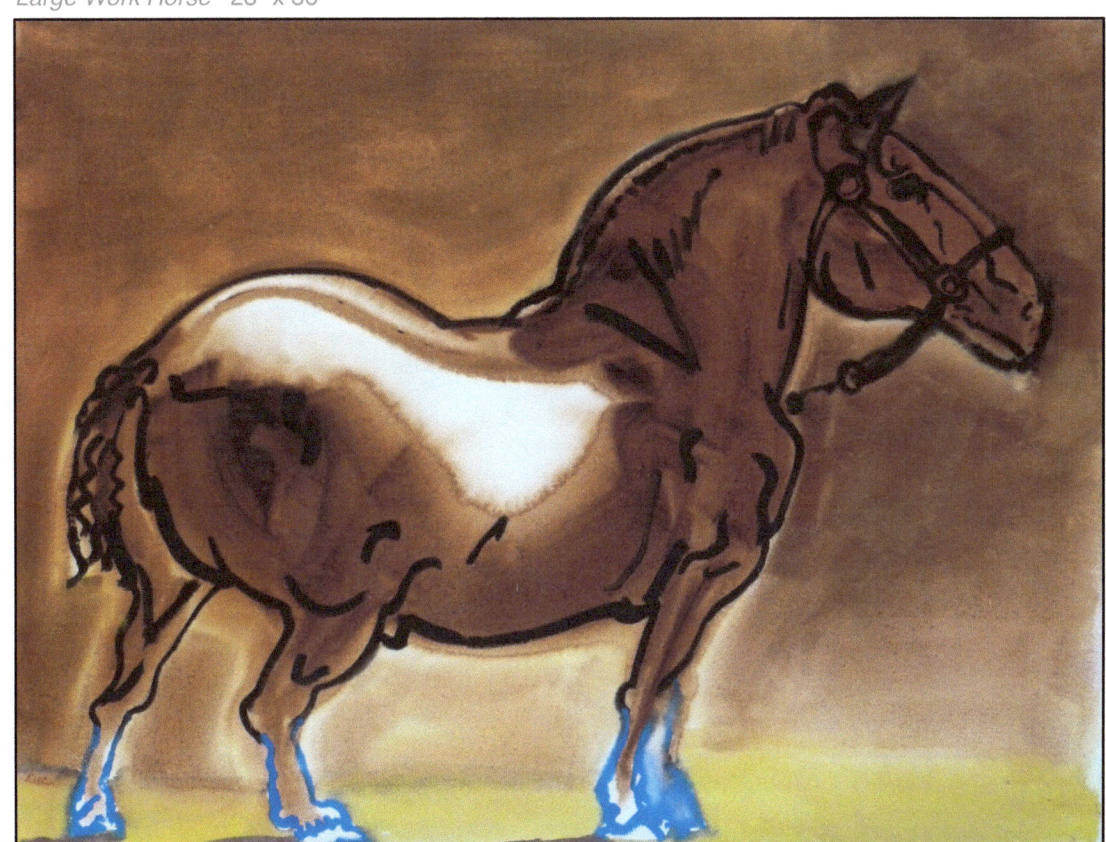

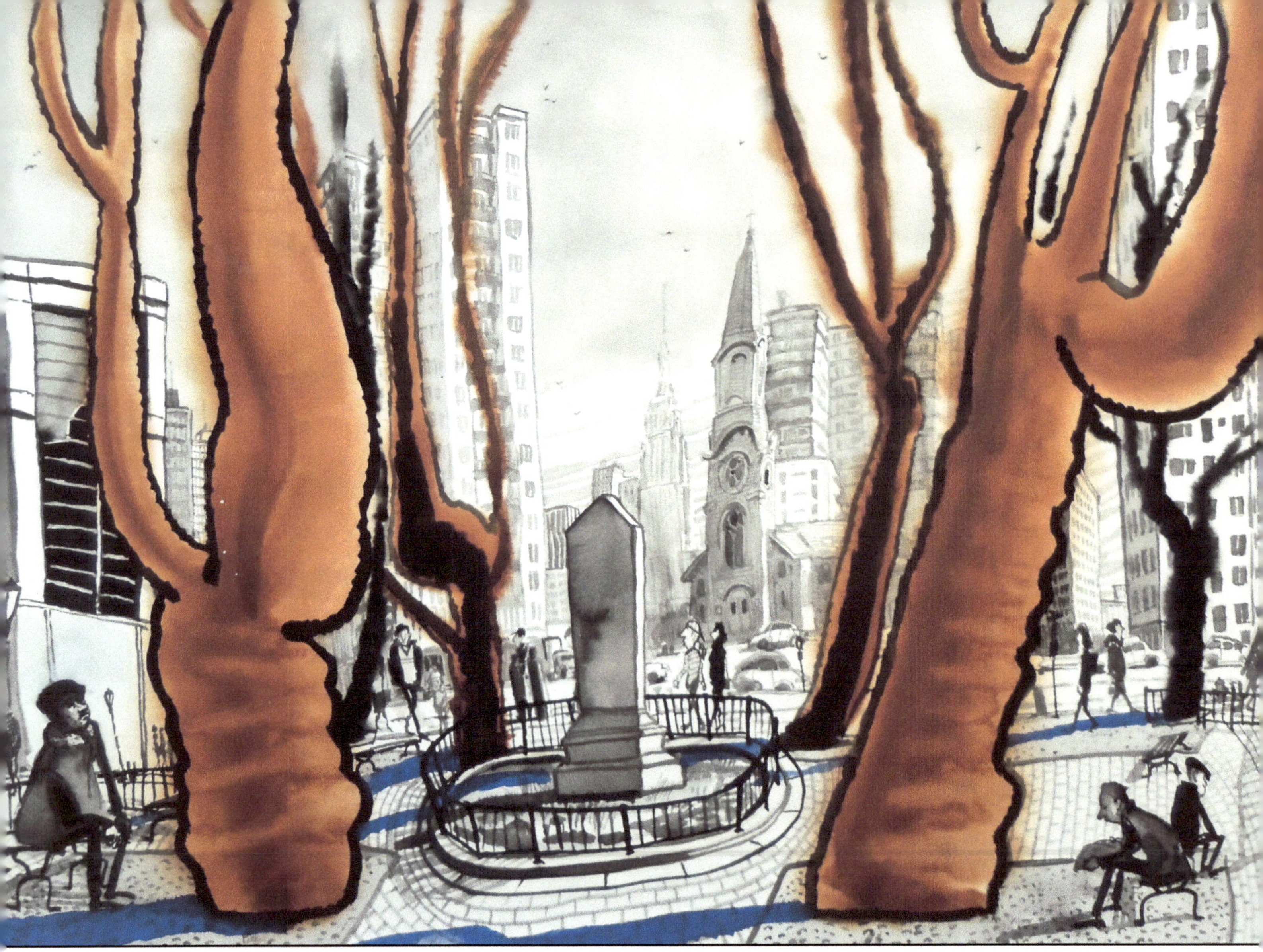

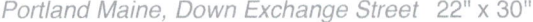

Chelsea, New York City 28" x 36"

Portland Maine, Down Exchange Street 22" x 30"

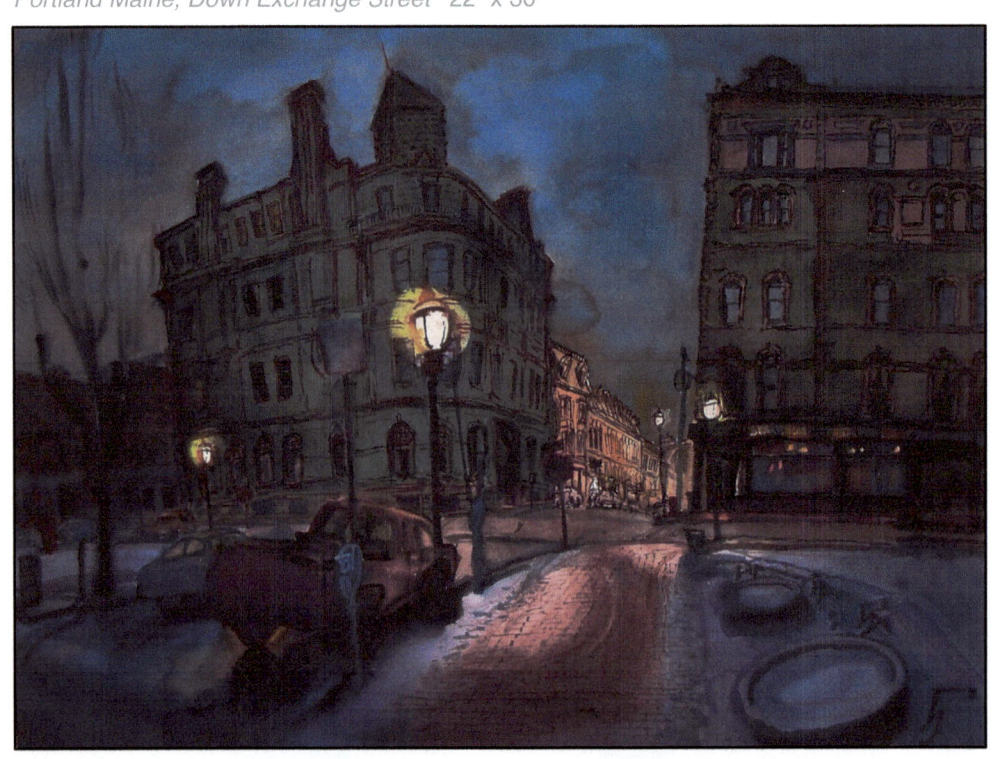

114

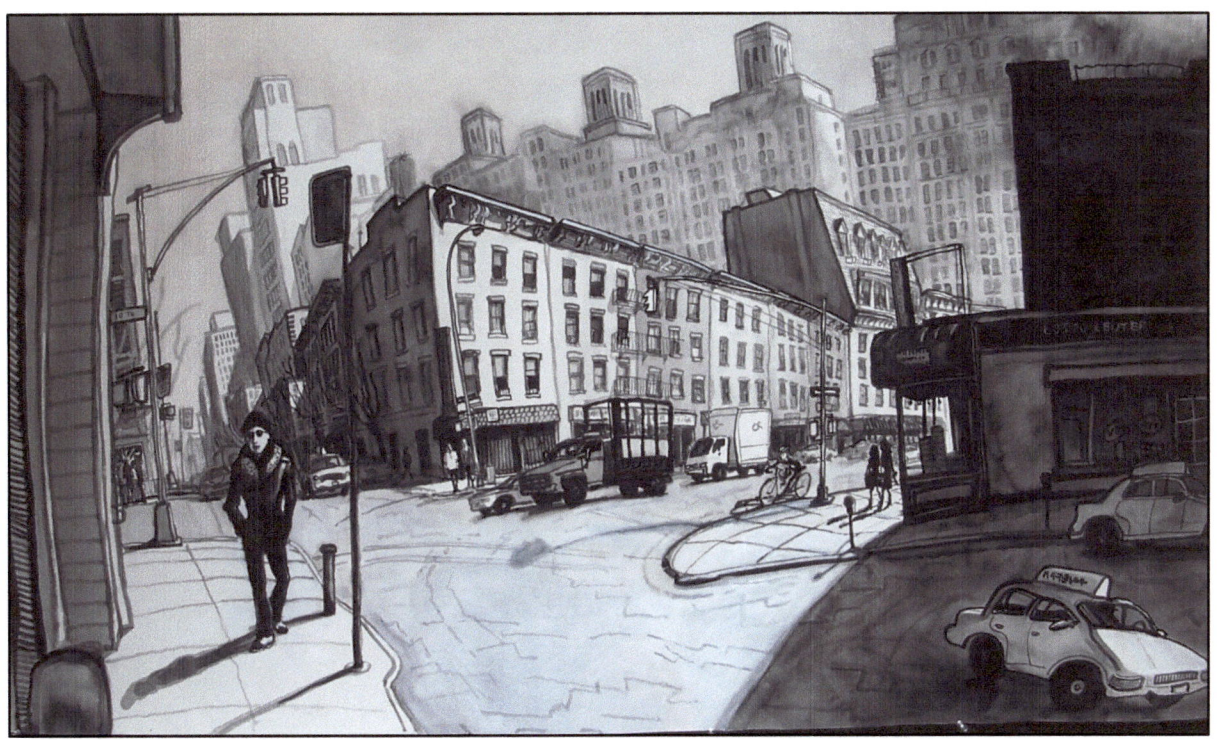

New York City   36"x 28"

city scenes

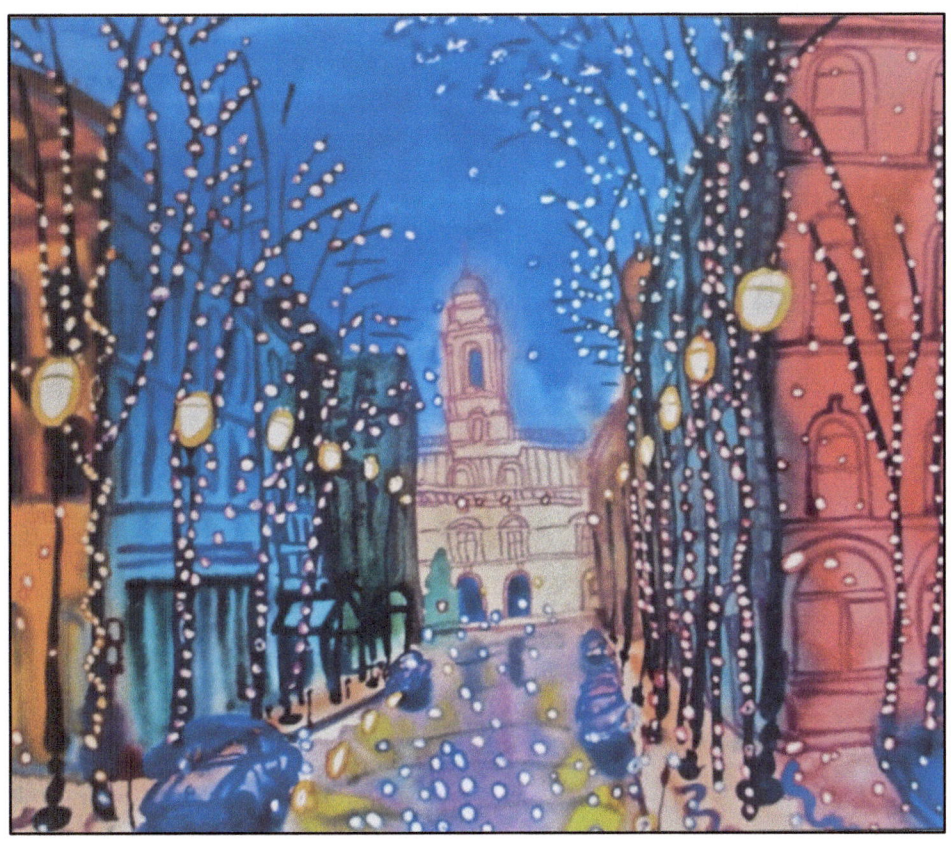

Up Exchange Street   18" x 24"

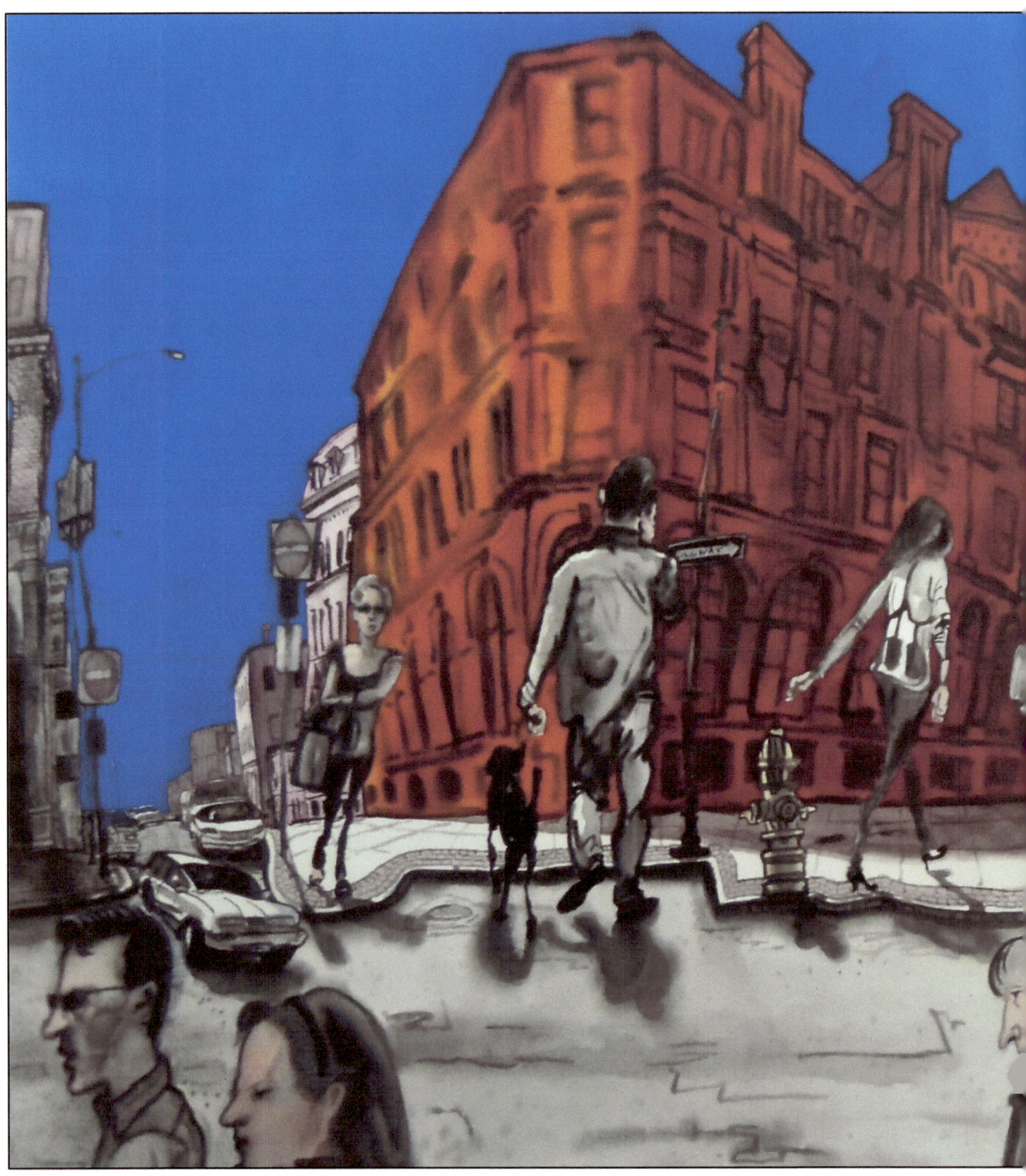

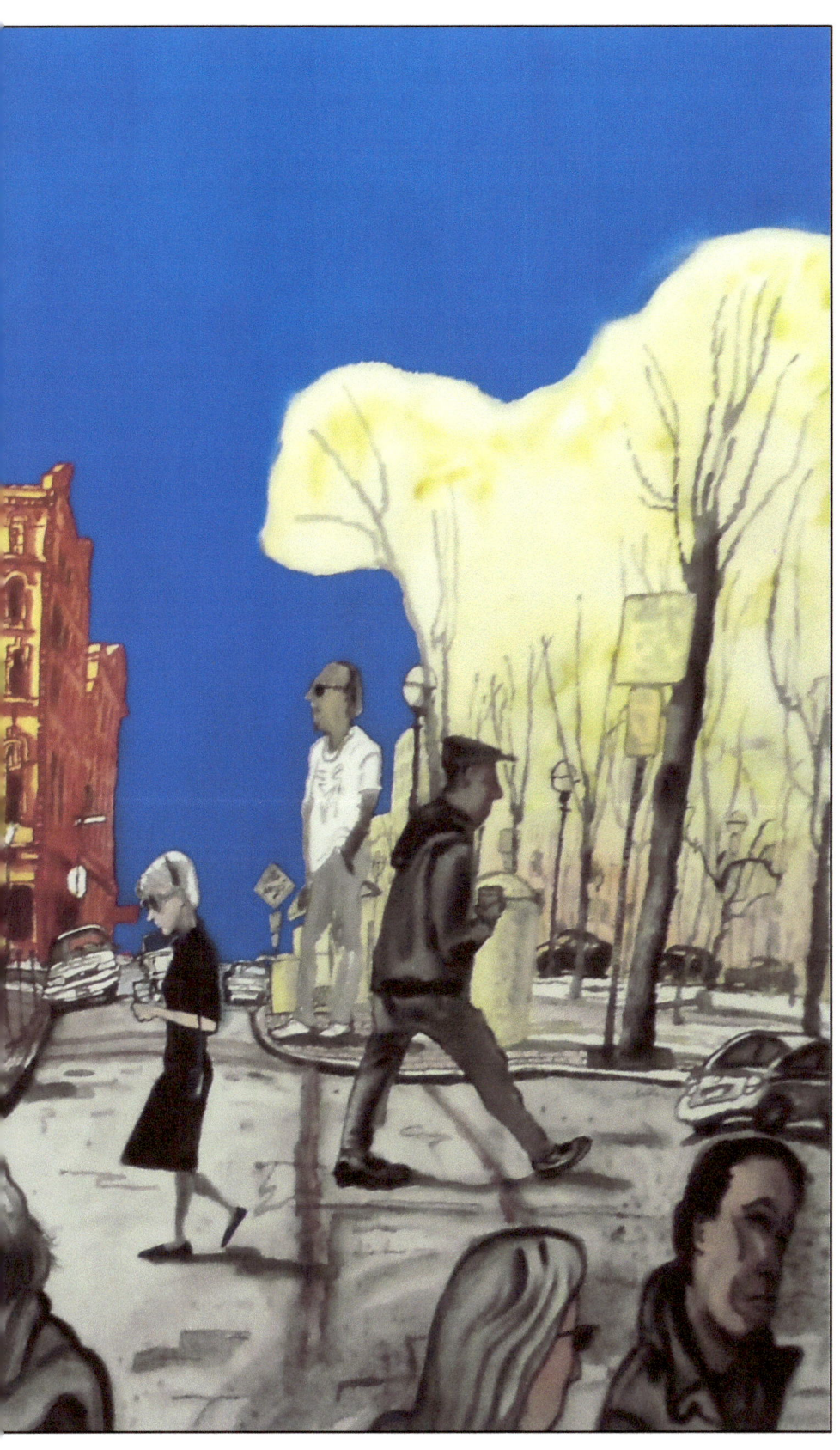

Middle Street, Portland, Maine 36" x 54"

Taos Mountain Storm   28" x 36"

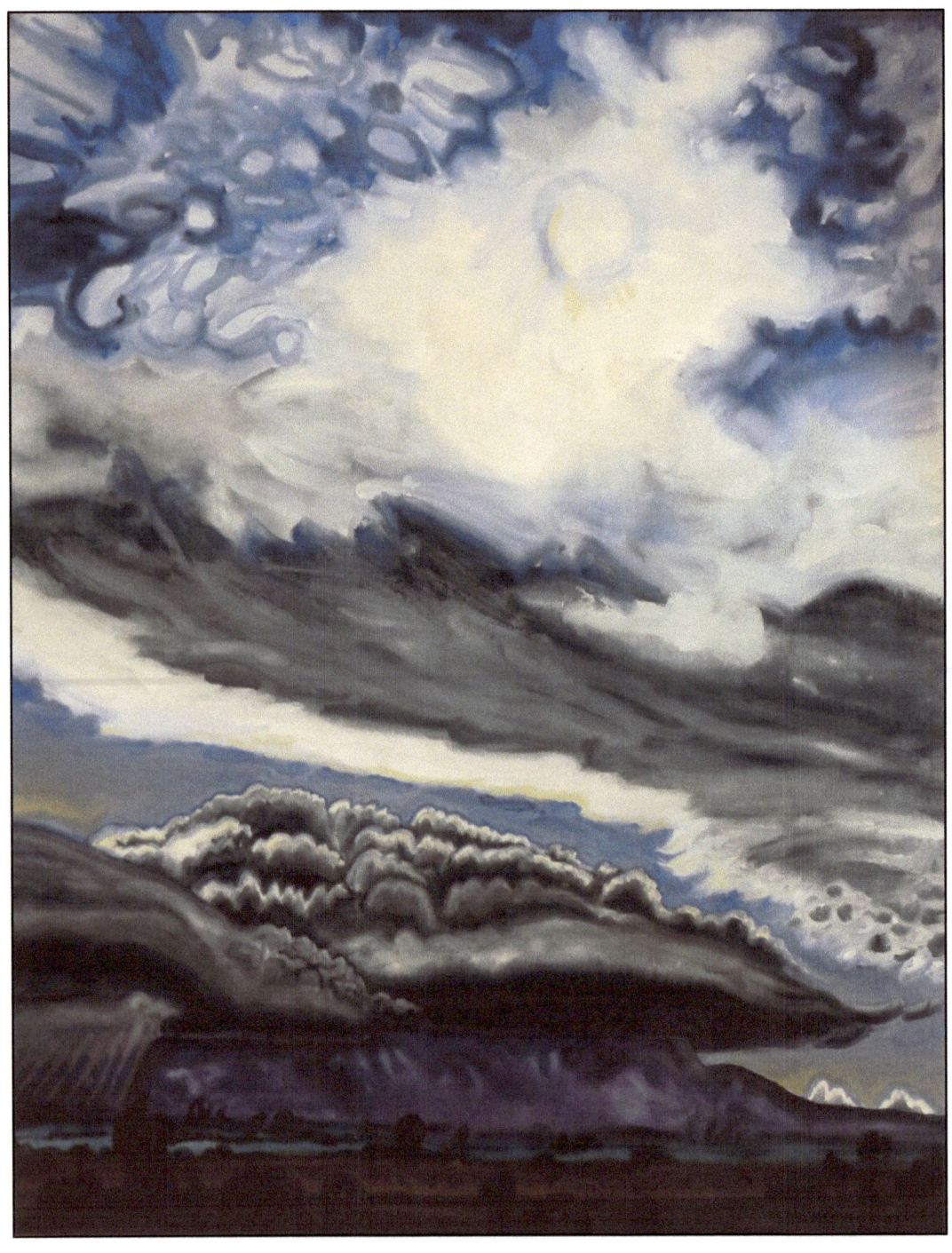

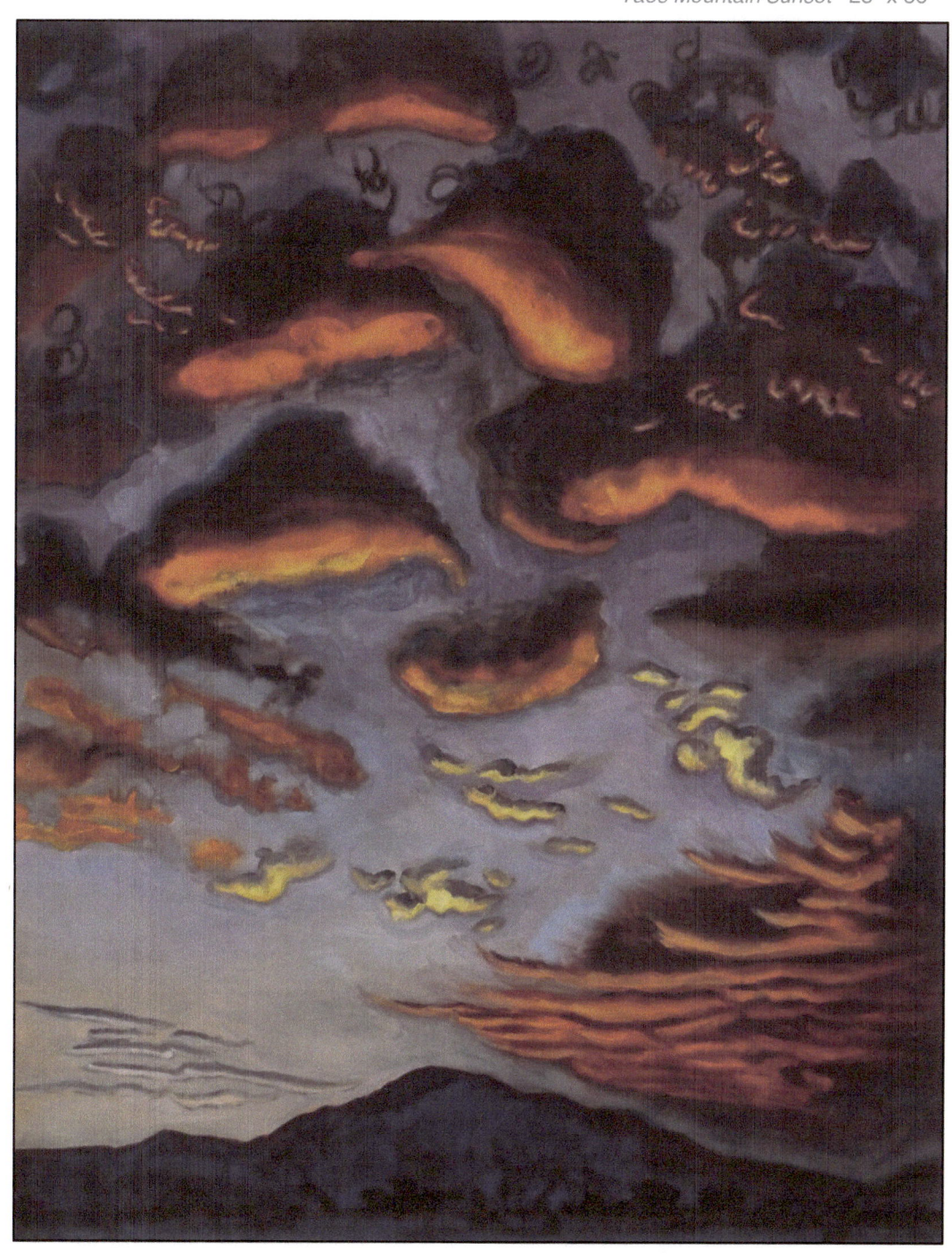

The West: Taos

Giants 22" x 30"

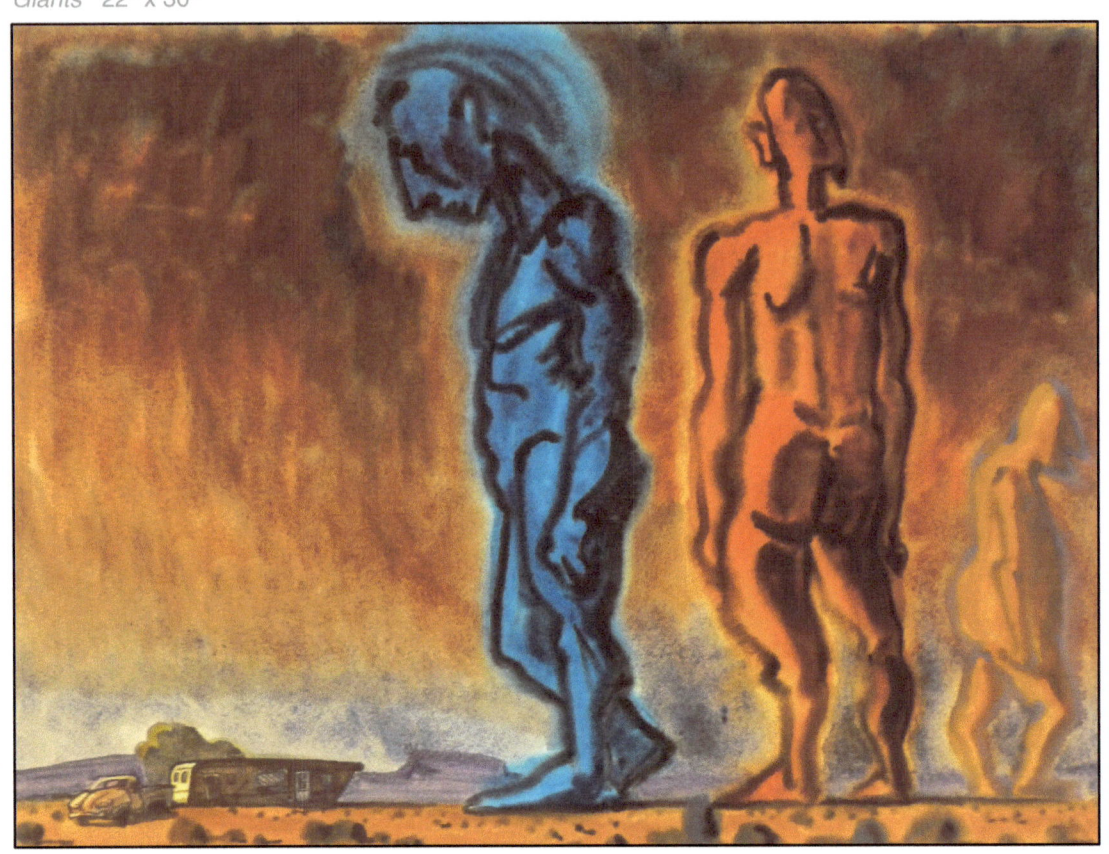

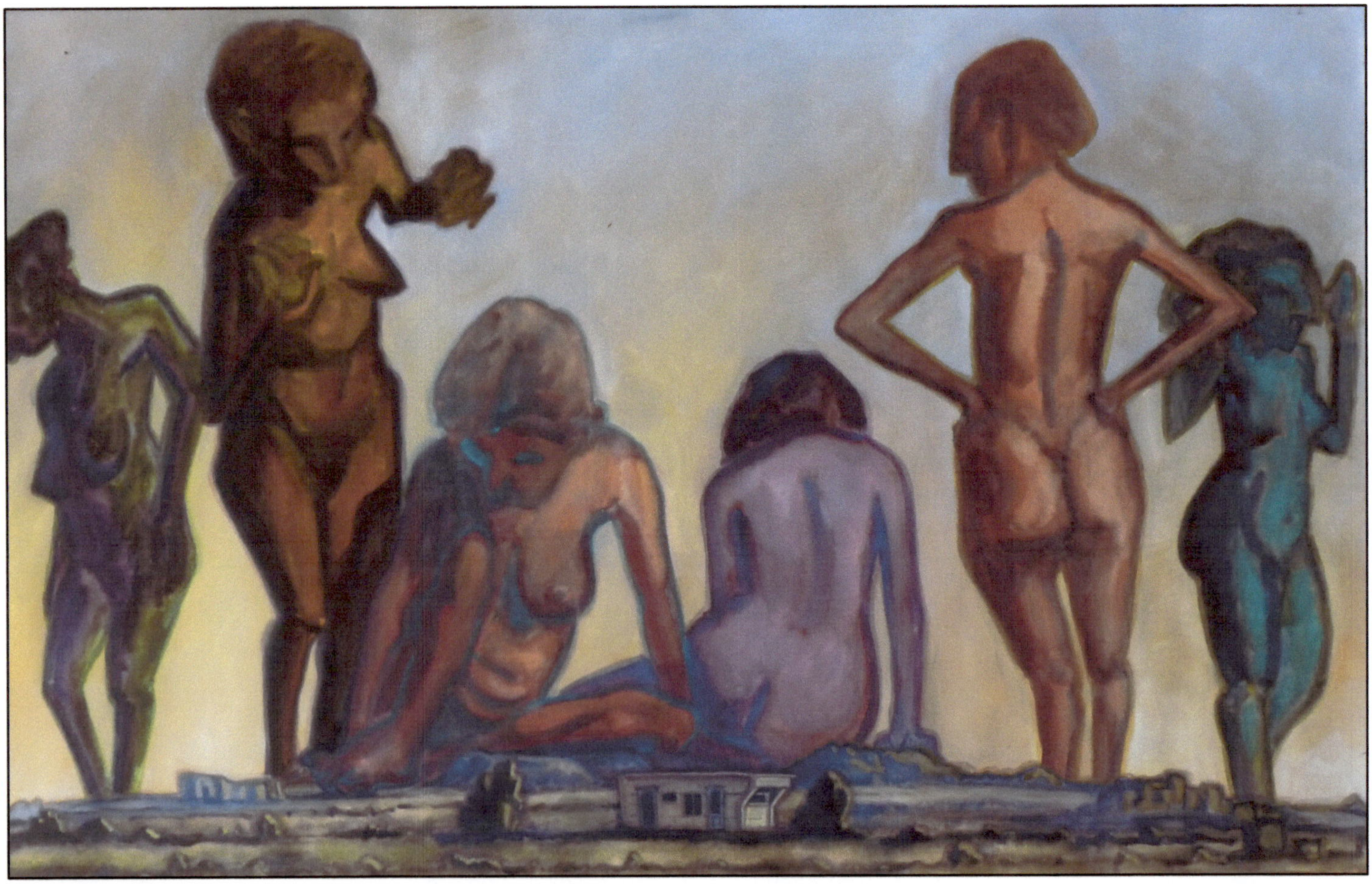

The Ladies 36" x 54"

Self Portrait 28" x 36"

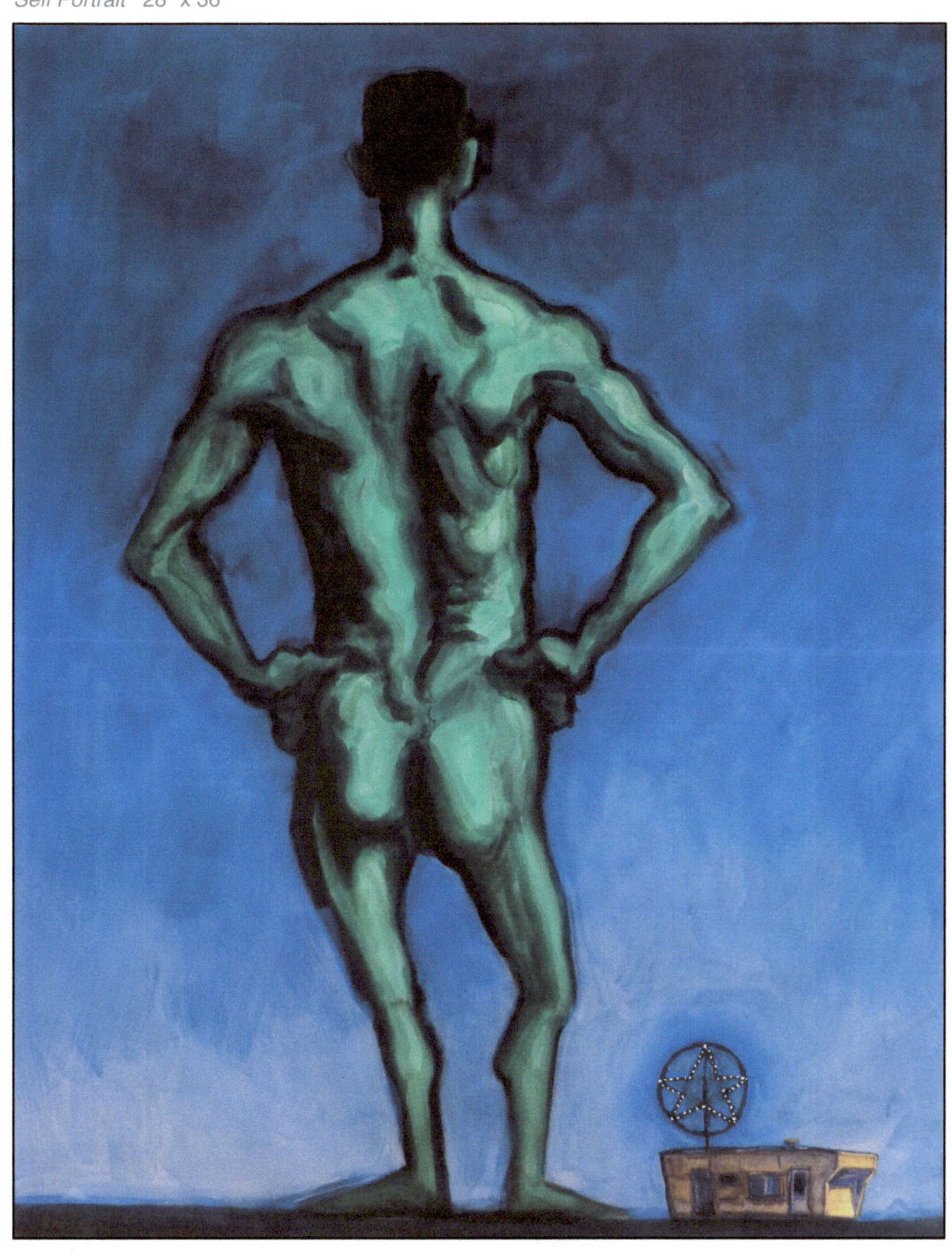

trailers

Cowboy Lament 28" x 36"

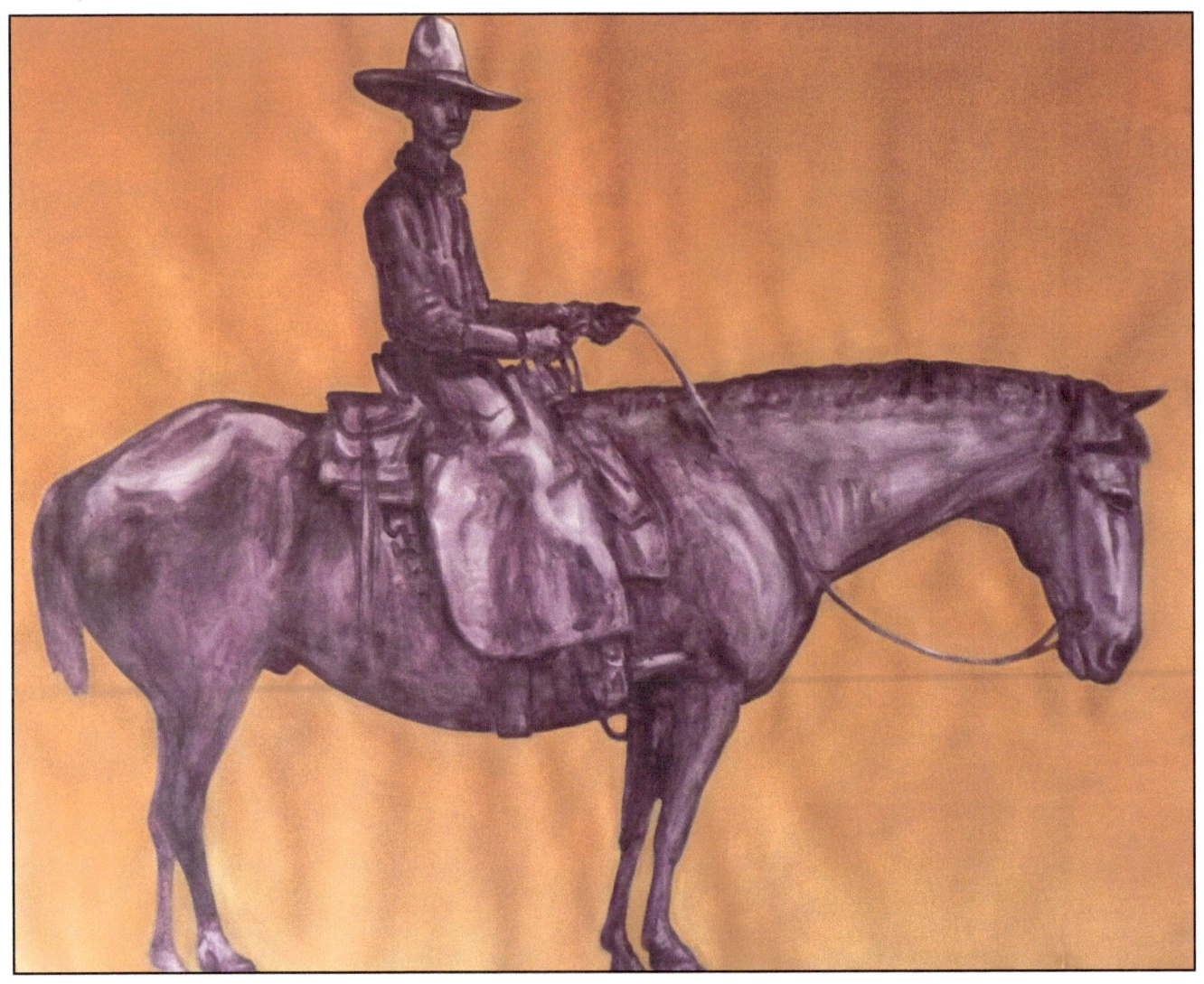

horses and cowboys

Wild One 28" x 36"

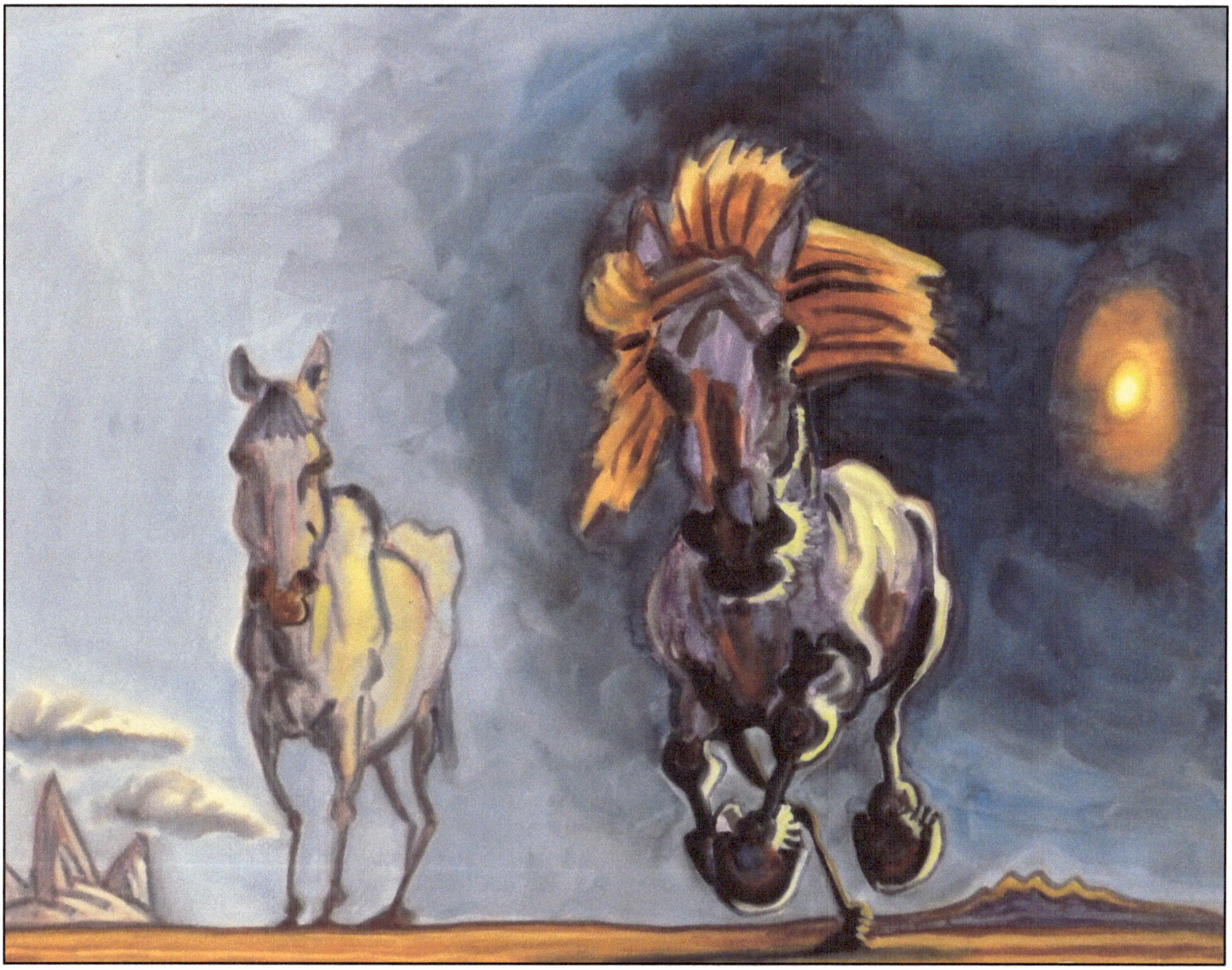

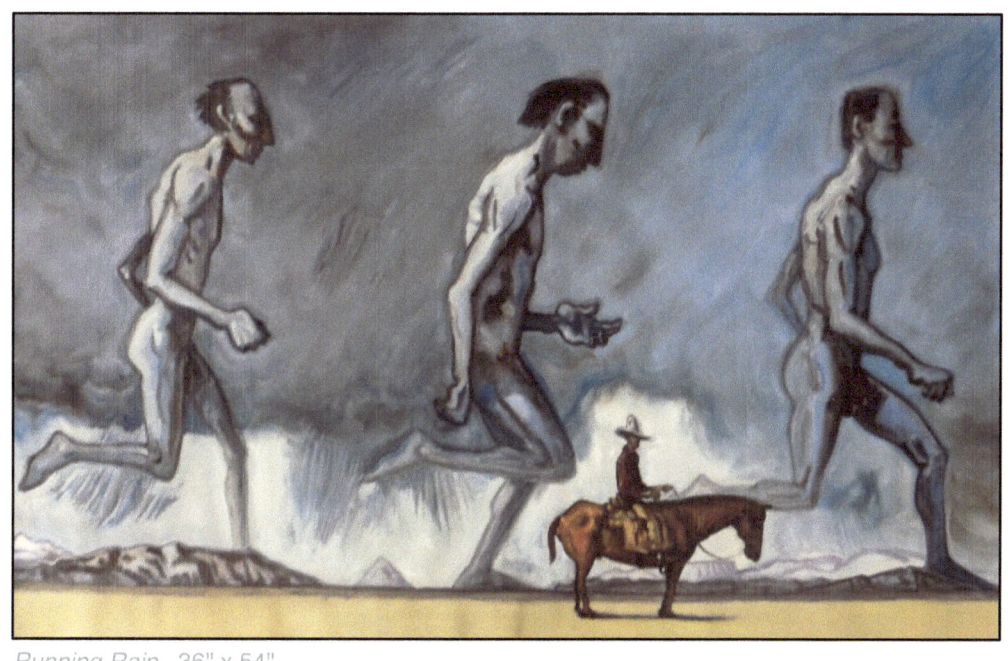

Running Rain 36" x 54"

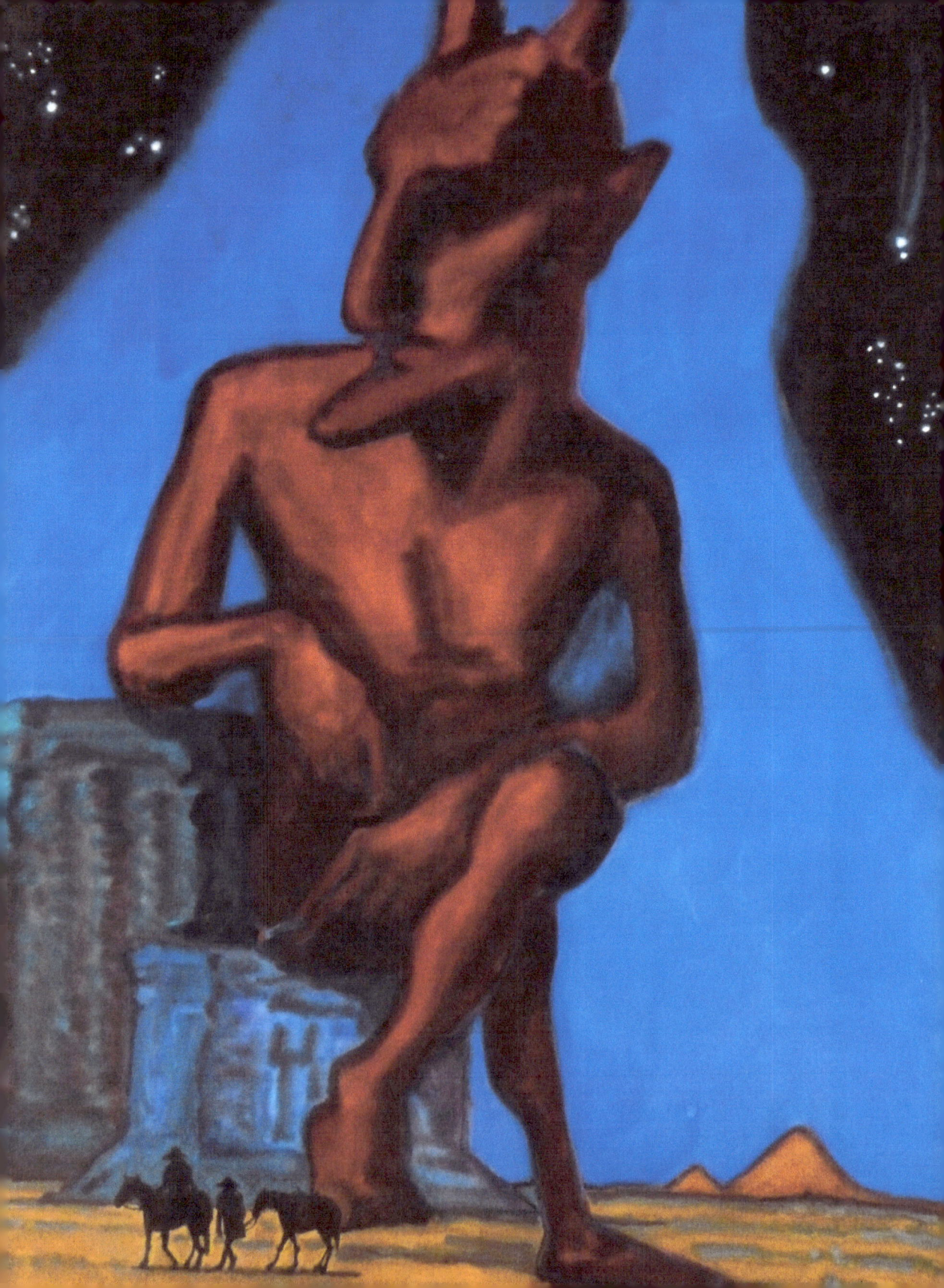

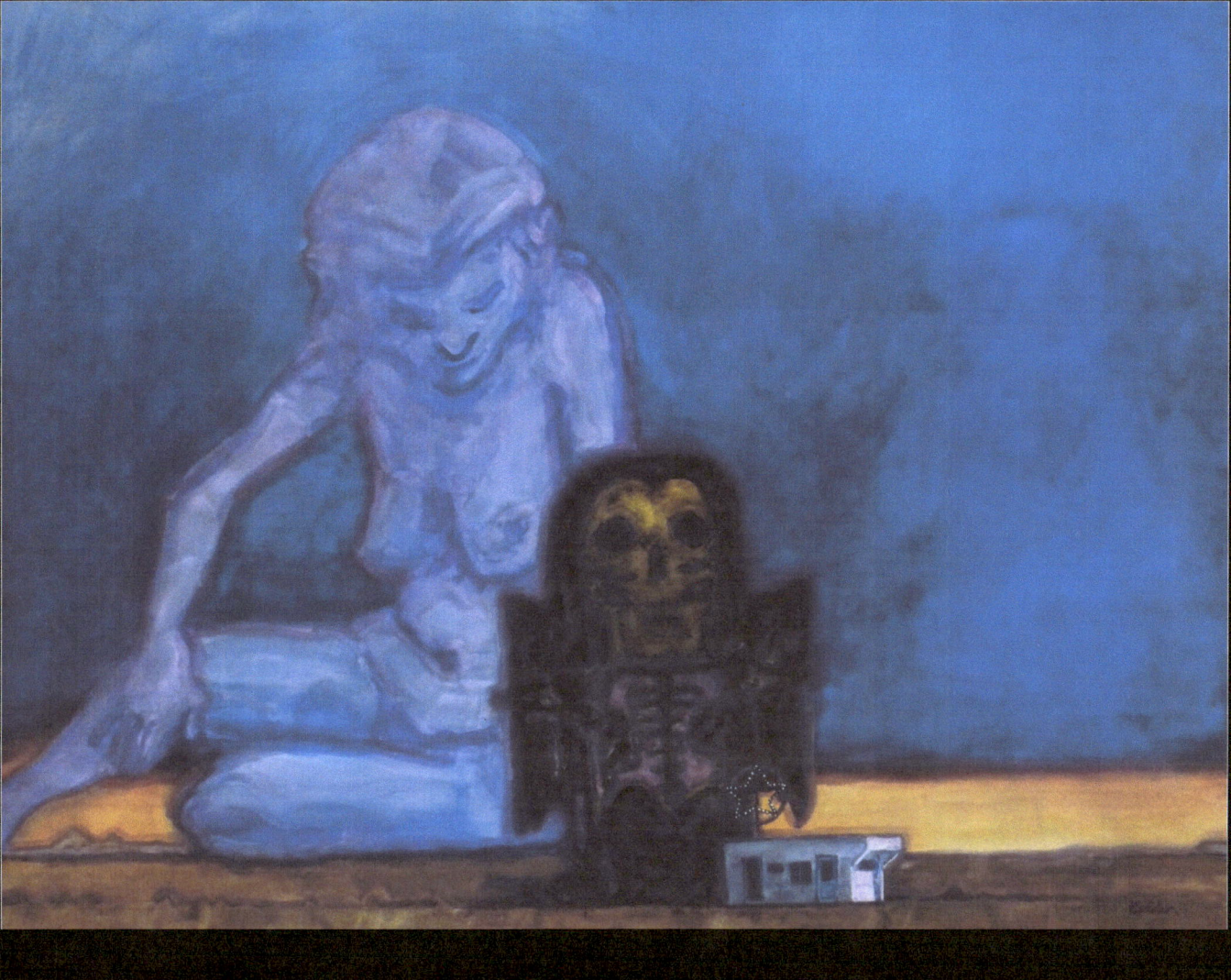

devils and death

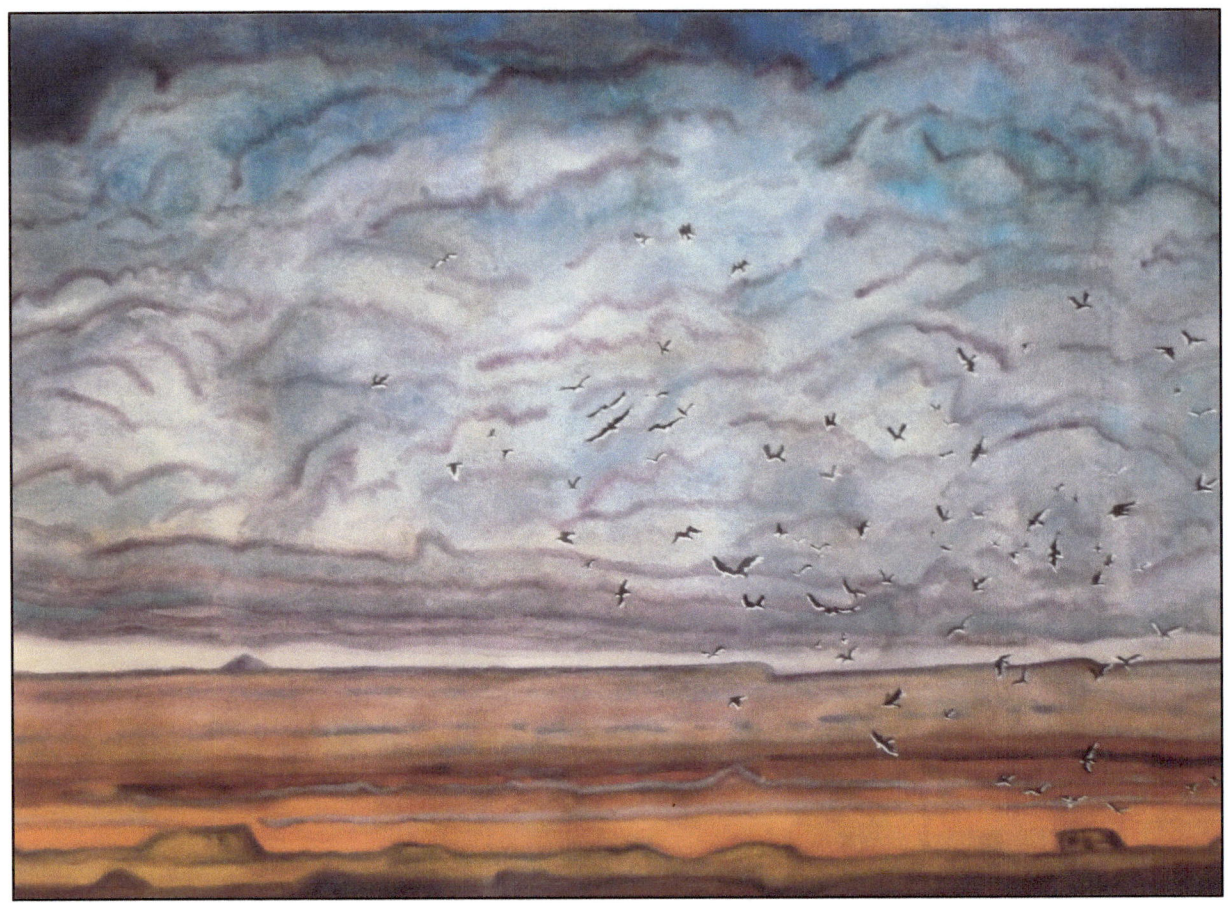

Crows #5 28" x 36"

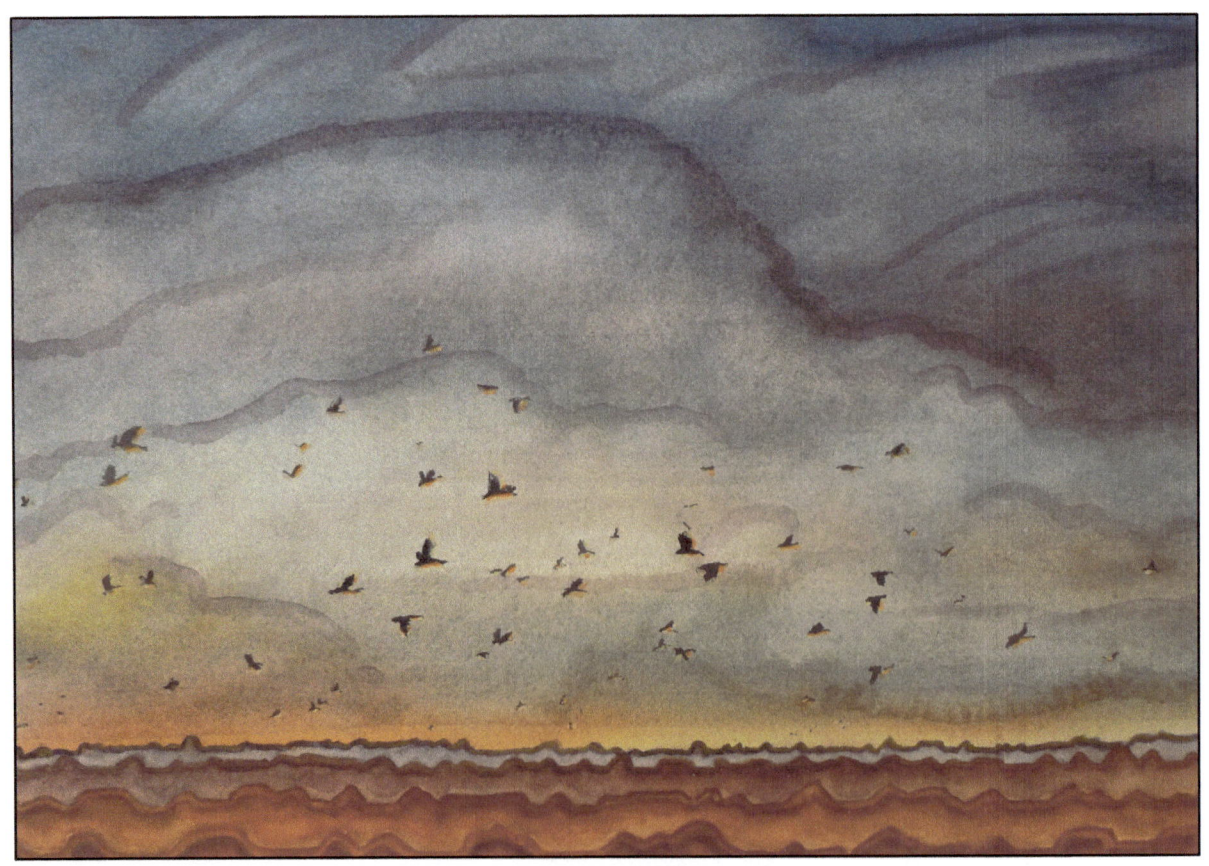

Crows #4 28"x 36"

crows

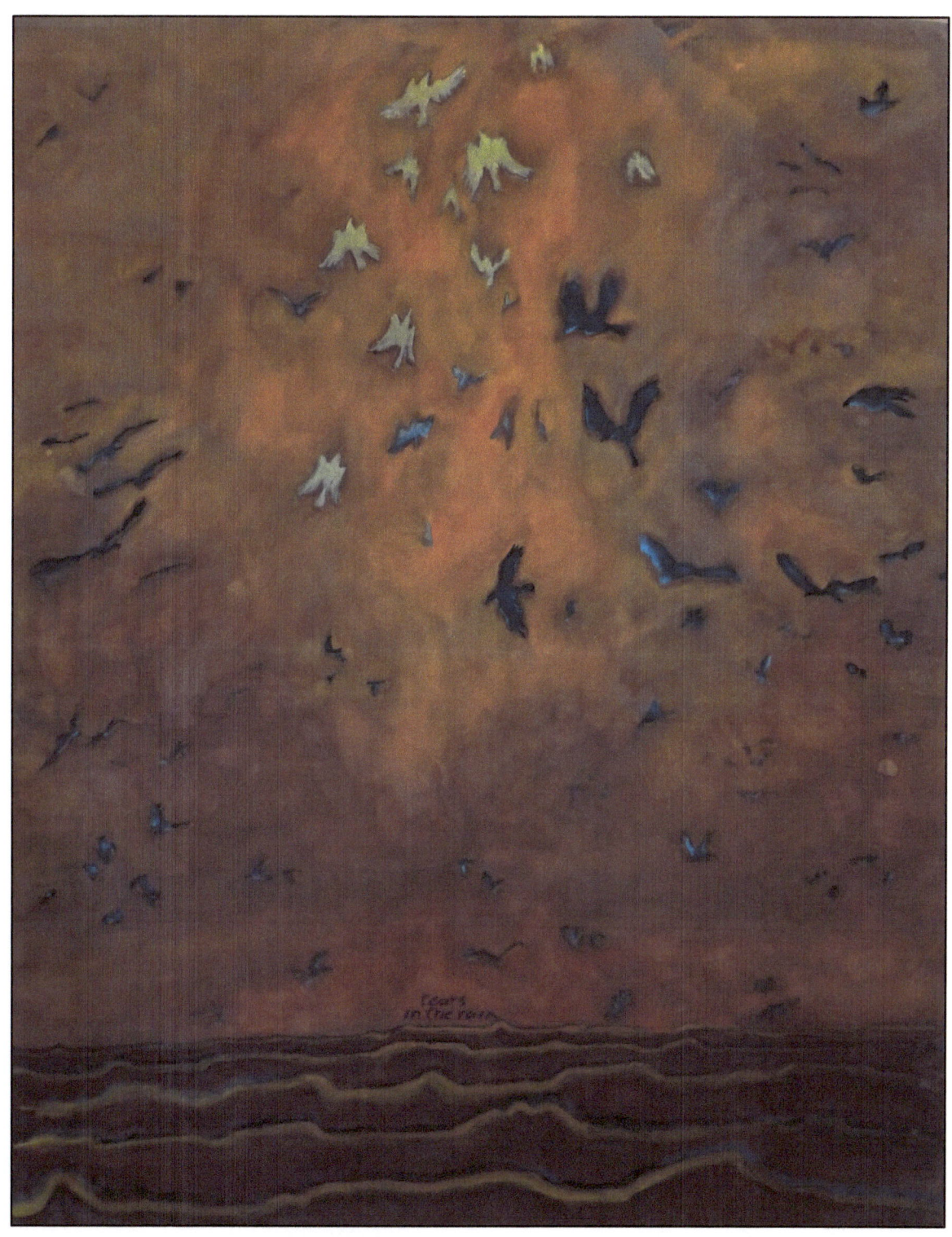

Tears in the Rain   28" x 36"

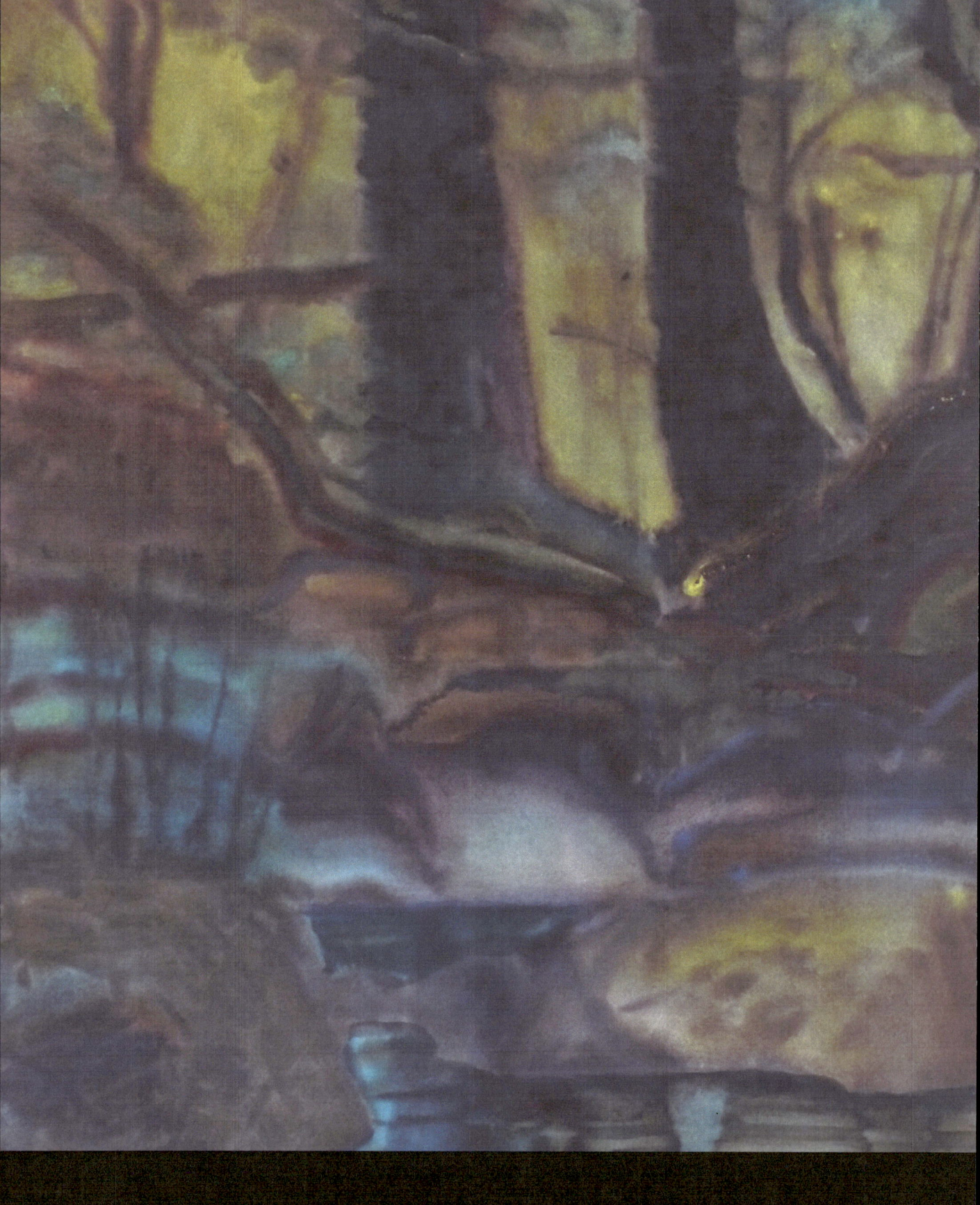

glimpses of the eternal

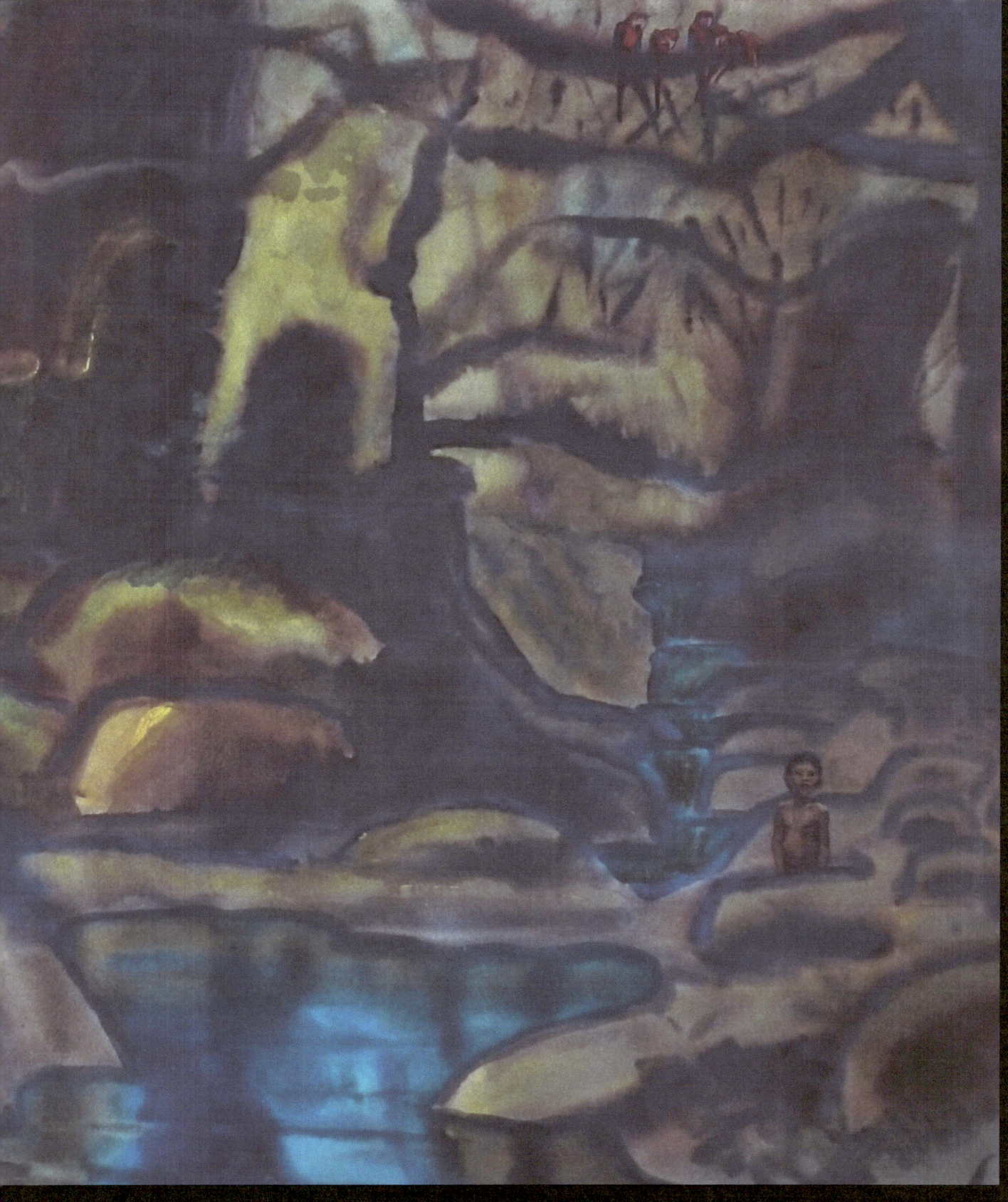

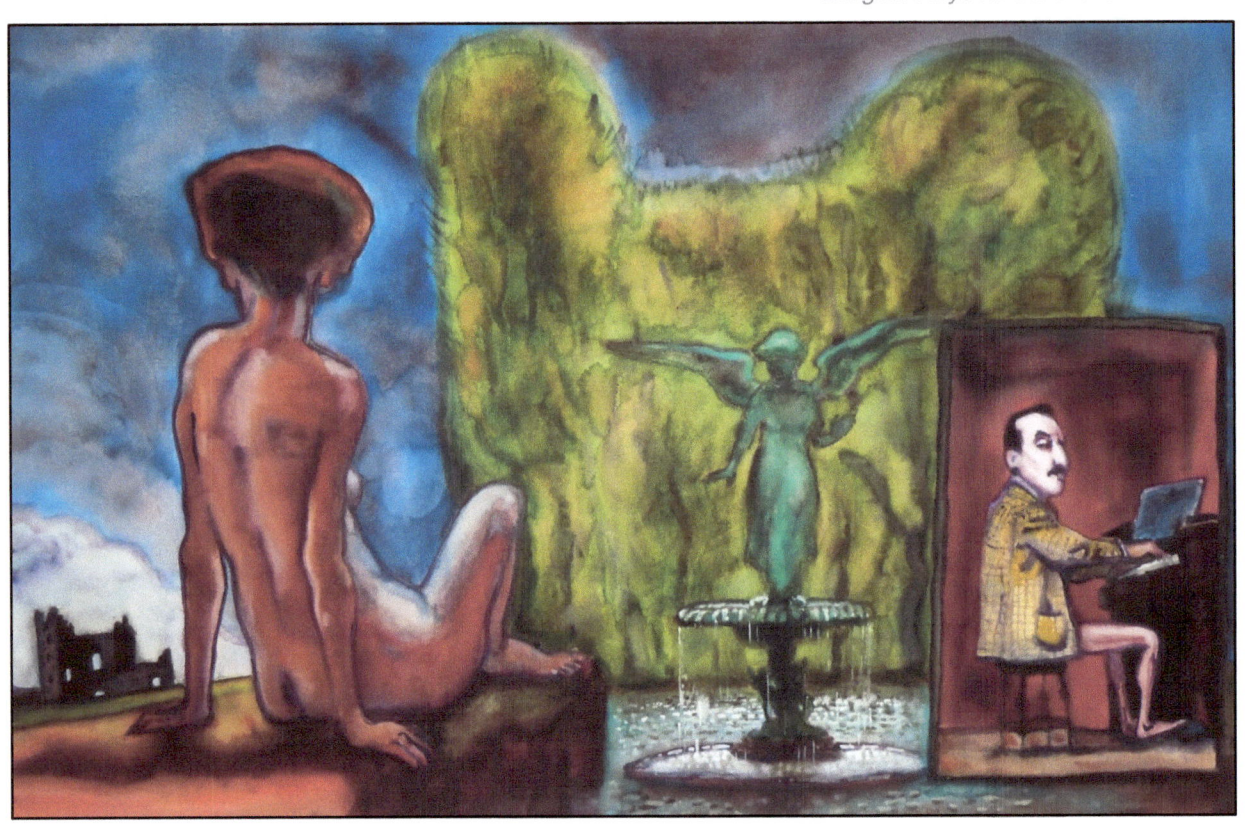

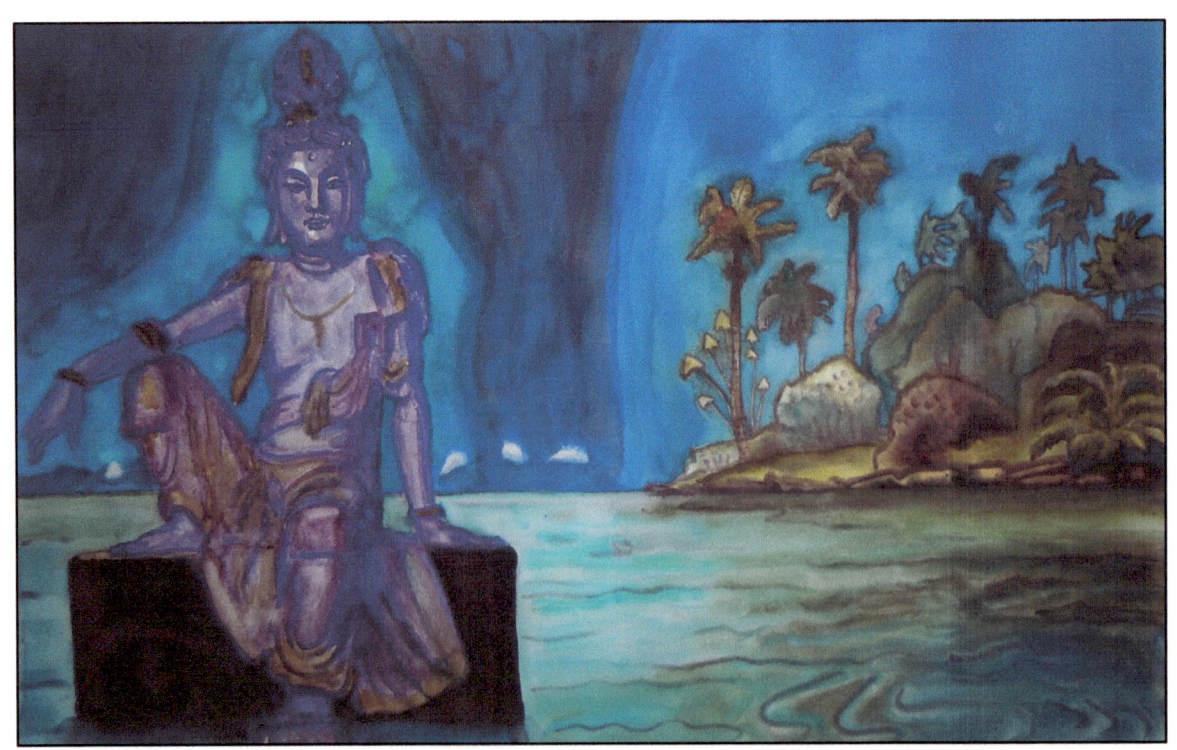

Have to Get Back to the Garden 28" x 38"

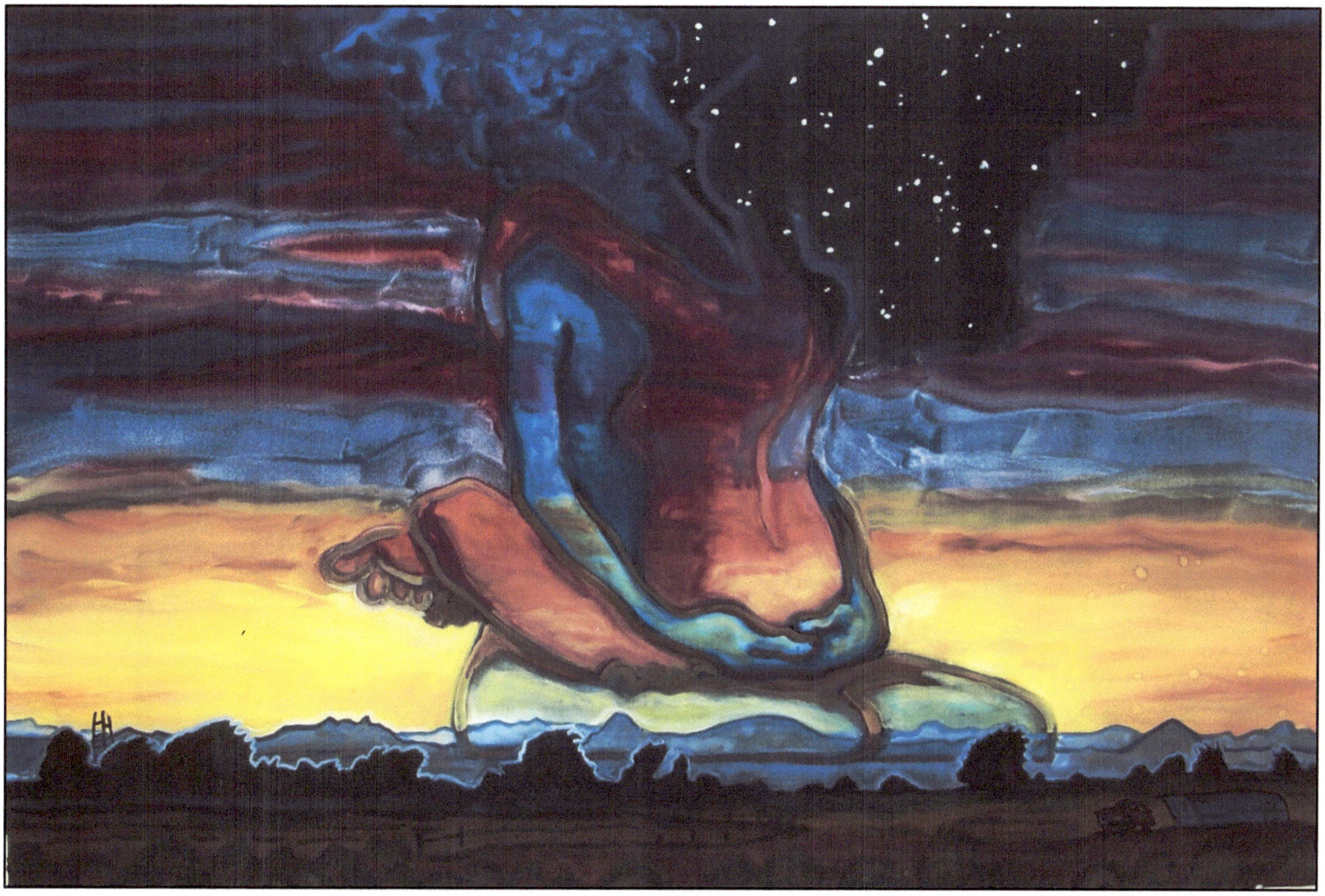

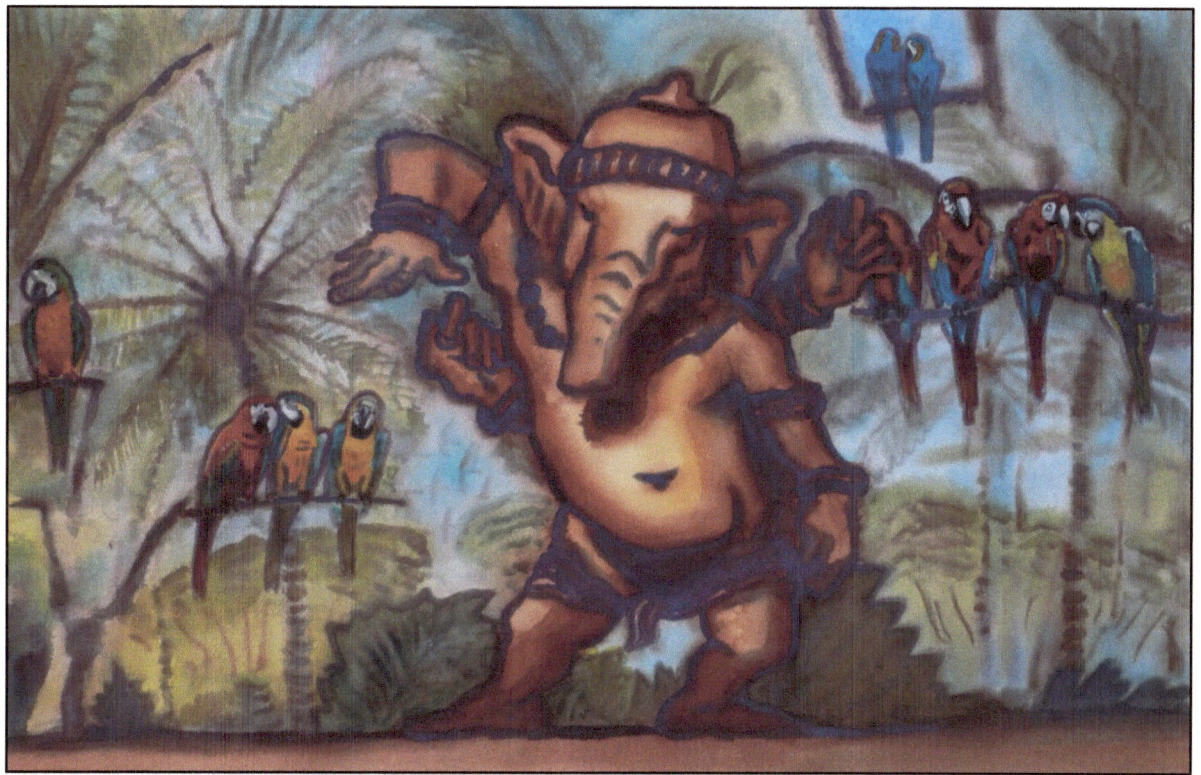

Ganesh Dances 22" x 30"

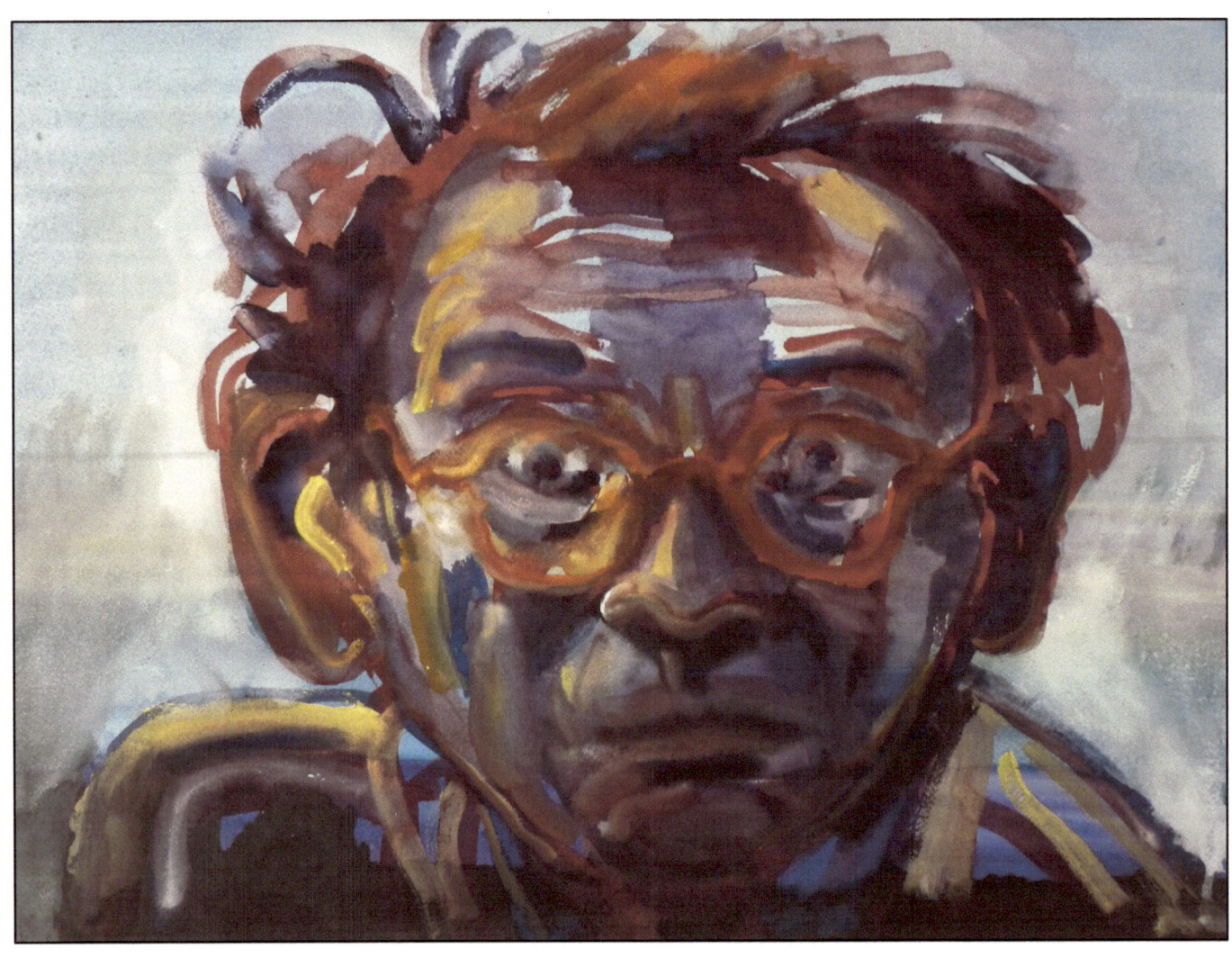

Self Portrait

THE ARTIST'S SECRET (a poem)

It doesn't matter what they are working on, or what they are working with.

It doesn't matter what they look like on the surface.

All artists are SUFFERING, DANGEROUS, RAVING, LUNATICS.

I'LL TELL YOU WHY

IT'S A SEXUAL THING.   More like an erotic thing.   The word "erotic" being Eros or love.

Like two lovers who can't stand to be apart, artists want there to be no space between themselves and what they are working on.

NO SPACE.

They are willing to risk a lot to get this to be.

But, because there will always be some degree of distance in this process, artists are slowly driven crazy.

Their work, to them, is never good enough, NEVER. This breaks their hearts.

The degree to which you are able to lessen the distance between yourself and what you are working on, IS the degree of value and success your finished work will achieve.

The broken crazy heart of an artist becomes a dangerous heart.

When a heart is dangerous it has value.

DANGEROUS PEOPLE TELL THE TRUTH.

Ted

About the Author

Ted Keller is an accomplished watercolor painter, as well as a master teacher of art.

As a boy, Ted loved to paint and draw and was enchanted by the smell of oil paints.

After earning his BFA degree from Syracuse University in Ceramics and Painting, Ted attended the University of Montana at Missoula where he graduated with an MFA in Ceramics.

To begin his career, Ted accepted a job as a professor of art at Oregon State University, where he taught for two years. Although his classes were always popular, he felt that he was too young to teach, so he made the decision to quit teaching and move to the coast of Maine. Once in Maine, he began a 30-year career in ceramics, supporting himself and his family by making and selling over 100,000 pieces of colorful stoneware and porcelain pottery.

In his early 40's, Ted restarted his teaching career at the University of Maine, while continuing his work in ceramics. He taught a variety of art classes for over 20 years. His classes were legendary in their popularity, and many students chose to take classes from him over and over again.

At age 53, with the family grown, Ted decided to stop making pottery and begin painting. He started with oil painting, but soon switched to watercolors, the medium that best fits his skills and interest. Over the course of the next three years, Ted continued to teach and to develop his watercolor skills, creating over 300 watercolor paintings. He then began to show and sell his work in Maine galleries. At this point he has completed about 1300 paintings.

Attracted by the sun, the mountains, and the incredible light of Taos, New Mexico, Ted moved there with his wife in 2009. At the same time he maintains his home, connections and friends in Maine and visits the Midcoast area often. He continues to paint in watercolor, and his work can be seen at shows in galleries in the Taos area, as well as the Carver Hill Gallery in Rockland, Maine.

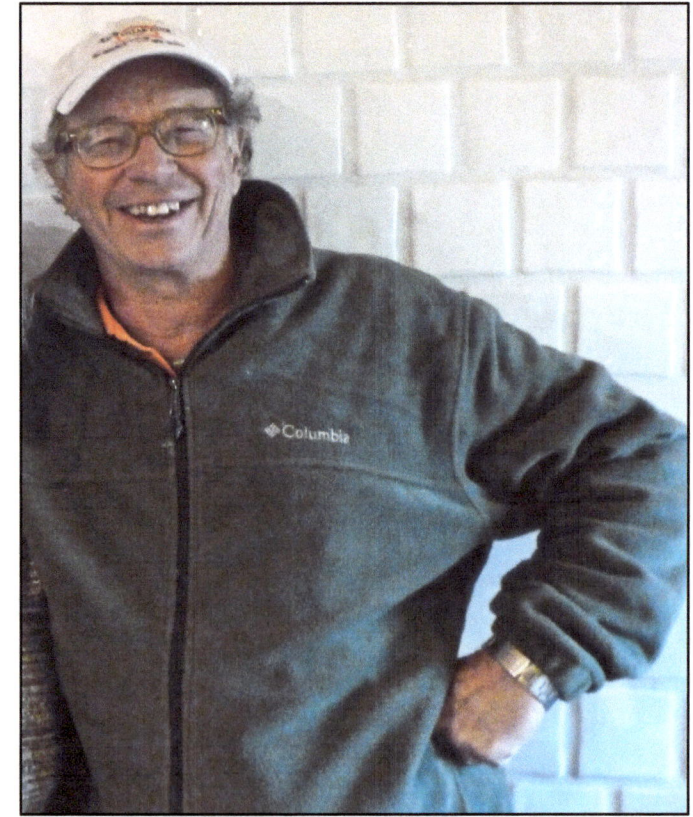

Ted Keller

Pale Green Jade Press
40 Camino A Realidad
El Prado, New Mexico, 87529

tedkeller77@gmail.com

Please visit us on Facebook